The University of Law
133 Great Hampton Street
Birmingham B18 6AQ
Telephone: 01483 216041
Email: library-birmingham@law.ac.uk

Birmingham I Bristol I Chester I Guildford I London I Manchester I York

D1092787

Praise for Online Courts and the Future of Justice

'*Online Courts and the Future of Justice* is a timely reflection on how technology has been embraced by various courts services around the world and how future technologies will be likely to significantly transform court processes as we enter the third decade of the twenty-first century. I strongly recommend this book to those who want to gain an insight into the opportunities and challenges that technology pose to the courts systems of the world.'

Mr. Justice Frank Clarke, Chief Justice of Ireland

'This book is an absolute must-read for lawyers and others interested in systems for making access to justice a reality in the digital age. It roams well beyond mere practical considerations of the functions of online courts in small civil claims. It raises (and suggests answers to) serious ethical questions relating to the extent to which machines can deliver outcomes for dispute resolution consistently with the rule of law. It discusses whether the role of judges can or should be assisted or supplanted by artificial intelligence. No judge or arbitrator providing dispute resolution services in today's or tomorrow's world can afford to be unaware of the issues it addresses.'

Dame Elizabeth Gloster, former Court of Appeal judge and
Vice-President of the Court of Appeal, Civil Division

'A timely and powerful book that every lawyer should read. Susskind makes a compelling case for online courts, both as a vehicle for increasing access to justice and as a means of securing better judicial outcomes. Online courts will soon handle all manner of disputes, from small claims to complex commercial matters, radically transforming the conduct of litigation.'

Bjarne P. Tellmann, General Counsel and Chief Legal Officer, Pearson

'I implore all who are interested or involved in the law to read this book with an open mind and heart. Written with Susskind's usual brisk pace, elegantly combining the erudite with the accessible, he tackles the fundamental issue of genuine access to justice. His vision is compelling and we owe it to the disenfranchised, vulnerable and disempowered to respond.'

Christina Blacklaws,
Immediate Past President of
the Law Society of England and Wales

'Susskind raises the bar again with a thought-provoking analysis of the pros and cons of Court as a Service or a Place and an inspiring vision of a justice system working for everyone. Horizon-scanning, Susskind paints a vivid portrait of the Court of the Future – a future where transformative technology, artificial intelligence and computer judges are the order of the day.'

Wim Dejonghe, Senior Partner, Allen & Overy

'With his characteristic insight, humour, and persuasion, Susskind takes us by the hand and leads us, some of us kicking and screaming, to the inescapable conclusion that online courts are our best hope for making justice systems relevant and accessible to the public. *Online Courts and the Future of Justice* offers a compelling call to action for anyone who cares about access to justice and is looking for a practical roadmap for fundamental change, based on successful case studies from around the world.'

Shannon Salter, Chair, Civil Resolution Tribunal

'Richard Susskind, our foremost guide to the future of the legal profession now provides the definitive guide to the future of the justice system. *Online Courts and the Future of Justice* is an eminently readable, insightful and astute analysis of how technology will provide new forms of dispute resolution and new opportunities for citizens to access justice. A must read for anyone interested in law, justice, and the social impact of technology.'

Ethan Katsh and Orna Rabinovich-Einy, authors of *Digital Justice*

'For more than three decades Richard Susskind has perceived what others would rather ignore: that most court users simply want their problems resolved and that online courts can be the best way of providing access to justice. This accessible, pioneering analysis will win over sceptics while enthralling admirers.'

Joshua Rozenberg QC (hon), legal commentator

'His radical proposals will no doubt trigger scepticism and fury from defenders of the status quo, but my money is on Susskind being vindicated yet again. This book is a must-read for anyone who wishes to look beyond prejudice, self-interest and conservatism in order to enhance the administration of justice both at home and abroad.'

Professor John Tasioulas, King's College London

'Susskind provides a blueprint for finally achieving one of the most noble and elusive ambitions of the legal profession: providing access to justice for all, without regards to means. Applied on a global scale, it could extend the rule of law to billions in need of justice, as called for by the Sustainable Development Goals of the United Nations. An exciting new chapter in the history of justice.'

Hugh Verrier, Chairman, White & Case

ONLINE
COURTS
AND
THE
FUTURE
OF
JUSTICE

ONLINE COURTS AND THE FUTURE OF JUSTICE

RICHARD SUSSKIND

OXFORD
UNIVERSITY PRESS

OXFORD
UNIVERSITY PRESS

Great Clarendon Street, Oxford, OX2 6DP,
United Kingdom

Oxford University Press is a department of the University of Oxford.
It furthers the University's objective of excellence in research, scholarship,
and education by publishing worldwide. Oxford is a registered trade mark of
Oxford University Press in the UK and in certain other countries

First Edition published in 2019

Impression: 1

Published in the United States of America by Oxford University Press
198 Madison Avenue, New York, NY 10016, United States of America

British Library Cataloguing in Publication Data

Data available

Library of Congress Control Number: 2019946450

ISBN 978–0–19–883836–4

Printed and bound in Great Britain by
Clays Ltd, Elcograf S.p.A.

To Rosa
my beautiful little granddaughter

ACKNOWLEDGEMENTS

I often joke that I write the same book every four years. Yet there is truth in this jest, in that my message has been consistent for almost 40 years – that we can and should find ways of using technology to improve the practice of law and the administration of justice. The enabling technologies change regularly, of course, and this periodically takes me back to the keyboard to write about what has most recently become feasible. As time rolls by, and our systems become more capable, I can see more clearly *how* the legal world is likely to evolve and transform.

In that spirit, this book brings together nearly four decades of work on technology and the courts. There is not space here to thank everyone who has helped me along the way, whether by championing or challenging my efforts, but now is a good time to call out those who have been especially supportive over the years, alongside those who have helped on this particular project.

My early interest in justice and in court technology dates to my time as an undergraduate in law at the University of Glasgow from 1978 to 1982. In the Scottish tradition, I was able to specialize in one subject in my final two years and my choice was jurisprudence, under the inspiring tutelage of Tom Campbell, David Goldberg, Gerry Maher, and Elspeth Atwool. It was they who gave me the initial freedom to imagine a legal world that might be radically changed by technology. I also studied philosophy during that period, and was privileged to be taught by Robin Downie. As a doctoral student at the University of Oxford, from 1983 to 1986, working on law and artificial intelligence, I was helped by several people who had a lasting influence on my thinking, not least my supervisor and the father of the field of computers and law, Colin Tapper, my principal collaborator and lifelong friend, David Gold, and my examiners, Jon Bing and Neil MacCormick, both of whom, sadly, are no longer with us. At Balliol College, Anthony Kenny and Joseph Raz were also of great support. At Oxford too, I met Phillip Capper, first as an examiner; later, from 1986 to 1988, we co-developed the Latent Damage System, the early AI system that is discussed later in these pages.

In the years that followed, many friends, collaborators, and clients offered me insight, guidance, expertise, and friendship. I have in mind Ruth Baker, Joan Bercovitch, John Bishop, Bruce Braude, Jonathan Brayne, Simon Carne, Orlando Conetta, Andrea Coomber, Stephen Denyer, Matthew di Rienzo, Neville Eisenberg, Amanda Finlay, Albert Fleming, Frances Gibb, Stephen Gillespie, Caroline Gould, Andrew Gwyther, Geoffrey Howe, Michael Ingram, Paul Lippe, Ian Lloyd, Ethan Katsh, Piet Hein Meeter, Christopher Millard, Michael Mills, Iain Monaghan, Alastair Morrison, Mark O'Conor, Alan Paterson, Tamara Quinn, Orna Rabinovic-Einy, Aviva Rotenberg, Joshua Rozenberg, Gail Swaffield, Martin Telfer, David Wilkins, Tony Williams, and Conrad Young.

Since 1998, I have had the honour of holding the position of Technology Adviser to the Lord Chief Justice of England and Wales, in which capacity I have been the personal adviser on technology matters to six successive LCJs – Lords Bingham, Woolf, Phillips, Judge, Thomas, and Burnett. Each of these remarkable men, in different ways, has generously and affably given me their valuable time and invaluable support. I cannot thank them enough.

I have also worked closely through the years with the small group of judges in England and Wales who have had specific responsibility for judicial technology. They came in two waves. The first were the pioneers – Sir Brian Neill, Sir Henry Brooke, and Lord Saville. They tirelessly advocated technology for the courts in the face of considerable resistance (judicial and political). And they were wonderful mentors to me. The computers and law community deeply mourned the recent passing of Brian and Henry but we remain warmed by the thought that they lived to see the early days of online courts. In many ways, this development was their legacy. The second wave of technology judges sought valiantly to embed a range of systems into everyday judicial practice. They were Lord Neuberger, Sir Stanley Burnton, Sir Anthony Mann, Sir Adrian Fulford, and now Sir Colin Birss. I have learned much from each. Very special thanks also to Dame Elizabeth Gloster and Sir Geoffrey Vos, whose ongoing encouragement is deeply appreciated.

Two senior civil servants deserve particular mention – Sir Alex Allan and Sir Ian Magee. They paved the way for much of the court technology that is currently being put in place.

Turning now to the book itself, it frequently builds on my previous thinking, most notably in *The Future of Law* (1996), *The End of Lawyers?* (2008), *The Future of the Professions* (2015, with Daniel Susskind), and *Tomorrow's Lawyers* (2017, 2nd edition), all of which were published by Oxford University Press. Chapter 4 of this book, on outcome-thinking, is an updated version of an article that appeared in the *British Academy Review* (Autumn 2018), while parts of Chapter 26 are taken from my submission on artificial intelligence (dated, 6 September 2017), to the House of Lords Select Committee on Artificial Intelligence. I have also been able to draw on letters of advice and reports on technology that I have written for the judiciary over the years.

Although I started writing and speaking about online dispute resolution (ODR) in the 1990s, this subject became a main focus for me in 2014, when Lord Dyson, then Master of the Rolls and Chair of the Civil Justice Council (CJC), invited me to assemble a group of experts and officials and to prepare a report on the potential of ODR for low value civil claims. This initiative is described in Chapter 9. The conclusions that our group reached underpin much that is written in this book and so I thank each member of the team - Mick Collins, Pablo Cortes, Adrian Dally, Andrea Dowsett, Peter Farr, Paul Harris, Julia Hornle, Matthew Lavy, Nick Mawhinney, Sue Prince, Graham Ross, Beth Silver, Roger Smith, Tim Wallis, and William Wood. While working on our report, as well as having the vital backing of Lord Dyson, I had the great good fortune to have the ongoing guidance and energetic support of Lord Thomas, then the Lord Chief Justice, and of Natalie Ceeney, then the Chief Executive of HM Courts & Tribunals Service. Lord Michael Briggs deserves special mention – his endorsement of online courts in his reports on the structure of the civil courts of England and Wales lent enormous credibility to the recommendations of the CJC report.

I also extend my thanks to the various individuals who provided background information for me while I prepared the case studies that now appear in Chapter 16 - Judge John Aitkin, Catherine D'Elia, Paul Embley, Richard Goodman, Justice Deno Himonas, Juthika Ramanathan, Shannon Salter, KenHwee Tan, Darin Thompson, Caroline Sheppard, Michael Fang, and James Prescott.

I am immensely grateful to three senior and exceptionally busy individuals for reading and commenting on the first full draft - Sir Ernest Ryder, the Senior President of Tribunals, Susan Acland-Hood, the Chief Executive of HM Courts & Tribunals Service, and Dame Professor Hazel Genn, immediate past Dean of UCL Faculty of Laws. Their feedback was of inestimable help. More generally, they are each, in different ways, pivotal to making online courts a reality in England and Wales. Hazel deserves an additional thank-you - for the title of the book. Quite late in the day, I found that the title, as it remains, was the self-same title of her Birkenhead Lecture at Gray's Inn in late 2016. Either great minds think alike or I unconsciously stole it. In any event, Hazel graciously said that she was happy for it to be re-used.

This is my seventh outing with Oxford University Press and it has been as agreeable as ever. I expect that it does not get any easier working with me, so I thank Dominic Byatt, Alex Flach, and Natalie Patey not only their expertise and their hard work, but also for their tolerance and indulgence.

Getting a book from manuscript to the finished item takes some time. I fully expect, therefore, that by the time this volume is in the hands of readers, the world of online courts will have moved on some. I have only been able to take account of developments up until the end of April 2019.

I submitted the final draft while on a golf holiday in Portugal with three remarkable friends with whom I grew up in Glasgow – Howard Beach, Lloyd Pinder, and Paul Robinson. Forty years ago, we spent a summer together in a kibbutz and have been an indivisible unit since then. It was somehow fitting that they helped me get the thing over the line.

As always in my life, in the background, I have had the love and backing of my father, Werner, and my brother, Alan. I do not tell them often enough how much their steadfast and unwavering support means to me. I wish my mother was still alive to enjoy the publication of this book.

My two sons, Daniel and Jamie, now considerable authors in their own right, commented extensively on the first full draft, and gave the kind of frank and forthright feedback that can only come from one's offspring. Their individual and combined intellects leave me daunted. I am more than fortunate to have their expert help at my fingertips and wholly blessed to have them as such loving and caring sons.

My wonderful daughter, Alexandra, is my youngest child but she is perhaps the wisest Susskind of all, always available with sensible counsel. Although she too is now in the world of tech, my thanks go to her, rather, for being such an undiluted source of happiness in my life. Every day.

Finally, I must thank my wife, Michelle. This is the tenth time she has vicariously endured the agony of finishing a book under stiff deadlines. She understands the ups and downs, my hopes and fears, as well as the thrills and, more often, the frustrations and chaos of my writing. She keeps me on the rails, she can empathize like no other, and for this I will always be grateful.

Richard Susskind
Radlett, England
28 April 2019

let justice roll down like waters

Amos 5:24

Before the law stands a gatekeeper. A man from the country comes to this gatekeeper and requests admittance into the law. But the gatekeeper says that he cannot grant him admittance right now ... The man from the country had not expected such difficulties; after all, he thinks, the law should be accessible to everyone at all times.

Franz Kafka

CONTENTS

PART III THE CASE AGAINST

PART IV THE FUTURE

Introduction

I often wonder what Rosa Susskind will think of this book in years to come. Rosa, to whom this work is lovingly dedicated, is my first grandchild. She was born in early 2018 and joined us at a time of remarkable technological change.

Projecting forward to, say, 2039, when Rosa will turn 21, I expect our world will be a very different place, in some ways as alien to us today as a distant planet. Our society will have been transformed by some technologies that already exist, by others that are emerging, and by many that are as-yet-uninvented. Perhaps Rosa will want to know, two decades hence, why her grandfather felt the need to waste his time writing a book that argued for the glaringly obvious—that in a digital society it makes sense for much of the work of the courts to be conducted online.

It will perhaps be evident in hindsight, from the comfort of whatever device serves as Rosa's armchair in 2039, that online courts were destined to become an integral part of legal systems around the world. But in 2019, as I write these words, many lawyers and judges are sceptical. This has led me here to make the case for online courts. I do so not because I worry that their future existence is in the balance but because I want to accelerate their development and uptake. My hope is to generate wider enthusiasm for a set of innovations that I am confident will greatly increase access to justice around the world. And Lord knows that greater access is long overdue.

By 2039, we will surely no more need to argue the case for online courts than we need to advance the case today for online shopping or, I expect, the case for autonomous vehicles a decade from now. This is not to say that the arguments for each are the same. It is to observe that human beings often take time to accept the merits of changes proposed by innovators and early adopters. Some may sympathize with the Nobel prize winning physicist, Max Planck, who once said that a 'scientific truth does not triumph by convincing its opponents and making them see the light, but rather because its opponents eventually die, and a new generation grows up that is familiar with it'.[1] But I see no reason to wait for a new generation to bring great change in the delivery of court service. If it is within our grasp to effect meaningful improvement now, then we should be applying ourselves today, rather than leaving the job to our descendants.

Some context

I spent much of the 1980s exploring the implications of artificial intelligence (AI) for the law. At the time, most lawyers claimed there would never be a place for this technology in their world. Today, most major law firms are working on AI.

The Future of Law, published in 1996, was my first systematic attempt to write about the impact of information technology on the practice of law and the administration of justice.[2] My predictions seem restrained in retrospect. I insisted at the time, for example, that email would come to be the main means of communication between lawyers and their clients. Officials at the Law Society of

England and Wales responded that I should not be allowed to speak in public and that I was bringing the legal profession into disrepute. Today that same Law Society is a leading advocate of technology for lawyers.

I also claimed in the 1990s that the Web would become the first port of call for anyone undertaking legal research. Lawyers and judges joined in denouncing this suggestion, saying that I did not understand the practical and cultural significance of law libraries.

I cite these examples to remind those who live in the legal world that they have been wrong in the past about the future use of technology in the law. All I ask is that my readers keep an open mind. In my view, most of what I say about online courts in the following pages is more likely to come to pass than my predictions about email in the mid-1990s.

Gut reactions

I also offer that preamble because the concept of online courts is stirring some emotion in legal circles, largely amongst lawyers and judges, many of whom—there is no escaping the truth—have not actually learned what is envisaged nor observed any kind of system in action. Their instinctive responses to the term itself range from scepticism to outrage. No matter the emotion, the premise is frequently the same—that online courts are misconceived and their deployment should be resisted. This visceral reaction is often an instance of what I call 'irrational rejectionism', which I define as the dogmatic dismissal of a technology with which a critic has no personal or direct experience. It is plainly not rational for lawyers to discard a proposed innovation without evidence or experience.

Some technologists regard lawyers' dismissal of online courts as crude protectionism. I think this is too cynical. Although the adverse reaction may sometimes be motivated by an inclination to protect traditional jobs, it is more often rooted in a firm commitment to the values and procedures of the conventional court system. It is based on a conviction that justice is best served when those in dispute assemble in the time-honoured set-up—a public, physical space where everyone accommodated can look fellow participants in the eye. The resistance can also stem from a concern that this introduction of technology is yet another ploy to reduce public expenditure on the justice system.

It is relevant too that lawyers and judges are steeped in tradition and contained by precedent. By disposition, they are often conservative and risk-averse. My research elsewhere suggests that in the great pantheon of professions, certainly in relation to technology, only the clergy are more cautious about change.[3] The comfort zone of lawyers is the courtroom rather than the online collaborative shared space.

We can therefore appreciate and even respect lawyers' aversion to radical technological change, and we might even enjoy poking fun at their irrationality, but we should not be deterred from exploring better ways of administering justice. We should be driven by the needs of society and of citizens rather than by the prejudices (even if well-intentioned) of the current cohort of providers, the influencers amongst whom are in their 50s and 60s and not always on top of digital developments. The future of our courts is too important to be left exclusively in the hands of those who currently work in the system (and, regrettably, those who sometimes work the system). At a time when technology is bringing great change in all corners of our social and working lives, we should welcome new perspectives on our most important social institutions. As Susan Acland-Hood, Chief Executive of HM Courts & Tribunals

Service, often reminds us, 'our processes don't need to be as old as our principles'.[4]

Our object of study

There is no avoiding, upfront, what has already become a hoary definitional question. What are online courts? Inevitably, because it is early days for the field, commentators and developers are still squabbling over this. Some are touting alternative labels. Others want to banish the term from the legal lexicon. Yet others want watertight definitions that would stand up in court.

My starting point as someone who advocates radical reform in our public dispute resolution systems is that the term itself is useful and should continue to be used, but I do accept that it is, in various ways, both provocative and fuzzy at the edges. That said, it has caught the attention of the legal and judicial worlds like no innovation I can recall in my near-40 years in the field of court technology. When people hear the term, everyone (lawyers and non-lawyers alike) rightly senses that it has something to do with some of the work of the courts and judges being undertaken on-line rather than in physical courtrooms. It might be more accurate to speak of 'online court services' or 'online court processes', but the term, 'online courts' has somehow stuck as a brand. It does roughly what it says on the tin and it prompts, in equal measure, the frissons of excitement and apprehension in which champions of change rejoice.

I am not persuaded at this stage that a tight definition of on-line courts is either possible or desirable. Nonetheless, for current purposes, to set our bearings at least in general terms and to give a taste of what is being contemplated, it is helpful to have in mind two broad senses in which the term 'online courts' is used. One is specific and the other more general. Both refer to some kind of public, *state-provided* dispute management and resolution service. Neither was conceivable until the birth of the World Wide Web in the early 1990s.

The specific sense of online courts, and the one that attracts the liveliest of debates, can be called *online judging*. This involves the determination of cases by human judges but not in physical courtrooms. Instead, evidence and arguments are submitted through an online service. In turn, judges deliver their decisions not in open court but again via an online platform. The proceedings are not conducted in one live sitting by video, audio, or real-time chat. There is no hearing, virtual or otherwise. Online judging is not appropriate for all cases but its advocates claim it is well-suited to many low value disputes that current courts struggle to handle efficiently.

The more general conception is of a system that takes advantage of technology and is able to extend its reach beyond the traditional remit of traditional courts. On this model, technology can and should enable courts to deliver more than judicial decisions. These *extended courts* provide tools, for example, that can help court users understand relevant law and the options available to them. They can guide users in completing court forms, and help them to formulate their arguments and assemble their evidence. They can also offer various forms of non-judicial settlement such as negotiation and early neutral evaluation, not as an alternative to the public court system but as part of it. Less dramatically, everyday techniques and technologies—apps, smartphones, portals, messaging, video calling, chat bots, livechats, webcasts—can help non-lawyers interact much more easily with the courts. The extension here, and it is a major change, is that the latest systems are being designed primarily for self-represented litigants (litigants-in-person in the UK, pro se litigants in the US) rather than for lawyers. And these court users can themselves file documents, track cases, engage with court officials and judges, and progress their disputes by using intuitive, jargon-free systems.

My aim in this book is to explore online courts in both senses—online judging and extended courts. I do not always address each separately because, in practice, the online courts that are emerging around the world are providing a mix of the two. I use the distinction here to give a flavour of what online courts are about and to spark some immediate thoughts about the issues to which they give rise. Are we seriously contemplating judges undertaking their mainstream work without courtrooms? Can it really be the responsibility of the state to stray beyond the provision of judges who decide cases?

In fact, online courts are already here. In England and Wales, Canada, the US, China, Singapore, and Australia, for example, operational systems are up and running.

In later pages of the book, I also try to look into the future, reaching beyond the first generation of online courts to a hazier but looming second generation. When I speak of the first generation, I have in mind online courts in which all authoritative directions or decisions are made by human beings. In contrast, I envisage a second generation which, in broad terms, draw on artificial intelligence (AI) techniques, so that some if not many of the formal directions and decisions are made by systems rather than flesh-and-blood people. Unsurprisingly, the prospect of this second generation gives rise to much greater debate than the first. Can we actually be spending valuable time, I am often challenged, on the idea of computers replacing judges? Although most of my book is in fact focused on human judges working online, I do think it important that we start now to confront some of the ethical and social questions that will inevitably arise as our machines become much more capable.

The case for online courts

The case for online courts can take many forms. There is the business case, often favoured by politicians in the current climate of public sector belt-tightening. This argues, in broad terms, that the investment and introduction of online courts will reduce the cost of court service, and that savings will accrue both to the state and the taxpayer. Another is a socio-technical case, tabled frequently by legal and court technologists, who claim that current court systems are antiquated, out of place in a digital society, and in urgent need of upgrade. Yet another case focuses on quality and is advanced by a wide range of disgruntled commentators and participants. They maintain that today's courts do not always deliver the best outcomes for their users and that online courts will resolve disputes more quickly and to a higher standard.

I touch on each of these cases in the chapters that follow but my main motivation in calling loudly for online courts is to improve *access* to court and legal services. I want it to be easier for everyone to understand and enforce their legal entitlements. It worries me deeply that, for most people, even in avowedly advanced legal systems, our courts are too costly, too slow, and largely unintelligible. In my 38th year of thinking about court technology, I am confident that online courts offer the most promising way of radically increasing access to justice around the world.

My case therefore is largely a *moral* case, based on what I believe to be right and good. It is rooted in a deeper set of convictions: that all human beings—whatever their capabilities, status, wealth, and wherever they live and work—deserve and should be accorded equal respect and dignity. This global entitlement for each and every citizen is important in and of itself, whether or not it leads to a more harmonious, prosperous, or happier life for all. Crucially for present purposes, this right to respect and dignity, I believe, should be enshrined in and enforceable by the law. But for this to be so, we need effective court systems and services that are genuinely access-ible to all. And we do not have these today. Anywhere.

I call for online courts in two ways. First, I am inviting policy-makers, judges, and lawyers in their own jurisdictions to look squarely at the shortcomings of their current court systems and to give serious thought to the introduction of online judging and extended court systems. Different countries will no doubt respond in varying ways. Some may consider that these systems make sense only for low-value cases. Others might predict, as I do, that once online courts are seen to work well for such cases, their use will be extended over time and will come to transform much higher value litigation as well.

Second, I invite readers to rise above the local challenges of particular jurisdictions and consider the bigger, global picture. Intolerably, more than half of humanity currently lives beyond the protection of the law,[5] in countries where there is scant oppor-tunity for people to understand and enforce their legal rights. In response, many diligent bodies seek to promote the rule of law as a central pillar of humane society, to increase access to justice, to introduce effective human rights regimes, to tackle corrup-tion and criminality, and to promote peace and security through effective legal systems. By and large, these efforts depend on the introduction of a series of traditional building blocks—public and charitable legal funding, human legal advisers, conventional law enforcement and court systems, with a smattering of basic websites, and some desultory public legal education. I believe that trying to scale up these techniques to tackle global inaccess to justice is doomed. I cannot imagine, for example, that the backlog of court cases in Brazil, 100 million in number, will be cleared by lawyers and judges beavering away in conventional courtrooms. And Brazil is a country in which the rule of law and courts are relatively well established.[6] Many countries have much less developed court systems.

My hypothesis is that one partial solution to the tragedy of global exclusion from the law could lie in online courts—in introducing online judging as a way of disposing of large volumes of disputes and extended courts to help people understand their rights and navigate court systems. Online courts, on this line of thinking, could empower and bring greater security and peace to great numbers of people.

Principles of justice

Although the main objective of this book is to make the case for online courts as a way of improving access to justice, I have a second, supporting aim which is to propose and apply a set of general principles that should underpin any court system, whether traditional, online, or a blend of both. If we can come to agree, more or less, on the principles and values that *any* court system should embody and the outcomes and benefits that any court system should bring, then we will be better placed to compare current with proposed systems. More, I want to provide a set of criteria against which future developments and recommendations can be assessed. Realistically, I am not suggesting that we can identify a set of principles for all court systems in all places at all times. Rather, my focus is based on systems in the western legal tradition (both common and civil systems), sitting, broadly, in democratic regimes. Some of these principles come from constitutional theory, others from legal philosophy, and yet others from public policy thinking. These principles are also stress-tested later in the book, when I come to consider a series of common objections to online courts. Although many of these doubts do not survive systematic scrutiny, they are fuelled by deeper concerns that do need to be unearthed and considered by reference to the general principles of justice that I propose. If we are striving to increase access to justice, we should be clear what we mean by 'access' and 'justice'.

Scope

My main focus is on online courts for the resolution of *civil* disputes, especially those of low value. If we can develop systems that can help resolve minor conflicts, then this can be a platform for wider deployment of online courts in years to come. This is consistent with widely accepted theory of 'disruptive technologies'—it is better to start with the introduction of systems for straightforward problems and evolve these later for more challenging tasks once the market has become used to the innovation in question.[7]

For non-lawyers, the term 'civil' can cause confusion. Sometimes in law, when the term 'civil law' is used, reference is being made to a particular type of legal system that is distinguishable from 'common law' systems. This is not what I have in mind when I speak of civil disputes (although I do say more about this distinction in Chapter 23). Nor am I referring here to Civil Law when it is used synonymously with Roman Law. This is not a book for ancient Romans.

My use of the term 'civil dispute' is to refer to the legal disagreements that arise when a party who has suffered loss seeks a remedy from another for conduct such as not paying a debt, causing a personal injury, firing an employee unjustifiably, breaching a contract, or acting negligently. This means that I do not devote much of my analysis to family law, administrative law (disputes involving public bodies), or criminal law, although I believe most of what I say about online courts is also applicable to each. I acknowledge up front, though, that criminality and its handling by court systems does raise some additional and difficult questions.

Although I work mainly in London and am an adviser in various ways to the major court reform project that is under way in England and Wales, this book is not directly about that initiative. It is true that online courts, in both senses just noted, lie at the heart of the £1 billion English and Welsh reform programme, but this present work is not premised on its success. Nor does it seek to chronicle its progress. Others are doing this.[8]

More generally, this book is not a detailed empirical study of today's operational systems. In thinking about the future of online courts, I am influenced much more by the challenges and frustrations I have observed as an adviser to judiciaries, governments, law firms, and in-house legal departments around the world since the early 1990s. In particular, my work for more than two decades as Technology Adviser to the Lord Chief Justice of England and Wales has given me a clear view of the strengths and shortcomings of contemporary court systems.

The future

It is frequently said that we cannot predict the future. This truism seems to embolden both the myopic and the unimaginative to reject any foresights as meaningless flannel. I take a different view. I accept that we cannot of course know about what I call 'as-yet-uninvented' technologies. But I line up with those who hold that we can anticipate the broad trajectory, if not the specific details, of the world yet to come. Inevitably we will miss some major break-throughs, but if we do no more than extrapolate responsibly from where we are today this takes us to a very different future; one from which long-term planners should not hide.

Another way of thinking about the future is to consider the sus-tainability of what we currently have in place. Given the explosive increase in the power and uptake of technology and the profound problems we have in offering access to legal and court services, I find it hard to accept that our current court systems, legal insti-tutions, and legal profession will and should remain substantially unaltered over the next couple of decades. On the contrary, it seems to me that the least likely future is that nothing or little will change. And yet, the long-term strategies (if they have strategies) of most judiciaries and governments make precisely this assumption of modest adjustment. Truth to tell, the prevailing model of court service is not sustainable. As I argue, it is already broken and in any event unaffordable, and so we should be thinking deeply about what might lie beyond.

Preview

The book is organized in four parts. In the first part, I lay the foun-dations for the rest of the work. I explain why courts matter and I lay out the case for change. I outline the remarkable changes we are witnessing in the world of technology and propose a mindset, 'outcome-thinking', that can help us to contemplate radical re-form. I distinguish between physical courtrooms, virtual hearings, and online courts. And I devote a few chapters to the concept of justice—analysing the concepts of access to justice and of justice according to the law, and proposing that our principal focus should be on tackling injustice.

In the second part of the book, I ask whether court is a service or a place. I present a generic framework for online courts. I set out my broad vision and standard architecture for online courts, and then devote chapters to looking at the central components—online guidance, containing disputes (rather than resolving them), online determination by judges, and assisted argument. I also ana-lyse the complex connection between law and code, and provide a series of short case studies of online courts that are already up and running.

The third part of the book provides responses to the criticisms that are most commonly levelled at online courts. I argue that on-line courts do much more than offer 'economy-class' justice and that they can be more rather than less transparent than traditional courts. I maintain that trials held online can be fair, that few people will be digitally excluded, and that they need not lead to a more li-tigious culture. I also address some specific jurisprudential concerns and suggest that public sector court technology projects are not so risky that they should be avoided altogether.

In the final part of the book, I look to the future, well beyond the current generation of online courts that help settle low-value civil claims. I discuss various emerging technologies—telepresence, augmented reality, virtual reality, advanced online dispute reso-lution techniques, prediction machines, and artificial intelligence. This leads me to consider the fraught concept of the 'computer judge'. Most ambitiously, I conclude by considering the possibility of deploying online courts globally as a way of securing much wider access to justice.

In summary, the book is an essay on the digital transformation of a central public institution and public service. I envisage a set of pervasive, technology-enabled changes to our courts that extend well beyond the piecemeal efforts at modernization of court and legal systems that are being made today in many countries. In truth, despite all manner of reform initiatives around the world, today's court systems—along with our legal professions and our law schools—remain fundamentally 19th- and 20th-century institutions. They are out of place and inadequate in the 21st century. It is time for radical change.

PART I

Courts and Justice

Chapter 1

Why Courts Matter

Modern courts can be traced directly to bodies that came into being around 900 years ago. Today, they sit at the heart of all democratic societies, undertaking a remarkable variety of work. They handle quarrels amongst citizens, disagreements within families, conflicts between individuals and the state, and disputes between businesses. They determine the guilt or innocence of people accused of crimes and they settle sensitive questions of national security. In resolving disputes, judges apply the law when it is clear, bring clarity when there is uncertainty, develop the law (to some extent) as changing circumstances require, and set precedents that influence later cases. The judgments of courts differ from all other decisions in society—they are binding, enforceable, and backed ultimately by the coercive powers of the state.

Our courts therefore bring peace and security in the personal lives of citizens, they promote stability in the commercial world, discourage and punish unacceptable conduct, and provide balance in the affairs and operations of governments. The daily activities of independent courts reinforce commonly held values and deepen social cohesion. Civilized democracies and market economies could not function effectively without them.

Courts matter.

The social, economic, and political functions of courts and judiciaries therefore extend well beyond their widely recognized role in publicly resolving disputes. Courts make vital constitutional and jurisprudential contributions that are often overlooked.

Constitutional significance

Constitutionally, it is often said that an independent judiciary is one of three elements that make up the modern state, the others being the legislature and the executive. Classical political theory speaks of a 'separation of powers' between these elements, so that none has sweeping capabilities than can be exercised without check or limitation by another. An independent judiciary, in England for instance, is commonly called upon to conduct judicial reviews of executive decisions. In some countries, such as the US, Supreme Courts can strike down legislation as unconstitutional. Judges hover at the shoulders of politicians and public officials, imposing legal conscience, poised to enforce the law of the land.

The courts are of constitutional significance in another way, relating to the 'rule of law'. I use this term tentatively because it is invoked today in many different ways. In his book, *The Rule of Law*, Lord Bingham explains why he chose in 2006 to give a public lecture bearing the same title:

> [B]ecause the expression was constantly on people's lips, I was not quite sure what it meant, and I was not sure that all those who used the expression knew what they meant either, or meant the same thing.[1]

I enjoy this passage because I do often wonder what people have specifically in mind when they speak enthusiastically and often portentously about the rule of law. Drawing on the work of Lord Bingham and others,[2] when I speak of the rule of law, I take the following five elements as constituting a working definition.

First, the rule of law requires that laws of the land should apply equally to everyone, to public officials as much as to private persons, and to all citizens, whatever their gender, religious, racial, or ethnic origin. Second, these laws should emanate from authoritative law-making bodies and should be available, understandable, consistent, relatively stable, not applied retrospectively, and generally observed by citizens and officials. Third, the state should provide an accessible, independent court service, underpinned by fair procedures with judges who settle disputes over the rights and duties of legal persons by applying and enforcing the law. Fourth, the powers of the state are limited by law and citizens are protected by legal rights that governments are under an obligation to uphold, and do in fact uphold. Fifth, the state should recognize and comply with its international legal obligations.

If all states ticked these five boxes, our world would be a much safer and happier place.

The courts and judges are central to the rule of law in two ways. First of all, any state or community that lacks an independent state-based dispute resolution service cannot be said to uphold the rule of law. Second, an independent judiciary is a daily public reminder of the importance of the rule of law. In regularly applying, upholding, and enforcing the law, the courts are emblematic of the authority and bindingness of the law.

The rule of law can be compromised in various ways. In some dictatorships, we see unambiguous breaches—arbitrary rule-making, institutionalized discrimination, officials who operate above the law, kangaroo courts, arbitrary detention, and frequent contravention of international treaty obligations.

Other infractions are less blatant. A court system that is antiquated, detached, unaffordable, slow, or unintelligible, can weaken confidence in the judicial process. In turn, the rule of law can be relegated to a nebulous and unrealized aspiration. Unless courts and judges are perceived to lie at the heart of social order—for example, in awarding damages, enforcing contracts, convicting criminals, settling divorces, and so forth—the rule of law runs the risk of being devalued. Likewise, if courts are not seen frequently to affirm the authority of the law over citizens and law-makers alike, then the rule of law no longer prevails.

Alternative dispute resolution (ADR), such as private sector mediation services, also presents a challenge to courts and the rule of law. As Hazel Genn notes, ADR services have often 'grown out of a *failure* of the civil courts' and moreover 'can be a means of citizens side-stepping legal systems in which the public have no confidence'.[3] The same can be said of private sector online dispute resolution services (ODR—Chapter 5). The threat here is to both aspects of the rule of law. If private sector service were to be routinely preferred to public courts, we would be in danger of being governed less by the law of the land than by compromise, unpredictable social norms, and the market itself, none of which seek directly and publicly to uphold justice. We can say of ODR what Hazel Genn says of mediation, that the outcome, 'is not about *just* settlement, it is *just about settlement*'.[4] And we should worry in consequence that we might lose the daily presence of the courts as confirmation of the authority and pervasiveness of the law.

Jurisprudential function

Turning now to what I term the jurisprudential function of the courts, I have in mind here, certainly in common law jurisdictions, the law-making function of the courts. In the world of legal philosophy, the actual and acceptable limitations of this function are hotly disputed. Some argue that the job of judges is no more than to interpret and apply the law, others contend that judges must have a role to play in clarifying the law where it is unclear or apparently silent, while yet others maintain that judges do and should have a wider mandate and responsibility to develop new legal principles. There are many respectable views in between. Even on the most restricted conception of judicial discretion, however, most judges, lawyers, and commentators would agree that the courts have played a central role in developing legal doctrine—in broad terms, when judges come to decisions in particular cases, they sometimes (depending on the level of court) also set precedents that bind or persuade later courts. And in a remarkable, often haphazard, evo-lutionary manner, a body of authoritative law extends at the hands of judges alongside that created by legislators. Ronald Dworkin likened this process (founded in England and exported across the world) to the enterprise of a group of authors collaborating in the production of a 'chain novel', each contributing a chapter:

> [E]ach novelist in the chain interprets the chapters he has been given in order to write a new chapter, which is then added to what the next novelist receives ... Each novelist aims to make a single novel of the material he has been given, what he adds to it ... He must try to make this the best novel it can be construed as the work of a single author rather than, as is the fact, the product of many different hands.[5]

In this spirit, judge-made law (case law) evolves. This is a vital function of courts, at least in common law countries.

Why disputes arise

It might be asked, more fundamentally, why disputes arise in the first place and whether they are in some sense an unavoidable and necessary feature of society. They may not be strictly necessary, but there is overwhelming empirical evidence to suggest that when human beings gather in communities and organizations, they do tend to have disagreements. Even in times of peace and in civilized communities, we find overlapping interests, frank rivalry, and outright competition, all of which can bring people into some kind of conflict, from mild to extreme. Because human beings are limited in their generosity, their natural resources are finite, and they often lack will power, disputes are bound to arise.[6] It would be an extraordinary society whose citizens were never in dispute and which, in turn, would have no need for law and courts. This would require a level of interpersonal accord that is scarcely conceivable. Aristotle points us in a helpful direction when he observes that, 'when men are friends, they have no need of justice'.[7] In contrast, when men are acquaintances, associates, strangers, or rivals, we might well expect that disagreements and conflicts are all but inevitable.

Disputes also arise because of the nature of the law. The wording of legislation and regulation can be unclear—for example, some pervasive terms like 'reasonable' can be vague, while other everyday words, like 'vehicle', can be 'open-textured', so that it may not be obvious, to use an old classic, if a rule prohibiting vehicles in public parks extends to skateboards or even to trucks being driven as part of a memorial ceremony.[8] At the same time, the interpretation of case law can be challenging, given there is no single, canonical way of determining what parts of any given judgment constitute the definitive rule or principle for which the case stands. Judges are often called upon to bring clarity where the law is uncertain in these respects.

However, it does not follow from humans' tendency to conflict and from the uncertain nature of the law that we should unreflectively embrace the current apparatus that our justice systems have in place for the handling of disputes—courts, lawyers, procedure rules, buildings. This apparatus should be understood in the context of the print-based society in which they evolved. But in the digital age, when conventional justice systems are creaking, we should be open to the possibility of fundamental change.

Chapter 2
The Case for Change

More people in the world now have access to the internet than access to justice. According to the Organisation for Economic Co-operation and Development (OECD), only 46 per cent of human beings live under the protection of the law,[1] whereas more than 50 per cent of people are now active users of the internet in one way or another.[2] Annually, one billion people are said to need 'basic justice care' but in 'many countries, close to 30 per cent of problem-owners do not even take action'.[3] As for public funding of legal and court services, it was found in a leading global study of legal aid, involving 106 countries, that around one-third 'have not yet enacted specific legislation on legal aid' and that the 'demand for legal aid for civil cases is largely unmet in most countries.'[4] Meanwhile, the courts of some jurisdictions are labouring under staggering backlogs—for example, 100 million cases in Brazil (as noted), and 30 million in India. Even in those legal systems that are described as 'advanced', court systems are under-resourced, and the resolution of civil disputes invariably takes too long, costs too much, and the process is unintelligible to ordinary people. The broad case for change is self-evident—in varying degrees, the court systems of our world are inaccessible to the great majority of human beings.

England and Wales

Take England and Wales as a case study. Here we have a widely ad-mired court system that is in many respects an international leader. We have an outstanding judiciary that is notably independent, and we have world-class barristers and solicitors. Our common law system has been central to law and order in our country and in-fluenced the development of many jurisdictions around the world. Our commercial courts are recognized as a global forum of dis-tinction, while the fairness of the British criminal trial is frequently celebrated. Our legal profession is a major contributor to the na-tional economy.[5] Moreover, we have a rich history of eminent judges, jurists, advocates, and a substantial body of long-standing and valued traditions.

And yet, our system is broken in many ways. Most judges and lawyers would agree with Hazel Genn's observations that our courts are under-resourced, in a 'sorry state', and that some public areas are even 'run down and squalid'.[6] A day in court in these buildings can be very challenging for those who are physically dis-abled. Meanwhile, in an era of ever more complex law and regula-tion, public legal aid has been reduced by around 20 per cent in the past five years.[7] Before this, '[i]n the 1980s, 80 per cent of house-holds were eligible for legal aid. By 2008 that figure had dropped to 29 per cent'.[8] For most potential litigants—citizens and organ-izations alike—our court system has certainly become too costly and too slow. The workings of the courts are indecipherable to all but lawyers. For everyday legal issues, the language and pro-cesses of the court are excessively complex and antiquated, despite various reforms over the past few decades. Parties who retain legal advisers have clear advantages over those who cannot. Judges are called upon to decide cases that often do not require their levels of knowledge and experience (I hear this regularly when training judges on technological matters).

Overwhelmed by paper and routine administration, the operations of the court system are increasingly out of place in a digital society in which so much other daily activity is enabled and augmented by the internet and advanced technologies. Conceived in the dark ages and reformed radically in the nineteenth century, our court system seems otherworldly for the generation of people coming through to adulthood, who socialize and work online, and for whom the expensive, slow, incomprehensible, and quite combative techniques seem outmoded. Consider also the estimate that disagreements arise in 3–5 per cent of online transactions which led, in 2015, globally, to over 700 million e-commerce disputes,[9] and bear in mind too that the UK is the third largest e-commerce market in the world.[10] A conservative extrapolation would suggest that tens of millions of online conflicts are already bypassing the court system of England and Wales, a system that in its current form is therefore ill-suited to the resolution of many twenty-first-century disputes.

This ineffective court system sits on a shaky foundation of law-making. The law of the land emanates largely from legislatures and subsidiary bodies that are under no obligation to alert citizens to new law or changes in old. And even if non-lawyers are able to determine what formal legal sources seem on the face of it to apply to their circumstances, the language of statutes, regulation, and law reports is impenetrable without legal training, and it is all but impossible to know whether a given law or case is still in force or binding.[11]

The impact of these shortcomings is profound. Justice is often not delivered. Entitlements remain poorly understood and invariably unenforced. Citizens are excluded and feel disconnected. In turn, public confidence in the system has diminished, along with morale amongst lawyers and judges. When only a minority enjoys access to an outstanding court service, the credibility of the entire institution is at risk and so, in turn, is the rule of law.

As Bertie Wooster might have observed to Jeeves, this is a rum state of affairs. Although I stand by the view of the previous chapter, that civilized democracies and market economies could not operate effectively without independent courts, it is hard to reconcile this with the everyday reality for most people. At a macro-level, most citizens live and work tolerably enough within a broad framework set by the law and enforced by the courts, but on a daily basis they do so in the pale shadow of the law rather than through any deep connection. Even if the funding were available to them, citizens are often not familiar enough with the law to recognize that they have reason to take legal advice in the first place. Most people sit somewhere on a spectrum from feeling consciously alienated from the law to muddling through unconsciously. Meanwhile, the lucky minority who understand the law and can afford lawyers and court service are greatly advantaged. The case for change in England and Wales seems unassailable, even though it is often held out as a paragon.

Globally, it is surely intolerable that more than half of the world's citizens live beyond the protection of the law. Traditional courts and lawyers may well remain necessary for our future, but they are certainly not sufficient.

What kind of change?

There are two broad ways that change can be effected in a court system. The first is evolutionary and incremental, and involves improving the current system, in part by introducing new efficiencies and partly by securing greater state funding. By and large, this is the tack preferred by most judges and lawyers. Their refrain is that the basic system is well-tested and well-proven, there are clear opportunities for running a much tighter ship, and it is a scandal that today's courts are so poorly resourced. On this view, the way to restore acceptable levels of service is to invest in process improvement, through a host of small, tactical adjustments and refinements, and to automate inefficient manual processes.

The second type of change to a court system is radical, and requires the current set-up or great parts of it to be superseded swiftly rather than improved over time. If technologies are involved, they should bring transformation, rather than simply automating conventional processes. This view is shared by a growing number of activists, within and beyond the legal profession, who are arguing for radical change, claiming that today's system is irretrievably broken or unfit for purpose.

These incrementalists and radicals are poles apart and come with their own phrase-books. The incrementalists advocate that we proceed in 'baby steps'. They maintain that reform is a more realistic aspiration than revolution, and warn against trying to 'boil the ocean'. The radicals, on the other hand, impatient with what they perceive as the short-term pursuit of 'low-hanging fruit' and 'quick wins', maintain that an incremental approach will, at best, only deliver 'mess for less', and they argue that grafting new technology onto antiquated processes delivers little more than 'putting after-shave on a pig'. While the two schools battle it out, most court technologists sit somewhere in the middle of the spectrum between them.

To put my cards on the table, I am much nearer the radical end. I expect the transformation to be incremental and ongoing but I fall short of being a full-on, fully bearded revolutionary.

Chapter 3
Advances in Technology

Many lawyers and judges are uneasy when speaking about technology. They bemoan the jargon of technologists, oblivious to the irony that legal experts are greatly superior purveyors of jargon. One of the difficulties here is that technology can be discussed at different levels. When some people talk about technology, for example, they are discussing particular systems that they use, packages and apps, such as PowerPoint and Twitter. This is not a book about packages and apps. Others speak about more general, enabling technologies, such as artificial intelligence (AI), robotics, natural language processing, and blockchain. I say quite a lot about various enabling technologies in the pages that follow because a failure to grasp their impact is to fail to grasp how court service is likely to change.

Another level of conversation about technology focuses on functions and tasks (what systems actually do) and what benefits should follow (cost savings, productivity gains, or the like). Much of this book proceeds at that altitude, as well as at a strategic level, looking at the overarching long-term impact of given technologies.

Automation and transformation

Technology can affect the work of courts in two broad ways, corresponding closely to the two types of change noted in Chapter 2.

On the one hand, systems can be used to improve, refine, stream-line, optimize, and turbo-charge our traditional ways of working. This is what most judges and lawyers (and most professionals, for that matter) have in mind when they give some thought to tech-nology. They reflect on routine, repetitive, and often antiquated tasks and activities in their courts and imagine (correctly) that some set of systems could be introduced to bring new efficiencies and make life easier. This first broad approach to court technology is a form of process improvement. I call it 'automation'. It involves grafting new technology onto old working practices. And it has dominated the theory and practice of court technology over the last 50 years or so.

On the other hand, technology can play a very different role. It can displace and revolutionize conventional working habits and bring radical change—doing new things, rather than old things in new ways. I refer to this as a specific type of 'transformation'.[1] This is about using technology to allow us to perform tasks and deliver services that would not have been possible, or even conceivable, in the past. The impact of transformative technologies can be pro-found. Online banking is an everyday illustration. As are online digital music services. These services are not trimmed and polished variations on old themes. They blast the old approaches out of the water. Transformation brings 'disruption' whereas automation sus-tains traditional ways of working.[2]

While automation is reassuringly familiar, the dominant general trend in the world of technology is very clearly towards transform-ation. This is apparent in transport, for example, with the advent of driverless cars, in manufacturing with its deployment of robots, in financial services with the introduction of systems like algorithmic trading and blockchain, in the professions with the increasing use of AI, and across government with the growing interest in 'big data'.[3] For now, the technical details of these technologies are less important than recognition that technology is bringing fundamental change across society. It is not simply automating practices of the past.

Online courts, as proposed here, are a clear illustration of transformation and not automation. The technologies envisaged will not simply sustain or streamline our current court systems. They will not simply graft new technology onto old processes. Instead they will transform, disrupt, and bring radical change. They will allow us to deliver court services in ways that were neither feasible nor imaginable a few years ago.

During my first decade of working on technology in law, from the early 1980s to the early 1990s, online courts and online dispute resolution were in no-one's contemplation, because the web had not yet been invented. Although enthusiastic legal technologists beavered away on their early PCs, Macs, and mini-computers, and some were even networked, the reality was that we were isolated islands, processing on our own. In that period, people of a practical inclination spoke of, wrote of, and developed systems in support of court administration while those interested in the future speculated, largely in the spirit of science fiction, about whether it might be possible for AI to replace judges and whether that might be a good thing.

It is understandable but wrong-headed to think that technologies that bring transformation must be advanced and complex, whereas automation is technologically simpler. In fact, many of the world's most sophisticated and advanced systems do no more than automate highly complicated pre-existing processes. Airline booking and scheduling systems are one example. At the same time, some of the highest-impact transformations are technologically quite primitive (ATMs and cash dispensers, for instance). So it is with the first generation of online courts, as introduced in this book. They rely very largely of course on the formidable technological infrastructure of the internet and the world wide web (online courts would not be possible without these technologies), but many of the basic systems that sit on this foundation are fairly primitive in technical terms. However, as envisaged in Part IV of this book, later generations of more advanced systems, based on machine learning and AI (and other technologies), are coming over the horizon. These are likely to bring much greater upheaval.

Technological developments

To understand online courts, past and future, it is important to have a basic grasp of the main developments in the world of technology. All technologists have their own ways of explaining the remarkable times in which we live, an era of greater and more rapid technological advance than humanity has ever witnessed. My own preferred way of introducing technology (by which I mean *digital* technology) was first laid out in *The Future of the Professions*, where we suggest that the great advances in technology can be understood under four headings.[4]

First, as is commonly observed, technology is advancing at an exponential rate. My starting point in understanding this trend is 'Moore's Law', which is not a law of the land, but a prediction made in 1965 by Gordon Moore, the man who co-founded Intel. In broad terms, he projected that, every two years or so, the processing power of computers would double. Doubters at the time claimed that this rate of growth would not last for more than a few years. But there have been more than 30 of these doublings since, and computer scientists, material scientists, and industry analysts say that processing power is likely to continue burgeoning for the foreseeable future (although not indefinitely using silicon). In his remarkable book, *The Singularity is Near*, Ray Kurzweil explores the future consequences of Moore's Law, if it continues to hold. By 2050, according to Kurzweil, the equivalent of an average desktop machine will have more processing power than all human brains on earth.[5] You may call me extreme, but it seems to me that if we can anticipate the day on which the average desktop machine has more processing power than all of humanity combined, then it might be time for us to rethink at least some of the working practices of our courts.

Notice also that this exponential growth in processing power is mirrored in many other aspects of technology (from the number of transistors on a chip to hard disk capacity, computer memory, bandwidth, and more). Consider the little memory card that we have in our digital cameras. In 2005, a good card had a capacity of 128 megabytes. Fast-forward less than ten years and, by 2014, a good card could store 128 gigabytes. That is more than a 1,000-fold increase in less than ten years. As I write, the first 1 terabyte card has just appeared on the market. The advance is relentless. So too with the amount of data. In 2010, Eric Schmidt, the former chairman of Google, said that every two years we create as much information as we did from the dawn of civilization until 2003. Extrapolating forward, by the early 2020s, we will be creating that much information every hour or so.

This explosive advance in underpinning technologies is fuelling a second trend, that our systems are becoming 'increasingly capable'. This is perhaps the most fundamental point to grasp, and it has profound implications for the future of professional work and public service. Scarcely a day passes that we are not assailed by news of some new innovation, technology, advance, breakthrough, or app. Our systems are able to do more and more. In the practice of law, for example, often at a higher standard than junior lawyers, we now have systems that can draft documents, undertake due diligence work, isolate the most relevant documents from litigation bundles, predict the outcome of deals and disputes, and offer legal guidance. And we now have more than 2,000 legal technology start-ups around the world (there were fewer than 200 but five years ago), many of which are focused precisely on extending the range of legal tasks that systems can take on. More generally, some entrepreneurs aspire to do to legal work what Amazon have done to bookselling.

Further, we can see our machines steadily taking on a growing number of capabilities that not long ago we thought were uniquely human, such as the capacity to solve problems and to answer questions; or systems that can perform psycho-motor or manual tasks (the province of robotics); or systems that can paint, or write poetry or symphonies; or systems that can detect and express emotions. There is a system, for example, that can look at a human smile and tell, more accurately than human beings, whether or not that smile is fake or genuine (this, from the field of affective computing). As I explain in Chapter 26, when I discuss AI, we must be careful not to assume that these systems operate in the same way as humans. They assuredly do not.

The result of these increasingly capable machines, in part, is what Daniel Susskind calls 'task encroachment' which means machines are taking on more and more of the chunks of work that people do.[6] More than this, though, given the explosive growth in the underpinning technologies—not least burgeoning processing power, their ability to handle truly vast amounts of data, and ever more sophisticated algorithms—emerging systems are able to take on tasks that cannot be done by humans at all. One illustration of this is the technology known as blockchain—'an open, distributed ledger that can record transactions between two parties efficiently and in a verifiable and permanent way'.[7] This much-vaunted technology does not automate some pre-existing human processes. While it might be thought simply to replace, for example, old-fashioned registers and filing systems, it brings so many new features that it would be misguided to think this is a substitute for some traditional human tasks and procedures. Likewise with virtual reality (VR, see Chapter 25) which provides online environments in which we can socialize, play games, trade, and much more. VR is not a displacement of some longstanding human service or task. The technology offers an entirely new experience.

The third major trend in technology is that our systems are becoming increasingly pervasive. I am not simply referring here to, say, the handhelds, tablets, and laptops that have come to dominate our lives. I also have in mind the 'internet of things', a term that refers to the presence of chips in everyday objects, so that they are directly controllable by humans and are connected to one another across the internet. By 2020, it is predicted that more than 25–50 billion objects will be linked in this way; and in due course that 99 per cent of physical objects will be connected to a network.[8] Buildings, parts of buildings, and furniture within structures will also be hooked up. Courts will not be exempt. We can also expect a growing number of embedded sensors in these same physical entities, capturing images, recording sounds, and monitoring, measuring, and scanning much else going on in the world around us. These chips and sensors will also be embedded in human beings, at first for medicinal purposes but in due course to enhance our capabilities. Over time, all these developments will lead us no longer to regard computing and technology as something that happens exclusively in sleek metallic objects with screens. Humans will be increasingly integrated with machines.

The fourth trend in technology is that human beings are becoming increasingly connected. There are many aspects to this. Using technologies from email to telepresence, humans are now able to *communicate* in ways that were not just unavailable but were unimaginable to our ancestors. At the same time, the web has become our first port of call whenever we want to undertake *research* on any conceivable subject. It has also provided many platforms, such as Facebook (over two and a quarter billion users) that enable users to *socialize* online. People who are connected across the internet tend to *share* online too—photographs, video clips, presentation slides—and so on (YouTube, for example, has 1.3 billion users, and five billion of its videos are watched daily). It is increasingly common as well for users to *build communities* online, both public (LinkedIn—over 500 million users) and private (in medicine, Sermo is a closed social network with over 800 thousand doctors, while PatientsLikeMe plays host to 600,000 patients).[9]

It is also increasingly common for users to *co-operate* online. Take Wikipedia, 'the free encyclopedia that anyone can edit'. Around 300,000 editors have edited Wikipedia with more than 1.8 edits per second. In all, the Wikipedia community has contributed 40 million articles in over 290 languages. In the same spirit is the phenomenon known as open source software. Linux, for example, the most commonly used operating system, is the result of mass collaboration amongst more than 15,000 developers from more than 1,400 companies.[10]

Another new way in which humans connect online is when they *crowdsource* which involves drawing on networks of people to carry out pieces of work or to raise finance for given initiatives. Huge numbers of humans also now *trade* online. Online shopping now accounts for around 18 per cent of retail spending in the UK. And eBay has become a global phenomenon—in the fourth quarter of 2018, there were almost 180 million active buyers on this platform, casual and accomplished users alike. A related set of networks enable and encourage people to *compete* with one other and to be ranked against their competitors.

In summary, when more than four billion human beings are on-line, new behaviours and activities blossom. People communicate and look for information in very different ways from a pre-digital world. More, they are also able to socialize, share, collaborate, build communities, crowdsource, compete, and trade in a manner and on a scale that was not possible in an analogue world.

No finishing line

Remarkable though these four sets of developments might be, what at once excites and unsettles me most is that there is no apparent finishing line. No-one in Silicon Valley, China, or South Korea is dusting their hands off, proclaiming, 'job done'. Nor is anyone there advocating that we might pause and take breath for a while, or plateau for a couple of years. No-one in the world of tech seems to be saying 'enough is enough'. Enough, it seems, is not nearly enough. In fact, the pace of technological change itself is accelerating. This follows from the scale of current investment in technology, both capital and brain power. It is huge and growing. With this in mind, the least likely future is that there will be no further breakthroughs; and that the technologies we see today represent the end-point in technological innovation (although at least one eminent scholar has argued to the contrary).[11] It seems to me much more likely than not that by say, 2030, our daily lives (and our courts) will have been transformed by what I call 'as-yet-uninvented' technologies. I cannot prove this to be so, but our trajectory, our general direction, is towards radical change rather than more of the same. In technology and in court technology, we are still at the foothills or, as Kurzweil would say, at the 'knee' of the exponential curve.[12]

Information sub-structure

Consider the law and court service from another perspective. At the heart of both is legal information (from legislation and case reports through evidentiary material to knowledge held in lawyers' heads). Now think about information. We are currently seeing a change in what I call the 'information sub-structure' of society. I introduced this term in 1996 in *The Future of Law* to refer to the principal way that information is captured, shared, and disseminated.[13] I agree with anthropologists who say that human beings have moved through four fundamental stages of information sub-structure: the era of orality, when communication was dominated by the spoken word; the age of script; then print; and today a world in which communication is very largely enabled by technology. (There will likely be a fifth—perhaps the epoch of transhumanism, when humanity, technology, robotics, nanotechnology, and genetics converge.)

For now, I suggest, we are reaching the end of a transitional phase between the third and fourth stages of development, between a print-based society and a digital society. For law, the big message is that the information sub-structure in society determines to a considerable degree how much law we have, how complex it is, and how frequently it changes. It also determines who is able, knowledgeably and responsibly, to advise upon it and administer it. If we study the way that the law has evolved through history, we can understand some of the changes in terms of transitions in information sub-structure. At its core, then, law and court work are information-based. And we live in an age when we are greatly enhancing our capacity to process information. It is not outrageous to claim that the work of judges and courts is unlikely to emerge unscathed. Today's courts were designed for a different epoch.

Back in 1996, this line of thinking led me to predict a 'shift in legal paradigm'.[14] By this, I meant that many or most of our basic assumptions about legal service and legal process would be fundamentally challenged by technology and the internet. At that time, I made a twenty-year prediction. Although it is not for me to mark my own homework, I venture that the direction of travel I plotted then has turned out to be fairly accurate, even if we are running about five years behind my schedule.

I accept that the radical change being brought by technology is unsettling and sometimes worse. Concerned parents and disillusioned students often ask me how I feel about a world in which the traditional work of lawyers and judges may be, as they see it, under siege. I take a different view. I believe it is a privilege to be alive at this time of unprecedented change, at a time when young aspiring legal professionals, along with their senior colleagues, can play a central role in shaping tomorrow's legal profession and court systems. I go further and say that it is the duty of all lawyers and judges to be involved.

Biases

No discussion of technology for lawyers and judges would be complete without acknowledgement of a set of biases that are encountered daily in conversation and in written materials. I have selected three that pervade debates about online courts. The first is 'status quo bias' which is a tendency to resist change, a preference for carrying on as we are today. Like all professionals, only more so, lawyers are conservative.[15] One manifestation of this bias is the special pleading at which lawyers are so effective. They accept that change is necessary, they see some scope for improving current processes, but they strongly resist any shifts that are transformative.

They are incrementalists rather than radicals, in the language of Chapter 2. More, they often claim that their own particular fields of endeavour are somehow out of scope. Often this special pleading is reinforced by a well-practised form of argument—the argument from 'hard cases'. For example, many lawyers challenge the idea of online courts by invoking celebrated cases such as *Donoghue* v *Stevenson*. How on earth, they ask, would an online court handle that case? The short answer is that in first-generation online courts, in which it is human beings who are making all the decisions, judges at first instance would likely deal with such cases much as they would do today. The bias point here, though, is that rather than conceding that many everyday challenges might indeed be handled in new ways, the critic focuses on the atypical. This can mislead and distract, and should be challenged. This bias, at its heart, I believe, is a failure to understand the needs of others.

A second common bias is 'irrational rejectionism', mentioned in the Introduction. I define this as the dogmatic dismissal of a system with which the critic has no direct personal experience. With no sense of embarrassment, lawyers frequently reject the idea of on-line courts having neither seen them in action nor taken the time to learn what is actually being proposed. Without reference to the problems that online courts might actually solve, appeals are im-mediately made to access to justice, problems and objections flow freely while operational systems are summarily dismissed. Without so much a glance at a screen. Sometimes this bias is rooted in a fear of the unknown or a sense that judges and lawyers know best when it comes to reform of the courts. Often it is based on an honest instinct that what is envisaged is neither possible nor desirable. But, there can be little doubt that an unwillingness to keep an open mind to new technologies is a serious obstacle to progress.

A third bias is 'technological myopia', which is the inability to anticipate that tomorrow's systems will be vastly more capable than those of today and to recognize the likely implications of the well-nigh inevitable advances. This bias is largely a failure of imagination. It is to frame the future in terms of the shortcomings of current systems. It is to underestimate the power of tomorrow's systems by evaluating them in terms of today's technologies. I try hard here to fight against this bias. My purpose is not to assess the future of justice in terms of the systems we have today. It is to project ahead to likely future systems and consider their impact. It is not to walk backwards into the future.

Chapter 4

Outcome-thinking

I was invited in 2017 to speak about the future to a gathering of some 2,000 neurosurgeons. My opening statement was that patients do not really want neurosurgeons. What they want, I said, is health. For a particular type of health problem, I acknowledged that neurosurgeons are undoubtedly the best solution we have today. But I went on to say that this might not always be so, because fifty years from now, give or take, we will probably look back and think it primitive that we used to cut people's heads open. I wanted to challenge those present who felt that the future lay only in robotic neurosurgery, because, I said, surgery will surely not be with us in the long run—the health troubles to which neurosurgeons currently devote their energies will in due course be sorted by non-invasive techniques.

In speaking this way, I was encouraging a mindset that I call 'outcome-thinking' and one aim of this book is to apply and encourage the use of outcome-thinking in planning court services of the future.

Outcome-thinking can be invoked when considering the future of all professions and professionals. Take the world of architects. People do not generally want these experts either. What they really want, as Vitruvius recognized in the first century BC, are buildings that are durable, useful, and beautiful. Nor do taxpayers want tax accountants. They want their relevant financial information to be sent to the authorities in compliant form. More than 50 million Americans are now using online tools to submit their tax returns. Few seem to be mourning the loss of social interaction with their tax advisers. In a similar vein, I spoke in 2017 to a group of generals of the British army. My theme then was that 'citizens don't want soldiers; they want security'. The same point holds in quite different fields. Patients do not want psychotherapists. Roughly speaking, they want peace of mind. You get my drift.

All of this echoes the apocryphal anecdote that I have told for nigh on thirty years, about the manufacturer of power tools that tells its new recruits that they sell 'holes' rather than drills, because it is holes that their customers actually want.

The disconcerting message here for all professionals is that clients do not really want them. They want the outcomes that professionals bring. These outcomes have two dimensions—practical results (a job done) and emotional effects (an appropriate feeling, perhaps of reassurance or confidence).[1] And when these outcomes can be reliably delivered in new ways that are demonstrably cheaper, better, quicker, or more convenient than the current offering, we can expect the market to switch to the alternatives.

What does this mean for lawyers and the courts? It follows that litigants do not really want courts, judges, lawyers, rules of procedure, and the rest. More likely, they want not to have a problem at all.[2] Or to have their disputes resolved fairly and with finality. Or they might want vindication. Or someone to listen to and empathize with their grievances. Or an apology.

Many lawyers and professionals baulk at this line of outcome-thinking. They insist that what a client surely needs, and will always need, is a trusted adviser—an empathetic and expert human counsellor. But this is to confuse means with ends, to muddle up *how* we work with *what* we deliver. It is to assume that there is something intrinsically valuable, indispensable even, in our current ways of working. It is to fixate on today's processes and disregard their broader *telos* (a Greek word which means purpose or goal). I challenge this. I am not denying that the work of many professionals (surgeons, nurses, dentists, vets, and physicians, for instance) is often admirable and heart-warming, as well as socially beneficial. Nor am I denying that these professionals find their work satisfying and stimulating, lending their lives meaning and purpose.

I am questioning, however, whether the working practices of these and other professionals, in and of themselves, are of such value that they should be retained at all costs in the face of alternative services that clients and customers find preferable. I find myself, in other words, favouring the interests of patients over doctors, of clients over lawyers, and of students over teachers. Adam Smith helps me here. In the *Wealth of Nations*, he argues that '[c]onsumption is the sole end and purpose of all production; and the interest of the producer ought to be attended to, only so far as it may be necessary for promoting that of the consumer'.[3] Spot on.

Consider this thought experiment. Imagine that medical scientists developed an affordable vaccine whose widespread introduction would prevent the development of all cancers. Would we feel that we should limit its deployment to protect the livelihood and self-esteem of oncologists? I pick an extreme example, precisely because of the great contribution that today's oncologists make to our lives. Even then, I suspect we would come to conclude, for the sake of the community's health as well as for economic reasons— for the sake of *outcomes*—that we should sensitively phase out this branch of medical practice. It is not the purpose of ill health to keep doctors employed.

More generally, there is no obvious reason that many of today's professionals will not be displaced by increasingly capable systems and then fade from prominence, much as blacksmiths, tallow chandlers, mercers, and many trades became redundant in their day. People still want transport, candles, and silk today, but we have found new ways of satisfying these demands.

In the face of this potential assault, many professionals take comfort from *task-based* thinking. They analyse the work they currently do, they break it down into a set of component tasks, and then identify those that they think might be undertaken by machines and those that seem to be beyond the foreseeable capacities of the most advanced systems. When they reckon that a significant proportion of their current tasks cannot be taken on by machines, they feel safe. And their task-based rationalization is supported by most of the reports on the future of work being published by academics and consultants, and reproduced daily in the mainstream media. My message is that this kind of task-based thought is deeply flawed.

Consider legal and court work. Commentators and practitioners often insist that much of the work of lawyers is beyond the reach of technology. They will suggest, for example, and not unreasonably, that the work of court lawyers cannot be replaced by machines. How could a robot possibly appear as an advocate before a judge? The answer, of course, is that we are nowhere near this happening. But the story does not end here, because these traditionalists are asking and answering the wrong the question. Mistakenly, they are focusing on current ways of working rather than on whether the outcomes that court lawyers deliver might be achieved in very different ways.

Now consider the possibility of conducting some of the work of courts not by physically congregating in courtrooms and arguing in person, but by submitting evidence and arguments electronically to judges. The idea, for the first generation at least, is that the final decisions of the judges (still humans) will also be delivered in electronic form. The outcome of the court (the binding decision) is unchanged but the methods by which it is reached are transformed, with oral advocacy or lawyers in a courtroom *eliminated* from the process. It is no comfort that machines cannot replicate the work of advocates and deliver a soaring closing argument in the courtroom. The irreplaceability of the work of oral advocates becomes an irrelevance. Most of the systems that replace us will not work like us.

In considering the future of work more generally, then, the big question is not whether machines can take on the work that humans do. It is whether the *outcomes* of today's human labour can be delivered in different ways with the support of technologies. Task-based analysis of the impact of machines, relying often on the outdated distinction of labour economists between routine and non-routine work, greatly understates the extent to which the work of human beings will be taken on by AI.

All of that said, I recognize that outcome-thinking has at least three significant limitations. The first is that it is conceivable, at least in principle, that some working practices and processes are intrinsically valuable and important to retain for their own sake. I struggle to find examples of this but I leave it open to traditionalists to argue this case. Some lawyers will say that the courtroom is inherently of value in this way—as a generality I do not accept this, as this book shows.

The second limitation of my consequentialism (as philosophers might describe it) is that any novel processes that deliver the desired outcomes must be sustainable. There is little point in jettisoning old ways of delivering outcomes, if the new system is destined to run out of steam. In other words, we might need to retain some of the old system (people and processes) to feed the new one. (In the context of courts, I return to this in Chapter 7, when I introduce the idea of 'sustainable justice'.)

Finally, we should accept that the outcomes that clients and customers *want* may not be what they actually *need* or indeed what their communities might need. Inexpert consumers, crudely speaking, may not know what is best for them. Nor indeed might expert consumers. Steve Jobs made an interesting related observation when he observed that 'consumers don't know what they want until we've shown them'.[4] There is much in this. Consumers, users, clients, and customers cannot be expected, for instance, to keep up with AI and other advanced technological developments. Their current conceptions of what is desirable are constrained by what they think is possible.

But these three qualifications are peripheral to my main point for judges and lawyers which is that people do not really want you. They want the outcomes you bring. In a digital society, our challenge is to think deeply about our *telos* and find new ways to deliver long-established outcomes. In the long term, we will find that these will increasingly call for systems rather than traditional institutions and advisers.

Outcomes and courts

In the pages that follow, I frequently rely on outcome-thinking. It helps me make the case for online courts, encouraging me to focus on the benefits that court systems should bring rather than preserving traditional practices and processes for their own sake. I also use outcome-thinking as a lens through which to scrutinize particular features of today's justice system (for example, the physical hearing). This encourages me to look at the deeper purpose of these features rather than the current surface processes.

But what is the *telos* of judges? What outcomes do court users seek? What are the social and political purposes of courts? What are the constitutional and jurisprudential functions of courts? Answers to some of these questions already appear in Chapter 1, from which it is apparent that there is of course no simple common rejoinder. Some judges speak of their role in terms of resolving disputes, clarifying the law, and developing the law. Others speak of their promotion of higher ideals like access to justice and the rule of law. Court users, on the other hand, often simply want their problem solved with authority and finality. Or, as noted, they would like a public apology. Still others just want to get on with their lives. A tiny minority seek binding precedents. Regarding the social purpose of courts, policy-makers conceive of the law as bringing certainty in the affairs of humans, of promoting social cohesion, of delivering social justice. As for their political function, the courts are thought to promote the rule of law, and serve also as a restraint on possible excesses or misdemeanours in the executive and legislative branches of government. What about justice? Is it not the role of judges to ensure that justice according to the law is delivered? It certainly is and I devote Chapter 7 to analysing this in some depth.

For now, we can say that there is no single overriding outcome that we should expect of courts. There is a family of outcomes. This does not mean that outcome-thinking is of no use. On the contrary, this technique is intended to increase our concentration on consequences, to work hard when thinking about change to be sure that we have all relevant results in mind, and to resist the preservation of old processes for their own sake.

The most challenging question of all is whether there are any features of our current courts systems that are so intrinsically valuable or important that their replacement should be resisted even if a different approach can yield better outcomes. Should we, for example, in the name of the 'humanity of physical presence' or the 'majesty of law' (Chapter 20) insist on maintaining the tradition of physical hearings, even if online courts could greatly and reliably increase access to justice?

Chapter 5
Physical, Virtual, Online

Modern court systems can be traced directly to bodies that came into being around 900 years ago. There were of course much earlier courts (for example, the rabbinical courts known as 'Sanhedrin', in the first century BC) and certainly there were people in antiquity performing decision-making roles that we would recognize today as judicial in nature (in the works of Aristotle, for instance, and the magistrates and jurists of classical Roman Law). But today's judges in England and Wales descend more directly from their predecessors of the twelfth century who, in the first instance, were court officials charged with the responsibility of advising the King on the resolution of disputes. Henry II (1154–89) formalized proceedings and laid the foundations for the modern justice system by establishing an assembly of twelve local knights to settle disagreements over the ownership of land.

Much has changed since, although many of today's court processes and sometimes even the buildings themselves have not altered greatly since the nineteenth century. Since the twelfth century, though, in script and then print-based societies (see Chapter 3), there have been three components at the heart of the judicial function—people called judges, following formal procedures, sitting in places called courts. It is hard to see how the service could have been rendered differently. The next phase in the evolution of courts will be heavily influenced by legal and court technologies: in a digital society, therefore, a fourth component will be introduced—the online environment—both supporting and challenging the traditional set-up.

Etymologically, the term 'court' comes from French, Latin, and Ancient Greek, in each case referring to an enclosed space or yard. As we move from physical courtrooms to virtual hearings and online courts, we need not jettison this meaning. To anticipate later themes, the online court may indeed come to be regarded as a safe online space in which justice can be secured.

Physical courtrooms

Most citizens have never actually been in a courtroom, and yet in their mind's eye they may well have a moderately clear, and frequently quite romantic, view of how such a place looks and feels. Based largely on television and cinema, the common conception is of a high-ceilinged, old-fashioned room, panelled in a rich dark wood, and dominated by a raised bench at which the judge sits, in a chair upholstered perhaps in a soft, lush burgundy leather. The wall behind the judge will be adorned with a great crest, denoting who knows what. Around the room there will be law books stacked neatly on robust shelving. In this great theatre, the main actors are the lawyers and judges. They will be envisaged, in the UK at least, in wigs and gowns, making and defending their cases on behalf of their clients in a language that is no more intelligible to lay people than an exchange amongst surgeons in an operating theatre. It is here, in sombre and forbidding surroundings, that justice is done.

There are many courtrooms of the sort just sketched, especially in upper courts around the world, but in the name of modernity or as a result of public sector cuts, the reality is often more prosaic—harshly lit canteens of chrome and pale laminate, littered with screens and cables, carpeted in coarse tiles with insufficient adhesive, with walls painted in dirty off-white, and populated by lawyers and judges in unglamorous business apparel.

In either event, whether romantic or prosaic, this everyday impression of a court is certainly of a room where serious legal work is done—court is very much a place.

Some would go further and say that a court is necessarily a place. For example, in their magisterial tome, *Representing Justice*, Resnik and Curtis's reverence for court buildings sometimes verges towards a metaphysic that posits courts not just as symbolic of justice but somehow as constitutive of justice; that justice without courts is unimaginable if not conceptually impossible.[1] Lawyers and judges may not go quite so far but, emotionally and psychologically, they often find it hard to imagine serious judicial work being carried out anywhere other than in a physical courtroom.

Virtual hearings

In the early days of court technology, before the birth of the world wide web, one great advance in the 1980s was the use of video links between hearing rooms. With limited bandwidth and primitive compression techniques, the quality was not great. The connections were frequently lost and the high latency (delay) meant the participants at the other end presented as juddering puppet-like characters, and the mouth movements and sound were seldom in synch. In truth, it was not easy to discern any kind of facial impression, because users appeared as small figures in the corners of screens. Nonetheless, in countries like Australia, when major travel was otherwise needed for minor court appearances, attendance in court by video link became a respectable option.

Since then, there have been breathtaking advances in video and related technologies. While the most sophisticated systems, such as immersive telepresence, create a remarkable sense of being gathered together in the one place (see Chapter 25), even more modest systems, running as basic apps on laptops and handhelds (for example, Skype and Facetime) enable a very high level of interaction. Systems that, technologically speaking, sit between telepresence and mobile phone video-telephony, are widely installed in courts across the world (when I was in China in 2017, I was told that 20,000 video conferencing systems had just been installed in their courts in a handful of months).

There are two quite different uses of video technology in the courts. The first type is in fact a physical hearing into which some participants are linked by video. On this set-up, there is an actual courtroom with a judge and at least some parties and lawyers but, at the same time, some people take part remotely. In one way or another, this has been happening for several decades. Expert witnesses frequently give evidence by video from half-way across the world while vulnerable witnesses have been able to offer testimony without being intimidated by the people and the surroundings. It has also become common for some criminal hearings to be virtual in this sense. Bail hearings, for instance, are often conducted by video connection between the court and the prison. Again, there is a conventional hearing in a traditional physical court—the virtual element is the accused appearing on a large screen in the hearing room which saves costs (transporting and securing the accused) and is said by many prisoners to be more convenient and less harrowing. Most observers think that virtual hearings make sense for suitable cases. But they do have their detractors[2] and I turn to some of their concerns in Part III. For now, I am simply introducing the concept.

The second sort of virtual hearing is much rarer today. Here there is no physical event into which some people are connected by video. Instead, all participants are using video, including judges, lawyers, court clerks, witnesses, as well as parties to the dispute and sundry others. There are various enabling techniques used for these virtual hearings. On one approach, at any one moment, all users can see and hear whoever is speaking. Another sort of system might always have the judge visible, hovering at the top of the screen like some 'brooding omnipresence'.[3] In advanced systems, all users might be visible, arrayed perhaps like participants in the TV quiz show, University Challenge. More sophisticated still would be systems that arrange all or many of those linked in a way that resembles the appearance of a court. Using immersive telepresence technologies, participants might in fact feel that they are all gathered together in the one place. For the future, we can easily imagine this simulated courtroom to be rendered in 3D and, in due course, for a court to be held in some kind of virtual reality (see Chapter 25). What all these configurations have in common, in this second type of virtual hearing, is that there is no physical room in which arguments are heard, evidence is laid out, and decisions are handed down. Nonetheless, for court users it may still feel like a 'place'.

Lawyers and judges who have used video technology and been unimpressed with the performance of the systems should bear in mind that the enabling technologies are rapidly improving. Even the best systems (using immersive telepresence) are the worst they are ever going to be from now on. There is a danger here of technological myopia—denying the future potential of these systems on the basis of current technology. In a decade or so, we are likely, at the least, to be using augmented reality systems or perhaps even three-dimensional holographic services (see Chapter 25).

Online courts

As I say in the Introduction, I find it helpful to distinguish between two aspects of 'online courts', as currently conceived. The first I refer to as *online judging*. This involves the determination of cases by judges but the parties do not gather together in a bricks-and-mortar courtroom. Evidence and arguments are presented to judges through some kind of online platform and the judges then deliver their decisions not in open court or in any kind of virtual hearing room but again through the online service. Court proceedings are *not* conducted in one hearing by video link, or telephone conference call, or real-time chat. There is no hearing. Rather, like an ongoing exchange of emails and attachments, cases are progressed and disposed of, over a period of time.

In the language of technologists, the communication in physical courtrooms and virtual hearings is *synchronous* whereas online judging involves *asynchronous* forms of interaction.[4] This means that, for the former, the participants need to be available at the same time for a case to progress. In contrast, with the latter, as with email and text messages, those who are involved do not need to be on tap simultaneously—arguments, evidence, and decisions can be sent without sender and recipient being physically or virtually together at the same time.

This shift from a synchronous to an asynchronous court set-up is not a mere exercise in process improvement. It involves and requires radical change. It represents a much greater leap than the swing from physical to virtual hearings. Although virtual hearings give rise to great consternation, they belong in the same broad paradigm as traditional courtrooms. Online courts are a different idea altogether. Even in the first generation, where human judges are deciding the cases, online judging takes away much that many people hold dear—the public hearing, the day in court, the direct interaction with other human beings. On the other hand, it is likely to make court service much more accessible and affordable, and will chime with those who cannot recall a pre-internet world.

The second sense of online court is more general. I refer to it as *the extended court*. The idea here is that technology allows us to provide a service with much wider remit than the traditional court. The additional services include tools to help users to understand their rights, duties, and options open to them, facilities that assist litigants to marshal their evidence and formulate their arguments, and systems that advise on or bring about non-judicial settlement.

ODR

A field of study and activity that overlaps with online courts is that of online dispute resolution, more commonly referred to as 'ODR'. This phenomenon emerged in the 1990s as a branch of ADR (alternative dispute resolution). ODR was regarded at that time as a form of electronic ADR, with many techniques falling under its umbrella, including e-mediation, e-negotiation, and e-arbitration. Rather than meeting in person to conduct, say, mediations and negotiations, a variety of techniques were developed to sort out a wide range of disagreements informally and on an online basis—from consumer disputes to problems arising from e-commerce, from quarrels amongst citizens to conflicts between individuals and the state.

Amongst ODR pioneers, the main aim was not to develop systems to support human mediators and negotiators. More ambitiously, they sought to develop systems that parties could use to resolve disputes themselves without recourse to the conventional court system. I have long believed this to be fertile ground.

Although ADR proponents may protest, I think it fair to say that ADR has not entirely fulfilled its early promise. One of the drawbacks of traditional ADR is that parties and the neutral (for example, the mediator) still need to assemble in the same room, with all the cost and time involved. Like the conventional court system, it is still a synchronous process. To some extent, to the lay person, it may even feel quite court-like, relying on people with specialist knowledge and standard processes. Perhaps ADR is not sufficiently different from court service to enjoy the success that many expected of it. Non-lawyers might not really know the difference between a judge and a mediator, or an ombudsman or an arbitrator. In contrast, ODR—online and asynchronous—is really quite unlike conventional court service.

However, ODR of the sort just described does not sit in the public court system. It is still a form of ADR. In contrast, advocates of online courts propose that some of the techniques developed for ODR might actually be used within the court system—see Chapter 9.

Today, people often and understandably use the expressions 'online courts' and 'ODR' interchangeably. This can be confusing. Whereas online courts belong exclusively to the public sector, the term 'ODR' is used in both a wide and a narrow sense. In its wide sense, ODR refers, broadly, to any process of resolving a dispute that is largely conducted across the internet. This broad definition, therefore, includes the dispute resolution aspects of 'online courts'. Online courts use ODR techniques. The narrower sense of ODR equates ODR with electronic ADR ('e-ADR'), that is, the systems that are an alternative to public, state-based court service.

To avoid the confusion, I now prefer to restrict my use of 'ODR' to the narrower sense, of private-sector, electronic ADR. That is the convention I follow in this book—ODR belongs in the private sector, while online courts are a public service.

Blend

In practice, court services of the future will be delivered as a blend of some or all of physical courtrooms, virtual hearings, and online courts. It will become common practice, as a matter of case management, to disaggregate or decompose disputes into their component parts and to allocate each part to the most appropriate (efficient and just) process.[5] In this way, in one case, part of the work might be undertaken online, some in a courtroom, and yet other tasks in a virtual hearing room. And, over time, I expect that more and more elements will be conducted online. As noted in Chapter 9, there will be a shift away from the default that court work is conducted in a physical space to a presumption that it is carried out online.

Terminologically, 'online court' may well turn out, in the long run, to be an interim concept. When court service becomes a seamless blend of online service and conventional courtroom activity, court users may not feel the need to refer expressly to the 'online' aspect of the service. In the short term, however, there are advantages, practical as well as linguistic, in the idea of creating a distinct online court—an online service to which appropriate cases will be allocated; a court with a simplified body of rules; constructed from the ground up on the back of technology rather grafting technology onto existing court processes; and designed to be accessible to non-lawyers. Over time, I expect more and more work will be allocated to the online court and its use will become commonplace rather than exceptional. In due course, as its workload increases, many outdated practices of the conventional courts will be displaced. In this way, the online court will lead the way to a fully integrated online and physical court service, well-suited to the twenty-first century.

Chapter 6

Access to Justice

Two related phrases are commonly used in discussions about the courts and judges. The first is 'access to justice' and the second is 'justice according to the law'. Like motherhood and *apfelstrudel*, these seem to be ideals whose merits are beyond debate. However, some deeper digging suggests that the scope and meaning of these concepts are far from self-explanatory. They are innocuous enough as terms of art, and often deployed to lend some force or lustre to arguments about social and legal reform. But if we are to be clear about online courts and the future of justice, we need to be clearer about these fundamental notions. Accordingly, in this chapter, I explore and extend the concept of access to justice, arguing that much of the literature and debate on this topic is too narrowly conceived. I defer until the next chapter the notion of justice according to the law, where I argue that this is also a more complex notion than is generally allowed.

Access to justice

At the start of this book, I include a passage from the work of Franz Kafka. For years, this has both haunted and inspired me. Kafka was a tortured soul and trained as a lawyer (probably in that order).

He wrote incomparably about bureaucracy, authority, and exclusion. The extract itself is from a short story, *A Country Doctor,* which is analysed at length by Joseph K and the prison chaplain in Kafka's celebrated book, *The Trial.* It tells of an inscrutable gatekeeper who, for no apparent reason, refuses to grant a man from the country access to the law. The beleaguered man had not expected any problems. Surely, he thinks, 'the law should be accessible to everyone at all times'.[1]

Precisely.

In this spirit, for more than two decades, it has been fashionable, amongst policy-makers, consumer campaigners, law reformers, and commentators, to talk about increasing 'access to justice'. While no-one denies increasing access is a good thing, it is not at all clear what this actually requires in practice. As a meme, 'access to justice' began to take flight in the UK in the mid-1990s, when Lord Woolf's seminal reports used the phrase as their title.[2] His preoccupation at the time, consistent with much of the theory and policy work that followed, was improving access to less costly and more proportionate ways of resolving legal disputes in the courts.

While I warmly embrace any changes that make our courts and other methods of dispute resolution more efficient and accessible, I do not think that optimizing our current methods of dispute resolution of itself will secure a fully satisfactory system of justice. To be entirely or even mainly focused on the *resolution* of disputes in our pursuit of justice is, I submit, to miss much that we should expect of our legal systems. A broader view is needed.

A broader view

For some years now, I have argued that the concept of access to justice should embrace four different elements.[3] The first, of course, is dispute resolution itself. This is the central service of courts and a crucial component of all legal and judicial systems. Any credible justice system will offer some form of authoritative *dispute resolution*, a forum for the vindication of people's legal rights.

At the same time, second, we should also have better methods for *dispute containment*. Once disputes have arisen, we should want to be able to nip them in the bud. Failing this, we should try to ensure that our justice system's response to any dispute is proportionate and in the best interests of litigants. Sadly, institutional incentives embedded deeply both in the legal profession and in the courts tend to encourage the escalation rather than the containment of disputes. Because the dominant way that lawyers charge for their work and think about their services is still in terms of hourly billing, it is in the commercial interests of lawyers for disputes to continue rather than be concluded. At the same time, once in the court system, judges are generally (but not always) committed, by procedure and adversarial process, to tolerating combat, and to progressing cases according to the law rather than encouraging their resolution informally and pragmatically. It is a damning indictment of our court systems that most judges and professional litigators will strongly discourage their friends and families from becoming embroiled in litigation. It is of little reassurance that this has been the case for many years. Consider what the American judge, Learned Hand, had to say in 1926, almost a century ago: 'I must say that as a litigant I should dread a law suit beyond almost anything short of sickness and death'.[4] In truth, our system too often intensifies and exacerbates disputes rather than keeping their tone and scale commensurate with the nature and value of the disagreement in question. This leads me to identify this second sense of access to justice—our system should be as much about dispute containment as it is about dispute resolution.

My third sense of access to justice, *dispute avoidance*, is inspired by the world of medicine where it is commonplace to believe that prevention is better than cure. Immunization and vaccination are everyday features of our lives. All manner of awful ailments and illness are thereby avoided. I suggest that we should share this mindset in law. Most people, I expect, would rather avoid legal problems altogether than have them resolved by teams of lawyers. Most people would prefer a fence at the top of the cliff to an ambulance at the bottom (no matter how responsive or well-equipped that ambulance might be). If this is the case, then access to justice is not just a matter of dispute resolution and dispute containment. It is also about dispute avoidance. If lawyers are able, because of their training and experience, to recognize and avoid legal obstacles then, in a just society (one in which legal awareness and insight is an evenly distributed resource—see the next chapter and my discussion of distributive justice) we should want non-lawyers to be similarly equipped. Vaccinations are available to the public at large and not just to physicians and their families.

In law, this will largely require the introduction of new ways of putting legal know-how at the fingertips of all citizens and to a greater extent than has been feasible in the past. This readier, cheaper, and wider access to legal guidance should lead to a more distributively just society in the same way that immunization leads to a healthier community. Another consequence is also probable— wider understanding of the law and greater access to legal remedies may well nudge the unscrupulous (some landlords, for example) towards more compliant and honest conduct or at least discourage them from behaving unlawfully or exploiting others. In the past, they may have proceeded as they pleased, regardless of the law, safe in the knowledge that those who were suffering as a result were disincentivized from taking legal action precisely because the law and the courts were too costly, complex, or forbidding.

The medical analogy also helps us to identify a fourth dimension to the concept of access to justice—*legal health promotion*. I draw here from the work in recent decades on health promotion. We are counselled today to exercise aerobically for at least half an hour, three or four times a week, not simply because this will reduce the likelihood of, say, a stroke or coronary heart disease but also because it will make us feel much better. The idea of health promotion is not focused on the prevention of ill-health but on improving our physical and mental well-being. Similarly, I suggest, the law can also furnish us with ways in which we can promote our general well-being, and not only by helping to avoid or resolve problems. Readers who studied jurisprudence at university will remember Herbert Hart's seminal book, *The Concept of Law*, in which he distinguishes between 'duty imposing' and 'power conferring' rules.[5] This is a fundamental division. Hart made the point that most people, lawyers included, when they think of the law, tend to regard the law as duty-imposing—it requires, it obligates, it prohibits. But so much of the law is actually enabling. It is empowering. The law allows us to make wills, to get married, to contract with others. It affords all sorts of benefits, even if this is not the way it is most commonly conceived. The aim of legal health promotion is to help people, in a timely way, to know about and act upon the many benefits, improvements, and advantages that the law can confer, even when there is no perceived problem or difficulty. It is unsatisfactory that people often have legal entitlements of which they are entirely unaware, that there are legal benefits which they could secure if only they had the knowledge. In a distributively just system, it seems to me, people would not be disadvantaged in this fashion. And so, in contrast, I look forward to the day when we will be committed to legal health promotion underpinned by community legal services that are akin perhaps to community medicine programmes, except that they will be available very largely online.

Providing access to justice, in this fourth sense, will mean offering access to the opportunities that the law creates.

My line of argument in summary is this—when I talk of improving access to justice, I am referring to much more than providing access to quicker, cheaper, and less combative mechanisms for resolving disputes. I am also speaking of the introduction of techniques that deeply empower all members of society—to contain disputes that have arisen, to avoid disputes in the first place and, more, to have greater insight into the benefits that the law can confer. Today, even very capable people can feel disempowered when involved in legal processes. Tomorrow, we should want citizens to be able to own and manage many of their own legal issues.

So much for 'access to justice'. What about 'justice according to the law'? What does this involve?

Chapter 7

Justice According to the Law

In both promoting and challenging the idea of online courts, appeals are often made to the concept of justice. Supporters generally say that online courts will bring about greater access to justice, while critics foretell that justice will be denied. Given that 'justice' is so widely invoked in debate about online courts, it is important to clarify what this notion itself is all about.

If you are neither a philosopher nor a political theorist, you may think that justice is a pretty straightforward concept. But it turns out that the term is used in many different and conflicting ways, and even when people have the same conception of justice in mind they can disagree strongly over what it requires.

What is justice?

In trying to understand what justice is all about, most students of philosophy and jurisprudence are encouraged at the outset to start with the Greek philosopher, Plato, and his great work, *The Republic*. The book is written as a set of dialogues, led by the main protagonist, Socrates (named after Plato's teacher). Often to the exasperation of those within earshot, Socrates is a man who doggedly asks question after question after question.

He is searching for the truth. The concept of justice, roughly speaking, is his preoccupation in the opening pages of *The Republic*. There, he systematically demolishes attempts by a succession of hapless disputants who try to shed light. As an early, tentative characterization of justice, it is posited that 'it is right to give every man his due'.[1] Tricky questions arise, however, when we try to pin down what precisely it is that people are due and on what basis.

These questions have dogged thinkers for 2,000 years and we are still without definitive answers. But we have come some way in understanding the concept of justice much better. Modern thinkers like John Rawls and Amartya Sen have helped us and I draw on their and others' insights here to isolate what we might mean by 'justice according to the law'. In so doing, I cannot claim to come close to answering the age-old question, 'what is justice?', but I do want to show why online courts will lead to improved access rather than a denial of justice.

When lawyers and judges speak confidently about 'justice under the law' or 'justice according to the law', is the claim that the law delivers a type of justice that is somehow different from everyday ideas of justice? If we embrace these expressions, how can we make sense of the idea of an unjust law or unjust decision from the courts? Lord Devlin put it well:

> The first ... duty of the English judge is to administer justice according to the law. In this commandment has the phrase 'according to the law' a qualifying effect or is it just added to give *embonpoint* to the word 'justice' which might look, if made to stand by itself, too thin to be impressive?[2]

One of the complexities of 'justice' is precisely that the term is central not just to legal language but also to moral and political discourse.

Principles of justice

My main plan of action now is to propose a set of principles that seem to me to characterize 'justice according to the law'. I believe these principles should apply to all court systems, certainly in the western legal tradition, whether physical, virtual, online, or any mix of these. I have derived these from a variety of sources, but primarily they are rooted in legal and political theory, judicial writings, and public policy thinking. They are also rooted in my personal conviction, as laid out in the Introduction, that every human being deserves and should be accorded equal respect and dignity; and this should be enshrined in and enforceable by the law.

No firm ongoing distinction is drawn in the following analysis between a court system that is just and the just resolution of particular cases. In practice, when we talk about a just court system, we are generally speaking of a system that delivers both. Figure 7.1 summarizes the various conceptions of justice that I believe combine to deliver justice according to the law. In the remainder of this chapter, I expand upon each.

Substantive justice (fair decisions)

Procedural justice (fair process)

Open justice (transparent)

Distributive justice (accessible to all)

Proportionate justice (appropriately balanced)

Enforceable justice (backed by the state)

Sustainable justice (sufficiently resourced)

Figure 7.1 Conceptions of justice according to the law

Substantive justice (fair decisions)

When I say of a court system that it should deliver substantive justice I am suggesting, in broad terms, that its decisions and outcomes should be fair. This first principle might seem self-evident and uncontroversial. On more careful analysis, however, it transpires that the notion of substantive justice as fairness is far from straightforward.

An obvious starting point is to maintain that for a judicial decision to be fair, it must align with and implement the law that is actually in force. It is only fair that we are judged in accordance with whatever legislation and case law require of us. It is important in our daily activities that the law is to a great extent certain and predictable. Justice requires that judges apply the law as it is, rather than what they or others think it ought to be. We rely on judges to enforce our legal rights, as embodied in the current law.

It might be thought that there is little to further be said about substantive justice—a decision is substantively just if it accords with existing law. I disagree. When I think of judges in the Nazi regime, for example, I do not accept that many of their decisions should be said to be substantively fair. Because the underlying laws were iniquitous, many of their decisions, although consistent with these laws, were nonetheless morally abhorrent. I do not want to suggest that these laws were not laws at all; but I do want to claim that these decisions were substantively unjust.[3]

More generally, this means that for any judicial decision to be substantively just it is necessary but not sufficient that it upholds the law. We should also insist that our justice system delivers outcomes that are themselves *just*. But this step in the argument raises new problems. For starters, we are taken back to the question of 'what is justice?'. And simply replacing the grave term 'substantive justice' with the homelier word, 'fairness', does not really help us.

We are simply led after a moment of reflection to ask what fairness involves. Most people find themselves hard pressed to offer a precise and crisp characterization of fairness, although many will say they know it when they see it and especially when they see its converse, unfairness. This instinctive sense of fairness seems to be based on our personal, moral convictions (of what is right or wrong, good or bad) as well as a whole set of emotional and psychological phenomena, some of which we can recognize but many of which are no doubt unconscious.

One big difficulty here is that, in many circumstances, people can strongly disagree about what fairness involves or requires. Plato was onto this more than 2,000 years ago. Today our conventional and social media overflow with diverging views on whether certain judicial decisions—for example, on liability, damages, custody, alimony, criminal convictions, prison sentences—are equitable. Reasonable people (as well as unreasonable people) often differ over the fairness or otherwise of court decisions. Some people, for example, insist that the punishment should fit the crime, while others reject this retributivism and say that two wrongs do not make a right.

Is there some authoritative way of settling whether a decision by a judge is fair? Philosophers (strictly, meta-ethicists) would tell us that this depends on, very crudely, whether you are an objectivist (who believes in moral truths), a relativist (who argues that conceptions of right and wrong vary in different times and places), or a subjectivist (who maintains that there are no absolute moral truths).[4]

Today, relativism has a popular appeal. It is hard to deny that reasonable and unreasonable people often do disagree over the fairness of judicial decisions. Some people might even with disagree my view that many of the decisions of Nazi judges were morally abhorrent. How then do we settle what is right or wrong, morally acceptable or not? Do we accept a majority view? Philosophers will insist that rightness and wrongness are not settled by voting—even if 99 per cent of people believe a decision to be unfair, this does not mean that it is unfair in some objective definitive sense.

Philosophers will also point out, however, that even if there are no moral truths, we might still strongly favour one ethical theory of decision-making over another. Some, for example, will argue that we should judge the goodness of a decision by its consequences, while others will claim we should look at the intrinsic value of a decision. We are in murky waters here.

When we think about the determinations of judges and whether or not they are fair, a further distinction lurks—between decisions that are based on the application by judges of law that is clear as compared with those that involve greater judicial discretion (or, potentially, both). An unfairness could therefore derive either from laws that themselves are unacceptable (as in my Nazi example) or from a decision-making process that is defective.

Where does all of this leave us? First of all, we should treat with great caution any dogmatic declarations that a court system must deliver substantive justice, as though this were a straightforward notion. People disagree on many moral questions. Likewise, we should be wary when lawyers, activists, and commentators, dogmatically contend that any particular decision is fair or otherwise. Others might have different views that are respectable. Nonetheless, we should generally want our laws and judicial decisions to resonate with a community's shared values and sense of what is morally acceptable.

I take the view, in summary and tentatively, that substantive justice is delivered when the decisions of our courts apply existing law, they reflect a popular sense of right and wrong, but at the same time they formally protect the interests of minorities (preferably through a human rights regime). There can be no guarantee of universal unarguable fairness but we should want a system that, as a matter of fact, delivers outcomes and results that are generally regarded as fair by those involved, not least by parties, witnesses, and victims.

Procedural justice (fair process)

A second principle of justice relates not to the substance of a given court decision but to the processes by which any decision is reached. Often when there are allegations of injustice, it is procedural justice that is being questioned. A decision is considered unjust because it was handled in a manner that was in some way defective and inequitable. This takes us back to outcome-thinking and its two components as introduced in Chapter 4—practical results (a job done) and an emotional effect (an appropriate feeling). In the context of court decisions, participants want both a fair decision (a result that is substantively just) and the feeling that the process was fair.

Regarding procedural justice, again we need to do some unpacking to clarify what is involved. One aspect of this concept is referred to as 'formal justice', which is often characterized by some such phrase as 'like cases should be treated alike'. A great sense of injustice arises when, in apparently identical circumstances, people are dealt with differently. We value consistency and equal respect for persons, alongside the predictability and certainty that comes with formal justice.

A second aspect of procedural justice is known as 'natural justice'. I am using this term in a technical sense, frequently captured in two Latin phrases: *audi alteram partem*, which requires that all litigants should be the given the opportunity to state and defend their cases and *nemo iudex in causa sua*, which means that no-one should be a judge in his or her own case. These are fundamental components of procedural justice that chime with most people's sense of what is just. It feels right that parties in a case should have the opportunity to be heard, to explain their position, not to be muzzled or ignored; and that judges should not be called upon to settle disputes in which they have an interest.

The latter can be generalized as a third dimension of procedural justice—that judges should be honest, impartial, independent, and free of bias. More, they should work in a court system that is itself independent and supported by processes and procedures that are balanced and free of bias, including the methods that are used to allocate cases to judges to specific cases, the appointment of judges (favouring diversity as well as integrity), rules of procedure, and operational court processes. Procedural justice also requires judicial decision-making to be conducted uninfluenced by public officials (ministers and government, central and local), the media, pressure groups, political parties, friends, and colleagues.

A fourth and final component of procedural justice is sometime called 'corrective justice', in the Aristotelian sense. As Richard Posner explains, this involves,

> judging the case rather than the parties, an aspiration that is given symbolic expression in the statues of Justice as a blindfolded goddess—blindfolded because she is not seeing the individual characteristics of the parties and their lawyers.[5]

This interpretation of Aristotle is not mainstream but the underlying point is clear enough. It is a special call for the elimination of bias.

In summary, procedural justice refers to the fairness of judicial and court processes and broadly aligns with what is known as 'due process' in the US and 'fundamental justice' in Canada and New Zealand. As understood here, it has four elements which, if fulfilled, should give rise to a sense amongst litigants that they have been treated fairly and to a perception that the system is fair.[6] People care deeply about procedural justice. As Tom Tyler explains, they want the chance to tell their story; they need to feel that those who judge them are neutral, sincere, caring, and trustworthy; and they want to be taken seriously and respected; and it matters to them that their rights are acknowledged.[7] These factors are especially important for those who lose in court. They may not like the outcome but we should want them to feel the procedure was fair.

Open justice (transparent)

Turning now to a third principle of justice, open justice, this requires that the work of our courts should be transparent on various levels. It demands a clear window on the court system. Courts are influential public institutions in which great power vests. They should be visible, intelligible, and accountable. We object to court systems whose workings are held in private or cloaked in secrecy. We call loudly for demystification.

The operation of the entire court system should be open to scrutiny, as should the conduct and conclusions of individual cases. In turn, this should build and enhance trust and confidence in the court system and in the rule of law more widely.

As for the court system generally, information about the processes, procedures, and operations of our courts should be made publicly available; as should data about the throughput and volumes of court work, the subject matter of actions, and the value, timing, and outcomes of cases. Subject to occasional reporting restrictions, the media should be able to report on proceedings, informing those who do not attend. Court lists should be published, and we should also be able to determine the cost of court services to the public purse.

In particular cases, transparency requires that there should be advance notice of any hearing, and publicly accessible information about the processes and procedures involved, the nature and content of the dispute, and the identities of the parties. There should be some kind of record of proceedings, some insight into the decision-making process of the judge, some details about case management decisions, and the substance of the determination itself. Traditionally, it has been expected that all hearings, other than in exceptional circumstances, should be held in a public forum. Justice, in this way, can be seen to be done and parties are publicly vindicated or denounced.

There are strong arguments in support of the view that open justice also requires any information and data findings about the courts, as well as the court proceedings themselves, to be understandable to non-lawyers. There is little point in having access to a process that is unintelligible.

Open justice also entails some degree of transparency in relation to the individuals in whom power vests, most notably the judges themselves. Different jurisdictions have different laws and practices for the appointment (and removal) of judges. For example, in the US, in a very public process, the Senate has to consent to the nomination of justices of their Supreme Court. In contrast, judges of the UK Supreme Court are appointed by a commission (with judicial and lay members) that works very largely behind closed doors.

On the face of it, the case for open justice looks unassailable. However, there should be no suggestion that it is an overriding precept that trumps all other considerations. In most jurisdictions, for example, when matters of national security are before the court or where there is a substantial threat to the welfare of children, we are comfortable about imposing limits on transparency. We also accept that there should be reporting restrictions in certain circumstances; for example, to protect the anonymity of people who have been sexually assaulted. And, as noted, some jurisdictions are content with a private system of judicial appointments.

I return to the idea of open justice in Chapter 19, where I explore in some detail the allegation that online courts are not transparent.

Distributive justice (accessible to all)

When people demand much wider access to justice, they are invoking a fourth principle, that of distributive justice. Michael Sandel, in his book *Justice*, offers a useful starting point.

> To ask whether a society is just is to ask how it distributes the things we prize—income and wealth, duties and rights, powers and opportunities, offices and honours. A just society distributes these goods in the right way; it gives each person his or her due.[8]

My contention is that access to justice is itself a good we should prize, and in a just society this access is due to each and every person. Distributive justice requires that court service is accessible and intelligible to all; that access to legal and court services is a benefit that is evenly spread across society; that rights and duties are equably allocated; that the powerful and rich are subject to the same law as the less well-off and less powerful; and that the service is affordable by all regardless of their means. No categories of user should be disadvantaged, whether disabled users, self-represented litigants, non-users of technology, and all should be entitled to secure just results and feel they have been heard.

The principle of distributive justice, to sum up, overlaps very largely with access to justice. In most legal systems, it is the most commonly *unimplemented* principle of all.

Proportionate justice (appropriately balanced)

My fifth principle is proportionate justice. This is not a term that is found in the classical literature on justice but it is a concept that has gained considerable traction in recent decades. Certainly, in

England and Wales, it was a central pillar of Lord Woolf's Access to Justice Inquiry in the mid-1990s.[9] The basic thinking here is that while the delivery of justice (in the senses noted above) must be a priority for our court system, we must also recognize that the courts provide a public service that is subject to practical constraints.

The principle of proportionality requires, first of all, that we should ensure that the cost of handling individual cases in our courts makes sense by reference to the nature and value of each dispute. Similarly, low value cases or those of modest social significance should be dealt with in good time. Justice delayed is justice diluted. At the same time, such cases should not require highly complex procedures that only lawyers and judges can understand. Relatively straightforward issues should be governed by appropriately straightforward processes.

In a similar vein, although our system is adversarial, this should not mean that all disputes are conducted in a highly combative spirit. Unwarranted escalation of disputes, especially in smaller cases, should be discouraged. Sensible alternatives to full scale battle should be available. And judges should be involved only as a last resort, called upon to resolve disputes when their experience and knowledge is genuinely required.

In summary, then, proportionate justice requires that the expense, speed, complexity, and the extent of the combativeness of any case should indeed be proportionate to the substance and scale of that case. In more prosaic terms, we should not be using a sledgehammer to crack (or miss) a nut. Or, as the late Sir Brian Neill used to say, 'you do not need a Rolls Royce to haul a water cart'.

Many judges and policy-makers seem to assume that proportionate justice is an indisputable and even overriding principle of justice. However, it is not free of difficulties. In the end, many arguments in its favour are, as philosophers would say, *utilitarian* in nature. They appeal to the greater good for the justice system generally that would follow from the pursuit of this principle. But, as with all utilitarian arguments, the individual can be left exposed, and we should be cautious about impinging on the rights of individual court litigants. For example, we can devise a system of disclosure for small disputes which discourages exhaustive review of all documents on the grounds of proportionate justice, but in particular cases, leaving some or many stones unturned may in fact result in crucial documents never being found. In turn, this might lead to substantive injustice.

Enforceable justice (backed by the state)

Judicial decision–making is unique in society. It is based on the law rather than on personal preference, morality, an inclination to compromise, commercial convenience, or mere whim. The determinations of judges are binding and can be enforced by the coercive power of the state. Courts have the remarkable capacity to deprive people legitimately of their money, property, liberty, and, in some countries, their lives. The authority and enforceability of the determinations of the courts are perhaps their most distinctive feature.

When I speak of enforceable justice, my sixth principle, I am referring to their impact. Judicial determinations, by and large, are final, so court users can get on with their lives. They command respect and have the tacit backing of society. Crucially, disregard of court decisions can have very concrete consequences in criminal cases, involving arrest, penalty, and even imprisonment.

The enforceability of court decisions gives the law its bite. As I discuss in the next chapter, there is a gulf between knowing one's rights and having them applied and enforced. The likelihood of enforcement often determines the likelihood of an entitlement being satisfied. Without enforceable justice, the law runs the risk of affording a rather weak set of protections.

Sustainable justice (sufficiently resourced)

A final principle of justice relates more to court and legal systems generally than to justice or injustice in particular cases. This principle calls for courts to be stable, secure, adequately funded, and aligned technologically with the societies that they serve.

Courts should be safe havens; solid and reliable; anchors to which, in times of need, people and organizations can confidently tether themselves. Court users should feel a strong sense of protection under the law and that their affairs are being handled with care and, where appropriate, in confidence. Modernization of the courts should proceed with respect for continuity, preserving all (but, in my view, only) those traditions that are meaningful and effective. Whatever outcomes court users expect and our political and economic systems require, it is hard to imagine a robust and well-regarded, evolving court system that lacks these characteristics.

It is also hard to conceive of a truly sustainable court system that is not technologically in tune with the communities that it serves. A system whose foundations lie in a print-based world, dominated by paper and meetings, will soon be out of step with the daily lives of citizens of a digital society. This incompatibility will both reduce confidence in the justice system and create the widely accepted inefficiencies that result when analogue and digital processes rub against one another.

However, this stability, solidity, and introduction of technology comes at a cost, and we have seen in recent years a steady and deeply disturbing global reduction in public funding for court and justice systems. Policy-makers should be clear that a sustainable court system cannot be maintained on a shoe string. No doubt, there are all manner of competing demands on the public purse but it is hard to see how they take precedence over the need for a sustainable judiciary which, as I explain in Chapter 1, underpins civilized democracies and market economies.

This call for sustainable justice should not be construed, however, as a stark demand for greater public investment. If we accept that our traditional system has patent inefficiencies or incurs disproportionate costs that are hard to justify, then throwing more money at the challenge is surely not the answer.

Above all perhaps, a sustainable system should be *scalable*, which means that its processes must be able to handle very large volumes of cases. In England, many of the processes that support high-value commercial litigation are also brought to bear in much more modest litigation. In very low-value cases, and here we draw on arguments of proportionality, it is hard to justify extensive use of lawyers, barely intelligible rules of procedure, and taking days off work for court appearances. The system is not currently scalable. Greater investment is surely needed, but to help introduce a proportionate and scalable system that increases access to justice, rather than to shore up the conventional ways of operating.

There is a danger, however, that technological innovations (and, of course, cost cutting) might leave court systems impoverished. Consistent with what I say about outcome-thinking, when I note one of its limitations in Chapter 4, it would not make sense to jettison traditional practice if the replacement system is going to run out of steam. We may well need to preserve some of the old system (perhaps certain judicial tasks and procedures, including an obligation on the judiciary to oversee online courts), to ensure the new system is sustainable. Likewise, we must be alive to more fundamental effects that change might bring. Modernization that might threaten, for example, the sustainability of our common law and system of precedent should clearly be approached with caution and humility (see Chapter 23).

Weighing the principles

There is a profound difference between writing about legal philosophy and making actionable public policy decisions. Philosophers
can endlessly analyse and clarify concepts, identify inconsistencies
and confusions, and introduce new concepts and classifications.
And lawyers do much of this too in their debates about justice. But
if you are in the arena, if you are a politician or a policy-maker, it
is not enough to keep the plates spinning by theorizing or pontifi-
cating. Choices need to be made. Decisions must be taken. While
these choices and decisions should, one hopes, be principled, at the
same time they must also be pragmatic. This often comes down to
preferring one unsatisfactory option to another.

In the context of online courts, policy-makers cannot simply
take the seven principles of justice set out in this chapter and apply
them mechanically in thinking about the desirability of bringing
fundamental change to the justice system. In truth, the seven principles overlap and interact in complex and subtle ways. In the many
calls for just systems, we can find traces of some if not all of these
principles. But the most practical challenge is that sometimes these
principles pull in different directions. For example, and commonly,
proportionate justice can conflict with open justice—sometimes
the cost of transparency (a day off work in a public hearing) may
seem excessive given the nature and value of particular kinds of
case (say, a dispute over a faulty microwave oven).

For the policy-maker, the unenviable task here is to weigh relevant principles in respect of proposed reforms. The balance that
is chosen will often be fine. To make matters more challenging,
none of the principles that I advance always has primacy over all
others; different communities may balance the principles in quite
different ways.

Chapter 8

Tackling Injustice

With the building blocks of 'justice according to the law' now to hand, the task in this chapter is to shift emphasis and argue that policy-makers and activists who seek beneficial change should focus as much on *reducing injustice* as pursuing justice. I do not wish to abandon or discourage the pursuit of justice, but I fear if that is our only strategy, we are running two risks. The first is that we will fail to bring about the just arrangements and institutions to which many philosophers and lawyers refer when they speak about justice. The second risk is that, if we set our sights only on achieving some broad aspiration of justice, we might not effect any meaningful change at all.

In contrast, we can realistically and immediately set about reducing *injustice*. In comparing the pursuit of justice and the removal of injustice, again I find a tension between the very different approaches of philosophers and lawyers on one side of the table who speak grandly about justice, and policy-makers on the other who talk more practically about taking steps to tackle injustice.

A shift in emphasis towards injustice chimes with everyday discourse. As Tom Campbell points out,

> [t]here is some basis for the belief that it is the sense of *in*justice or grievance that is at the core of our ideas about justice and explains its powerful emotive force. Justice is normally the language of complaint, and sometimes of revenge.[1]

There is much in this. In the context of judicial work, Lord Devlin writes similarly when observing that the 'social service which the judge renders to the community is the removal of a sense of injustice'.[2]

Transcendental and comparative justice

A useful starting point in exploring the idea of injustice is *The Idea of Justice*, by Amartya Sen, a Nobel Prize winner in Economics. Early in this work, Sen draws a distinction that he suggests 'has received far less attention than ... it richly deserves'. Indeed, he describes it as 'quite momentous'. And I think he is right. Referring to the great contributions to philosophical thought of the European Enlightenment in the eighteenth and nineteenth centuries, he identifies one approach, supported by Hobbes, Rousseau, Kant, and Locke, which he calls 'transcendental institutionalism'. This concentrates on identifying 'perfect justice' rather than 'relative comparisons of justice and injustice'. It also concentrates largely on searching for 'perfectly just institutions'. In contrast, Sen identifies a second approach, 'realisation-focused comparison', exponents of which, instead of 'confining their analyses to transcendental searches for a perfectly just society' are 'involved in comparisons of societies that already existed or could feasibly emerge'. In this second camp are Smith, Bentham, Marx, and Mill, who 'were often interested primarily in the *removal of manifest injustice* from the world that they saw'.[3]

I accept that Sen's terminology is rather forbidding. But I am with him in favouring a *comparative* over a *transcendental* framework for the analysis and pursuit of justice. As much as the next academic, I enjoy metaphysical and philosophical debates over what perfect justice and perfectly just courts might look like, but these discussions offer little practical guidance when social choices must be made, when one arrangement must be preferred over another, when it is proposed that an old set-up might be replaced by something new.

In my work on online courts, my prime motivation is 'the removal of manifest injustice' from societies. In the context of the previous chapter, therefore, I am driven more by a desire to reduce substantive injustices, procedural injustices, open injustices, and so forth, than I am by an aspiration to secure some perfected forms of these conceptions of justice.

Most critics of online courts are romantic transcendentalists rather than pragmatic comparativists. When confronted with the idea of online courts, they swiftly isolate the shortcomings both of online judging and of extended courts and seek to show how they fall short of some idealized, perfect model of the court system. For long, I have observed their reactions at demonstrations of impressive new technologies. Invariably, their initial reaction is to assert, 'well, of course, your system can't do x, y, or z', apparently oblivious to the fact that today's set-up also cannot achieve x, y, or z. They choose to compare what is envisioned not with what is actually available today but with some imagined ideal system. And once they find fault, their inclination is then to reject online courts wholesale. This is transcendentalism hard at work. In response, comparativists must remind the critics that the proposed new system, *overall*, takes us to a better place. Transcendentalists often stand in the way of advance. In the name of justice, they miss the opportunity to reduce injustice.

Voltaire

Voltaire, the eighteenth-century French philosopher, once observed that 'the best is the enemy of the good', meaning that people are often unhelpfully discouraged from bringing positive change because what is proposed falls short of ideal. If we want to make progress, we should, in other words, seek improvement rather than perfection. The lure of some idealized or romanticized realization of justice obstructs straightforward advance. I have no objection to setting sights high, except when this discourages or precludes any kind of sensible advance. Perhaps Voltaire should have said 'the best is the enemy of the better'.

In the context of online courts, critics should therefore be cautious about comparing online courts with some ideal and yet simply unaffordable or unattainable conventional court service. In their enthusiasm to dismiss online courts, they often forget the many shortcomings of what is currently in place. The comparison that should be made is with what we have today—court services that are too expensive, take too long, are barely intelligible to the non-lawyer, and so exclude countless potential litigants with credible claims. Our focus, in other words, should be as much on practical steps to remove injustice than defaulting to the current set-up.

In the end, transcendentalism reflects an upmarket form of status quo bias (Chapter 3). While philosophers dance on pin heads and lawyers weave hifalutin arguments in opposition to online courts, I believe that we should keep our eyes on the prize—embracing technologies that, in modest increments, can help remove all manner of manifest injustices.

As we arrive at the end of the first part of the book, and with this focus on the removal of injustice as the backdrop, let me summarize the other main strands in the argument so far. Our courts are indispensable institutions whose daily work is central to our social and economic lives. Around the world, alarmingly, our court systems are creaking. They cost too much, they are too slow, and are unintelligible to all but lawyers. In an era of dramatic technological advance, it makes sense to explore how these current shortcomings might by overcome through existing and emerging technologies. Our aim in deploying technology should not simply be to automate and streamline our traditional processes but to deliver outcomes we expect of our courts in entirely new ways. This should take us beyond physical courtrooms and virtual hearings (trials by video conference) to asynchronous online judging and the provision of a wider range of services that help court users understand their legal positions and settle early, if possible and desirable. Our ambition should not stop at improved and more accessible dispute resolution. Our justice systems should also encourage the containment and avoidance of disputes, and empower and promote the legal health of citizens. We should be driven by the seven stated principles of justice to ensure we provide accessible, transparent, sufficiently resourced, appropriately balanced court systems, that are backed by the coercive powers of the state, and whose decisions and processes are fair.

PART II

Is Court A Service Or A Place?

Chapter 9
The Vision

'Vision without execution is hallucination.' It is not entirely clear who first said this, but it is an aphorism that is usually attributed to Thomas Edison, of lightbulb fame. And it is an invaluable insight. We can talk endlessly about a newly imagined world but unless we know how we can get there, it is daydreaming. Accordingly, in this part of the book, after setting out my vision for online courts, I go on to propose an architecture for these systems. My hope is that this provides practical guidance to those who want to implement operational systems.

The vision that I share in this chapter was developed in collaboration with others in 2014 and 2015. I tell the story here of its evolution and then build on this early thinking. Underlying the vision is a basic question. Is court a service or a place? When people and organizations are in dispute and call upon the state to settle their differences, must they congregate in physical courtrooms? The vision introduced here suggests not.

History of a vision

In February 2015, the then Master of the Rolls (the most senior civil judge in England and Wales) Lord Dyson, in launching the publication of a report on the subject of online dispute resolution, described it as 'an exciting milestone in the history of our civil justice system'. The report, entitled 'Online Dispute Resolution for Low Value Civil Claims' had been written for the Civil Justice Council of England and Wales by its Online Dispute Resolution Advisory Group, which I had had the privilege to chair.[1] We were set up by Lord Dyson, then Chair of the Civil Justice Council, in April 2014 and our remit had been to explore the potential and limitations of various online techniques for the resolution of civil claims of less than £25,000.

From the get-go, we recognized that we had a battle on our hands relating to mindset. Although the European Commission's ODR Regulation (No. 524/2013) had come into force not long before (in July 2013), few lawyers had heard of online dispute resolution (ODR), and those who had often wore sceptical frowns.

Early in our discussions, we anticipated that our findings might be seen as threatening the work of litigators. But we resolved that this should not divert us in our search for better ways of resolving disputes. It is not the purpose of the courts to provide an income for lawyers or judges, nor to lend their lives meaning.

We therefore asked at the start of our report 'for a willingness to contemplate that civil disputes, in the future, may need to be managed and resolved in ways quite unlike those embraced by our traditional system'.[2] We said explicitly that our report was a call for further work, rather than a blueprint. Nonetheless, I believe we laid out there, for the first time anywhere, the fundamental vision for the widespread introduction of online courts to justice systems around the world.

Our starting point was the widely shared view that our traditional court system was too costly, too slow, and too complex, especially for self-represented litigants with small claims. Lord Dyson put the point more memorably, when he said at the launch that 'any system that has a 2000-page user guide has a problem'. He was referring to the civil court system of England and Wales and to the mountainous body of rules that governs its operations.

The general expectation had been that our group would assume online dispute resolution (ODR) was an electronic sub-set of alternative dispute resolution (ADR), and that we would identify the most promising opportunities for diverting cases out of the court system into some kind of private-sector ODR services. Early success stories in the world of ODR gave hope that this might be the answer to those who asked how we might reduce the case load of our overworked public court system. Quite early on, though, we came up with a very different idea—rather than exporting cases from the courts into the fledgling ODR industry, why not import techniques from ODR and make them part of the court system? This was a big leap. But why not? If ODR held such great promise, why not embrace these technologies, with a view to widening and improving court service and, in turn, increasing confidence in the public courts and the rule of law. We wanted some of the kudos of innovating to be attached to our beleaguered courts as well as to the ODR entrepreneurs.

In our preliminary brainstorming, we therefore allowed ourselves to envision a very different future. We imagined an electronic court system that was as easy to use as Amazon, a service that was affordable to the overwhelming majority of citizens, accessible for the disabled who cannot easily attend physical hearings in courtrooms, a set-up that was more natural and intuitive for the internet generation. We were driven also by the possibilities of taking ill-suited cases out of the courtroom and so saving money, and of meeting hitherto unmet legal need and so increasing access to justice. We envisaged a system that was fair, fast, efficient, and proportionate. But we were sensitive as well about the need for safeguards, not least that there should be appropriate rights of appeal from any online court to the traditional process.

Systems that inspired

Our ideas were not plucked from the ether. We were inspired and emboldened by related services that had been unearthed by our initial research and thinking and, in our report, we provided mini-case studies of twelve in all. One of the more dramatic advances that caught our attention was the dispute resolution system embedded in eBay. We learned that a breathtaking 60 million disagreements amongst traders were resolved each year using two forms of online dispute resolution—structured online negotiation with no third party intervention, and an online adjudication process led by eBay's staff and leading to a contractually binding outcome.[3] On social media, when our report appeared, and since then in numerous discussions, there has been some considerable agitation about our reference to eBay. Sceptics should be assured that we were not suggesting that the court system of England and Wales, or indeed any state-based service, should employ eBay adjudicators. Our interest in eBay, rather, was that it showed there were already technology platforms that could process large numbers of disputes online and there seemed to be a willingness for parties to seek solutions without invoking traditional legal and court processes.

We were also much impressed by early news of the Civil Resolution Tribunal (CRT), an online service that would come to be launched in July 2016 in British Columbia, Canada. This was to be an online tribunal, regulated under the Civil Resolution Tribunal Act 2012. The service was not, strictly, being designed for the court system, as we were thinking for England and Wales, but it was very much in the public sector and not a form of private sector e-ADR. It was to offer a state-provided system for small claims (under CAN$25,000), relating to damages, debts, recovery of personal property, and certain kinds of condominium disputes.

A several-stage process was anticipated. The first would help users explore possible solutions to their differences. The second would be an online negotiation platform. Then, third, a case manager would try to mediate online or on the phone, failing which, fourthly, an adjudicator would engage with the parties—online, by phone, or by video link—and deliver a binding decision. This approach has since been implemented successfully and is discussed in more detail in Chapter 16.

The UK Financial Ombudsman Service (FOS) had also developed a service that we felt was significant. FOS was set up by statute in 2000 as the mandatory ADR body in the financial services sector. Its function was informally to resolve disputes between consumers and banks, building societies, and other financial-services businesses. The value and complexity of these disputes were similar to the low value civil disputes that were our object of review. We were struck by some key statistics—in the previous year, 2013/14, FOS had resolved 518,778 disputes, 487,749 of which were settled not by ombudsmen (the quasi-judicial decision-makers) but by case-handlers (known then, slightly misleadingly, as adjudicators)—informally, and quickly. Of the 31,029 disputes that were advanced to the ombudsmen, fewer than twenty required face-to-face meetings. The work of FOS offered some confirmation of some of our early intuitions—that large volumes of cases could be handled at relatively low unit costs, that many cases could be sorted out informally without needing formal disposal, and, vitally, that physical hearings were by no means indispensable.

Another service that informed our report was Resolver, a UK-based online facility that helped consumers raise and sort out disputes with suppliers and retailers. Using online forms and with the support of some boilerplate text, users were given assistance in drafting their complaints which were emailed directly to the complaint departments of (then) 2,000 major organizations. Resolver provided a platform on which consumers and businesses could discuss their disagreements in a structured way. What impressed us was the way in which fairly simple techniques could be used to help lay people formulate their grievances coherently.

Our recommendation

Excited by the idea of bringing ODR techniques into the courts and emboldened by these successes, our principal recommendation was that HM Courts & Tribunals Service in England and Wales (HMCTS) should establish a new, internet-based court service, that we named 'Her Majesty's Online Court'.[4] We suggested that this should be a three-tier court service for the resolution of low-value civil disputes. The first tier would provide what we called 'online evaluation'. This would help users with problems to categorize and classify their grievances, to understand their rights and obligations, and be guided on the options and remedies available to them. In the language of Chapter 6, this tier would help with 'dispute avoidance'.

On the second tier would be 'online facilitation', as we named it. Here, human facilitators would bring disputes to speedy, sensible conclusions without the involvement of judges. Communicating largely across the internet, these facilitators would review papers and statements and help parties by mediating and negotiating. Where necessary, they would also use telephone conferencing facilities. A key role of the facilitator would be to prevent disputes from escalating, failing which to direct cases to online judges or normal judges, as appropriate. In addition, and in the spirit of much historical ODR work, there would be some automated negotiation tools. This tier would provide 'dispute containment'.

The third tier would involve judges, working online rather than in courtrooms. They would be fully fledged members of the judiciary who would decide suitable cases or parts of cases, based on papers submitted to them electronically. This would form part of a structured process of online pleading and require users to submit their evidence and arguments across the internet. Again, this would be supported by telephone conferencing and, in the future, by video links. At any stage, though, online judges could decide to refer cases to traditional hearings. This third tier would provide 'dispute resolution'.

We also recognized that for online courts to be usable and work effectively, they would need to be governed by a new, simplified set of civil procedure rules, many of which would be embedded in the system itself. If the new system was to be accessible and intelligible, it could not rest on the current and very large body of rules.

On this model of online courts, our hypothesis was that two major benefits would flow from online courts. First, they would give rise to an increase in access to justice, a more affordable and user-friendly service that would be available to many more people. Second, they would yield substantial savings in costs, both for individual litigants as well as for the court system—fewer cases would reach judges and many of those that did would cost less because they would no longer require the expense of physical hearings. For litigants, this would offer a route to resolution where many otherwise had none; and a more convenient, less costly, speedier, more understandable route for people who litigated without lawyers, as well as for those who were represented but would prefer not to be.

Our hope from the outset was that online courts would be sufficiently easy to use that self-represented litigants would be able to understand and enforce their entitlements without retaining lawyers to work on their behalf. This would be especially attractive when the expense of lawyers would be disproportionate relative to the value of the case. That said, we never thought it appropriate to seek to exclude lawyers from participating from online courts. We also insisted that online courts would not be suitable for all cases, so the traditional court system would still be in play for many cases.

Aside from those who with good reason would be 'unable' to use online courts on their own (see Chapter 21), our view was that online courts would be mandatory for cases within their remit. We drew a distinction here between being 'unable' and 'unwilling'. We recognized that some people might prefer a traditional hearing but we did not generally conceive of online courts as optional for disputes within their jurisdiction.

Responses

We knew that this was challenging stuff. Judges without court-rooms. Justice without lawyers. The very idea. But the initial response was heartening. There was considerable media interest and much favourable coverage, although we knew that this was not of itself a definitive confirmation of anything. The buzz on social media was also sympathetic—again, though, not a decisive indicator.

Within the court and legal worlds, the response to the report was generally positive. HMCTS described it as 'important and thought-provoking' and seemed committed to taking the idea forward (as indeed it did). The Law Society of England and Wales (the professional body for solicitors) described the report as an 'exciting and interesting proposal that clearly calls for further detailed consideration'. The Bar Council (representing barristers) was more circumspect, warning that 'we must be wary of creating a system which is over-simplified'. Justice will not be served, they went on, 'if people with complex claims find themselves funnelled down routes that are designed for a quick result at the expense of proper consideration of relevant facts'.[5]

This concern was echoed by some practising solicitors. However, nowhere had we suggested that complex claims should be settled by the proposed online court. If such claims were to come before online facilitators or judges, our expectation then was that they would be assigned to the traditional court system. Online courts, we said again and again, would not be suitable for all cases.

We were generally not deterred by criticism from within the legal fraternity. We expected that lawyers and policy-makers might find online courts to be outlandish or alien, because few of them belong to the internet generation for whom, we believed, courts of the future should be conceived. Tomorrow's citizens, for whom socializing and working online is second nature, we said, are likely to look upon online courts as an entirely natural facility, a set-up indeed perhaps more conducive and convenient than conventional courts.

Not long after our report appeared, our recommendations on online courts were endorsed in a publication by JUSTICE, entitled 'Delivering Justice in an Age of Austerity'.[6] Although I was a member of the group (chaired by a former Court of Appeal judge, Sir Stanley Burnton) that produced this report, they needed little persuading that it was time for some technological transformation in the courts.

When we published the Civil Justice Council report, we also knew we had the backing of many of the top judges in England and Wales. As well as Lord Dyson's ongoing sponsorship, I also had the almost-daily support of the indefatigable Lord Thomas, the Lord Chief Justice at the time. But we argued that the successful introduction of an online court service would also need strong political endorsement. This came in June 2015, when the then Lord Chancellor and Secretary of State for Justice, Michael Gove, spoke publicly in support.[7] It was a good week because, on the previous day, Lord Thomas had also validated the idea in a major speech.[8]

Cynics said that the inevitable stumbling block would be investment. Surely the Government would never put hard cash behind a major technology reform project for the courts. These doubters were flabbergasted in November 2015, when the Spending Review of HM Treasury announced that the UK Government would in fact be investing 'more than £700 million to modernize and fully digitize the courts'.[9] I was pretty amazed myself. On Twitter, I wrote that, 'I have waited for this day for 34 years'. At long last, after countless under-funded false starts, there was serious commitment to upgrading the court system, even if only a fraction of the £700 million was to be directed towards online courts.

We then received a major boost during the following month, in December 2015, when Lord Briggs, then a Court of Appeal judge and now a Supreme Court Justice, in his interim report on the structure of civil courts, explicitly endorsed and built on the concept of online courts that our Group had proposed.[10] And he went further, in July 2016, in his influential final report in which he even more insistently advocated online courts while deftly addressing the many objections that lawyers and others had raised during his consultation exercise.[11]

The final official stamp of approval for the development and deployment of online courts in England and Wales came in 'Transforming Our Justice System', a joint statement by the Lord Chancellor, the Lord Chief Justice, and the Senior President of Tribunals.[12] In that document and in the £1 billion court reform programme which is being pursued as I write, the original vision of our advisory group is largely followed.

In a nutshell, then, the core vision was of a fundamentally new approach to the provision of the public court service for the resolution of minor civil disputes; a simplified service that would be affordable, quick, and intelligible, enabling non-lawyers to conduct their own cases not by congregating physically in a courtroom but by communicating electronically with human judges. More, court users would be given various tools to help them assess and formulate their claims while their cases would be handled in the first instance by facilitators who would encourage parties to settle without involving judges.

Although our focus was on small civil cases, we also said that some of our recommendations could extend to appropriate tribunal, family, and criminal work too. Since then, leading tribunal and family judges[13] have approved this suggestion and in fact some of the most advanced developments in online courts are taking place in these jurisdictions. On the other hand, there is understandable hesitation about the scope for technological change in criminal courts. Indeed when people are instinctively troubled by the idea of online courts, it is most often criminal cases that they have in mind. Some feel that it is important to have a physical place to play host, in the words of Lord Denning in a different context, to the community's 'emphatic denunciation' of a crime.[14] As I say in the Introduction, criminal cases are beyond the scope of this book but my instinct is that for minor offences there is considerable scope for the systems and techniques discussed here. I call on others to consider this possibility systematically.

In the Civil Justice Council report, because they were beyond our terms of reference, we steered clear of larger-scale commercial disputes. I have since come to the view that, in the long run, online techniques will also prove to be applicable and invaluable in more complex and higher-value cases. While litigators from major law firms will likely approach this book with the firm conviction that it has little bearing on heavy duty commercial dispute resolution, I expect at the very least that the work of courts will be disaggregated—routine parts of large cases will be handled online while some components will be conducted much as today, in person in courtrooms (where, for example, face-to-face interaction is genuinely thought to be needed). This already happens today in large-scale arbitrations when, for instance, submissions are made by parties and some decisions by arbitrators are conveyed via email.

The wider vision: bridging the gap between entitlement and enforcement

Since working on the Civil Justice Council report, we held a hackathon in July 2017 to involve the wider legal community in coming up with ideas for the design of online courts[15] and we also convened the First International Forum on Online Courts, in London, in December 2018.[16] Both events were remarkably well attended, suggesting genuine enthusiasm in the UK and around the world for the introduction of online courts. These events strengthened my view that there would indeed be a shift in the future in most advanced justice systems from the presumption that all disputes before the courts should be held in a physical space to the reverse—by default, cases in due course will be conducted online unless there are compelling reasons to assemble in a courtroom. And these reasons will be based on principles of justice like the ones I propose in Chapter 7 and on a drive to avoid myriad injustices, rather than on the personal preferences of judges, lawyers, and litigants. In the great majority of cases, once online courts are successfully installed, I believe that distributive and proportionate justice will generally require the use of these rather than traditional courts.

Over the past year or so, I have concluded that, ambitious though this may appear, online courts might also provide the basis of a

significant solution to some of our global access-to-justice problems. The challenge here is stated in Chapter 2, where I note that
only 46 per cent of human beings live under the protection of the
law and, annually, only 30 per cent of the one billion people in
need of 'basic justice care' take action. In 1996, in my book, *The
Future of Law*, I suggested that one way of increasing access to the
law and justice would be to make the law available online.[17] At that
time, I had in mind both primary materials (such as legislation and
case law) and well as secondary sources—guidance or commentary
on the law. This idea has gathered force over the years and now lies
at the heart of many worthy projects around the world that seek
to make the law more accessible and to help people understand
their rights. Often under the heading of 'public legal education'
or 'legal empowerment', all manner of systems and services are
now available—not just websites, but chatbots, livechats, document
automation, flowcharts and decision trees, guided pathways, text-
message reminders, visual guides to legal process, animations, triage
systems, webcasts, and much more.[18]

I now recognize, however, that online legal guidance can take
us only so far, no matter how friendly and well-designed. In truth,
there is a gulf between knowing one's rights and being able to enforce them in a way that delivers results. It is this yawning gap that
is the core of the access to justice problem.

Many people in advanced jurisdictions have at one stage or another caught a glimpse of the issue. For example, when in dispute
with recalcitrant insurance companies, airlines, major retail outlets,
or mobile providers, highly capable individuals discover that understanding one's legal position is not enough. Real progress, such
as being compensated, seems to require an immediately credible
ability and willingness to launch legal proceedings which carries
with it the prospect of enforcement backed by the state. In practice, this means instructing lawyers. Historically, the chasm between

entitlement and enforcement has been bridged by the legal profession. Even highly resourceful and committed individuals who have managed to establish their legal positions still find it difficult to translate their apparent entitlements into a final resolution without instructing lawyers. In advanced legal systems, lawyers are needed to translate rights into practical consequences. They know how the system works and their involvement sends out signals to the evasive and intransigent. Here, lawyers currently bring great value. Their involvement in a dispute lends teeth that no website or advanced technology can yet bring. Online guidance systems can offer insight into rights and process but they are a little like medical diagnostic systems that tell users what their problem is, when there is no medical or surgical treatment then available. When people learn their legal position, this can be an empty revelation if they have no realistic means of then taking action.

As for voluntary advice workers, they often provide wonderful counsel but they are not officers of the court. What makes everyone sit up and take notice is when a lawyer writes a formal letter or starts proceedings. Yet, most people cannot afford lawyers and, even if a claimant has the wherewithal, when a problem is minor, it is invariably disproportionate to engage solicitors or attorneys.

My vision and hope is that online courts can bridge this gulf between people knowing the law and enforcing their entitlements. In some ways, they will give the law the bite and immediacy that in the past has been the sole province of lawyers. Online courts will create a nexus, a connection, between legal understanding and remedy. This has two aspects. On the one hand, it will be empowering for those with entitlements that might otherwise go unenforced. Online courts should give the self-represented the institutional clout of the client with a lawyer. On the other hand, and perhaps as important, the prospect of more imminent enforcement by the state will incentivize those with duties actually to fulfil them. No longer can they be protected by the law when its main effect is to pass the too-weighty burden of legal action to the underdog. Perhaps now the playing field can be levelled, and many inequalities removed—between rich and poor litigators, between those who have lawyers and those who do not, between those who have the court system at their disposal and those who are excluded. Online courts are the answer, on this view, to some of the global problems of distributive and proportionate injustices.

In England and Wales, we have for some years seen a glimpse of the gulf being bridged in this way, with the service known originally as Money Claim Online. Launched by the Ministry of Justice in England and Wales in 2002, this online service (an early 'extended court' service, in the language of this book) was originally designed to enable users, with no legal experience, to recover money owed to them without needing to handle complex forms or set foot in a County Court. The idea was to allow claimants to request claims online, to keep track of the status of the claim and, where appropriate, to request entry of judgment and enforcement. Once a claimant completed his or her claim, the defendant received official notice from the court. This notice of itself urged many otherwise defaulting or procrastinating parties to sit up and pay up. In this way, the shadow of the coercive powers of the state is cast much further. And it can extend well beyond money claims, to help people, for example, who have been fired or evicted, or are being deprived of some state benefit or discriminated against. This is surely what a public court system is for. This is access to justice.

Chapter 10

Architecture

I often advise my law firm clients that 'you can't change the wheel on a moving car'. I say this in response to the exasperated look that appears on leaders' faces when they contemplate the scale of technological change they are soon likely to face. Daily, I meet senior lawyers who recognize that transformation is needed but cannot see how they might move seamlessly from their current business—successful, already over-stretched complexes of people and processes—to the new world. It would be fine if they could press a pause button for a couple of years and put in place a new business at their leisure. But they cannot imagine in what they frequently call 'the real world' how they can fundamentally change their business while keeping it running along or, to be honest, while squeezing every last drop out of the old economic model.

Not long ago, a litigation partner from a leading US firm who had attended one of my talks, sent me a link to a YouTube clip. It was a remarkable video of a truck, being driven precariously on two wheels while its mad passengers are—no joke—changing the wheel while in motion. His point, I think, was that, contrary to what I had said, you can in fact change a wheel on a moving car and, somehow, by implication, that all else I had to say about the future of law could safely be disregarded. He may well be right on both fronts but that two-wheel balancing act did not look to me like a solid business proposition.

The challenge of change

Court systems around the world face the same challenge. Wide-ranging technological change has to be brought about without interrupting the existing daily service. A failure to resolve the wheel-change dilemma often leads top management in both law firms and court services to opt for the compromise of committing to technology but simply grafting it onto current ways of working. In the language of Chapter 3, this invariably means that the technology *automates* rather than *transforms*—the systems streamline and optimize traditional working practices rather than enabling entirely different ways of working and of meeting the outcomes that users seek. The end result—marginal process improvement rather than comprehensive transformation—tends to be a disappointment for everyone involved. The promise of radical change is unfulfilled.

My solution to the wheel-change challenge, to stretch the metaphor a little further, is to build and launch an entirely new vehicle. In law firms, this might mean setting up a new legal technology venture or, under the English regime, an 'alternative business structure'.[1] In the context of court systems, I suggest this means designing and introducing online courts. Whether in firms or courts, the spirit is the same—start with a blank sheet of paper (no legacy systems or working practices), establish guiding principles, design with a focus on the outcomes that the market or public wants, introduce a new set of rules or working practices and not an edit of the old ones, use technology to deliver services and facilities that are not possible in a non-digital environment, and start modestly in the expectation that, over time, more and more work will move over from the old to the new vehicle. In due course, the old vehicle will be used less and perhaps even discarded as redundant.

In that spirit, my purpose in this chapter is to lay out a fairly formal architecture for thinking about online courts. I am not proposing a set of facilities to overlay traditional court systems. Nor am I describing any particular system that is planned or in existence. Instead, I sketch out a new and different way of conceptualizing and providing public, state-provided dispute resolution, exploiting existing technologies and anticipating future technological developments. The architecture builds on the vision laid out in the previous chapter and on the analysis of access to justice introduced in Chapter 6.

Four-layer model

The formal architecture that I propose for online courts is best understood, initially, against the backdrop of the 'richer' model of access to justice discussed in Chapter 6 and then by comparing the options we have today—traditional court service in physical courtrooms, virtual hearings, alternative dispute resolution /online dispute resolution—with the online courts I am advocating.

The access-to-justice component can be represented as a four-layer model, as depicted in Figure 10.1. Following the terminology of Chapter 6, the first layer denotes legal health promotion; the second, dispute avoidance; the third, dispute containment; and the fourth layer represents authoritative dispute resolution.

If we map traditional court service onto this model—see Figure 10.2—we can see immediately that this age-old form of authoritative public dispute resolution sits almost exclusively on the lowest layer, with a very minor presence on the one above. On the lowest layer, there are human judges working in the institutions we call

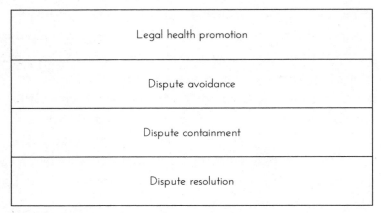

Figure 10.1 Four layers of access to justice

Figure 10.2 Traditional courts

courts. Insofar as judges seek to encourage alternatives to court-based resolution, whether, for example, by recommending mediation or by trying to inject common sense at case management meetings, the traditional court system does creep a little onto the dispute containment layer. In truth, though, this incursion into dispute containment lies at the margins and not the heart of the adversarial system. The traditional court system plays no role in dispute avoidance or legal health promotion.

Virtual hearings, as shown in Figure 10.3, occupy pretty much the same space on the architecture. As defined in Chapter 5, these are hearings in which some or all of the participants appear by

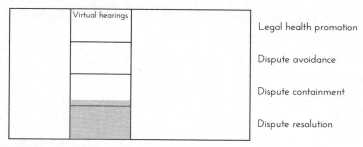

Figure 10.3 Virtual hearings

some kind of video conferencing. As such, virtual hearings are largely in the business of dispute resolution with occasional but relatively minor forays into dispute containment.

We can also map alternative dispute resolution (ADR) and on-line dispute resolution (ODR) onto the model. ADR, as noted in Chapter 5, includes techniques such as mediation, conciliation, negotiation, and early neutral evaluation. As compared with traditional courts, these are conceived as better, quicker, cheaper, more convenient, or less public ways of sorting out disagreements—not by the state but in the private sector, or by charitable or educational organizations. ODR services, in the narrower sense discussed in Chapter 5, are ADR facilities that are delivered electronically. For example, a negotiation or mediation is not conducted at a face-to-face meeting but is carried out with the support of some kind of online tools. As Figure 10.4 shows, ADR and ODR services

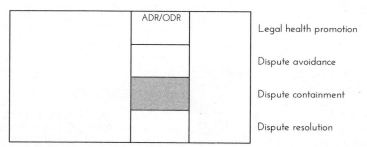

Figure 10.4 ADR/ ODR

both sit on the dispute containment layer of the model. When successful, they contain disputes, preventing them from proceeding to authoritative judicial resolution. Like traditional courts, ADR and ODR are not involved with dispute avoidance (by definition, a dispute has already arisen by the time ADR and ODR are engaged). Nor do they support legal health promotion.

Three-tier online court

Figure 10.5 shows the range of online courts—a three-tier service that maps onto the dispute containment and dispute resolution layers and part of the dispute avoidance layer of the framework. This three-tier construct follows the approach adopted by the Civil Justice Council in our report of February 2015 and endorsed and extended by Lord Briggs in his reports. I am not suggesting that this structure is canonical or definitive. Rather, I am introducing it as *one* systematic way to understand the nature and scope of online courts.

Looking more closely, on the dispute resolution layer we have Tier 3, which provides *determination* by the authoritative decisions of judges.[2] In the language of Chapter 5, this is 'online judging', one of the two core aspects to online courts.

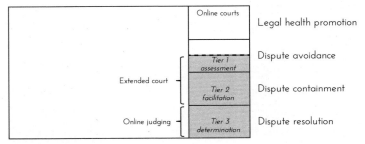

Figure 10.5 Online courts

In the first generation of these Tier 3 services, these are deter-minations made by human judges, but not in a traditional, phys-ical courtroom. Rather, arguments and evidence are submitted via some online service, and judges deliver their decisions, again, not in open court but through the online platform. As explained in Chapter 5, in contrast with physical and virtual courts where the communication and interaction is synchronous, the process of judging involves asynchronous forms of engagement. A second generation of these systems can in principle be envisaged, as dis-cussed in Chapters 26 and 27, when the determinations will be made by some form of artificial intelligence (AI). Today this may seem outrageous. Within two decades or so, the use of AI may well be commonplace for appropriate cases, not least where traditional court service is not available.

Tier 2 lies on the dispute containment layer, providing *facili-tation* services that help to contain disputes, inhibiting the escal-ation that traditional legal and court processes can often encourage. Human facilitators whom I now prefer to call 'case officers' play a central role in the first generation of these systems, for example, by negotiating or mediating across the online platform. The aim of these case officers is to bring about some kind of non–judicial settlement without assembling people in the same room to do so. Crucially, this service is provided not as an alternative to the public court system but as an integral part of it. When second generation online courts are in place, much of the facilitation will itself be en-abled by technology, using tools such online negotiation and ma-chine learning systems (Chapters 25 and 26).

Tier 1 of online courts occupies some but not all of the dispute avoidance layer of the framework. This layer is devoted not to re-solving or containing disputes but to preventing them from arising in the first place. In this spirit, Tier 1 provides online *assessment* (a term which I now favour over 'evaluation' which has misleading

moral overtones), helping users to categorize and classify their problems, to understand the law applicable to them, and to guide them
on the options and remedies available to them. The dotted line that
appears on Figure 10.5 marks the boundary between services that
are provided by the state within the court system and complemen-
tary services that are offered by others, from charities and educational bodies to private sector suppliers. The state cannot be the
exclusive provider of online help for those with legal grievances.
Some will want to claim that the state should not be in this space
at all. Yet this would be to deny the possibility of 'extended courts',
the second core aspect of online courts (see Figure 10.5). The central idea here is that technology enables us to deliver a wider court
service. For those who concede this new role for the public service,
the interrelationships between providers and services below and
above the line present interesting new challenges, not least whether
the state might integrate its systems with those above the dotted
line. This issue is discussed in more detail in the next chapter.

By way of summary, Figure 10.6 offers a comparison of the four
different approaches to dispute management and resolution, and
clearly shows that online courts have considerably greater scope
than the others. As noted in Chapter 5, the distinction between
the three public services (traditional physical courtrooms, virtual

Traditional courts	Virtual hearings	ADR/ODR	Online courts	
				Legal health promotion
				Dispute avoidance
				Dispute containment
				Dispute resolution

Figure 10.6 The four approaches compared

hearings, and online courts) will fade over time, as court service becomes a blend of all three.

In the four chapters that follow, I focus mainly on first-generation systems, and unpack and discuss each element of the online court architecture in more detail. This is presented largely from the point of view of someone pursuing rather than defending a claim.

Chapter 11

Online Guidance

If online courts are to work effectively and at scale, self-represented court users will need tools to help them assess their legal entitlements and the options available to them. In this chapter, I introduce some of these tools and discuss how we might design and implement them. My main focus is on Tier 1 of the online court, but I close with a digression that looks more broadly.

Navigating Tier 1

Tier 1 of the online court, as introduced in Chapter 10, provides 'online assessment' in the hope that when some problems are analysed and better understood, then disputes can be avoided altogether. This tier is the entry point into the online court and, ideally, two basic facilities should be offered to help users evaluate their circumstances from a legal perspective—a system to assess the nature of the grievance, and a system to offer substantive legal guidance. These can provide an early form of 'triage', to use the term popularized by Lord Briggs in his analysis of online courts.[1]

The grievance assessment system should help users to organize and classify their problems. This assists users in turning an unstructured grievance into a recognizable, justiciable problem.[2] A grievance here is a sense that there is a wrong that needs to be rectified while a justiciable problem is a more systematic expression of the circumstances in which the law provides a remedy. Equally, this part of the system can help users recognize when what they have is not a justiciable problem at all.

Judges often tell me that self-represented litigants arrive in court carrying plastic carrier bags overflowing with unindexed documents that are thought to lie at the heart of their cases. Without legal or administrative skills, these litigants often struggle to organize their papers and their thoughts, and then to classify them in a way that captures the issues at stake. The challenge is to move from the plastic bag of documents (actual or metaphorical) into a scoped and defined legal issue and an indication of what channels for resolution are open to the litigant. For many practitioners and theorists, this initial step is the most fundamental of all, and one that is far from trivial. This may be regarded as the heart of legal method. How can this be done by machine? The suggestion is not that the techniques introduced below combine to be a general purpose legal problem classification tool, able to handle the hardest of cases. Instead, pragmatically, it is assumed that the great majority of low-value disputes do not raise novel or complex legal questions, and the issues arising in most can be categorized uncontroversially.

In the same spirit, the second facility is one that offers legal guidance, support, and diagnostics. This part of the service helps people come to a legal view—to understand their legal rights and duties, to assist them in determining the likely legal merits of their situations, and so whether it makes sense to proceed at all. Even if they have to hand a succinct summary of the central points at issue they are unlikely to know enough about relevant law (legislation, regulation, case law, common practice), to understand their entitlements and obligations and, in turn, the legal remedies available to them. Legal guidance systems plug this gap.

Design thinking

If users of online courts are not lawyers, however, they will clearly need some help in navigating the systems. One of the crucial distinctions between traditional and online courts is that the former have largely been developed by lawyers for lawyers, while the latter are conceived as services for use directly by people with no legal training. Two sorts of sceptic argue that it is fanciful to suppose that non-lawyers might easily use such systems. There are lawyers who say that the substantive law and court procedure are too demanding for the non-legal mind. And there are others who say that most users will lack the confidence, ability, technological skills, and general literacy to use online courts effectively. For many cases flowing through the online courts, the answer to both categories of doubting Thomas lies in *design*. We can learn much here from the increasingly popular and successful field of 'design thinking'— techniques, methods, processes, and technologies that, in this context, can help identify and satisfy the particular needs and wants of court users. As Tim Brown and Roger Martin explain, design thinking extends not just to the design of the 'artifact' itself (the online court) but also to the design of its 'intervention', that is, its 'introduction and integration into the status quo'. They go on to say that, 'a sophisticated designer recognizes that the task is first to build user acceptance of a new platform and later to add new features'.[3]

Design thinking takes us way beyond the development of systems that are simply 'user-friendly', although user-friendliness will remain of great importance. Rather, it informs the actual content and substance of these systems and their assimilation into the lives of their users. Design thinking will lead us to develop systems that can: guide users through complex areas of law; replace the great volumes of court procedure with much leaner rules, many of which will be hidden from users; break down the process into non-forbidding, manageable chunks; and reach beyond the use of text to interact with users, taking advantage of animations, cartoons, videos, flowcharts, and other visual guides to legal processes. Work at Stanford Legal Design Lab, much of which is open-source, is leading the way in this field.[4] Using such techniques, and no doubt many methods that are as-yet-uninvented, court users will be supported every step of the way, as they navigate through the court system. For the self-represented litigant, this will be a radically different experience from the overwhelming challenge today of preparing one's case alone and then visiting a bricks-and-mortar courtroom.[5]

At the same time, we should not forget lawyers. It would be tortuous for them to be compelled to use the same interface as self-represented users. Sophisticated online courts will have alternative pathways for lawyers, bypassing the parts of the system that are intended to educate the non-lawyer; although there are compelling arguments from beyond the law, in medicine for example, that suggest experienced practitioners might well benefit from using basic checklists.[6] In any event, design thinking should also be used in developing the interface and experience for more advanced legal users.

Tools and techniques

The most advanced tools available for implementing online grievance assessment and legal guidance systems date back to the 1980s—rule-based expert systems. This technology underpins most of today's document automation systems as well as the multi-billion-dollar corporate tax compliance systems that are widely used. In Chapter 26, I discuss these in some detail. For now, imagine a huge decision tree or flowchart that represents complex areas of law or legal process. The basic idea is to enable inexpert people to navigate easily around these trees and charts, breaking complexity down into manageable chunks and leading users through an otherwise unnegotiable maze.

Using one or more of a variety of tools, as discussed below, the grievance assessment process will seek, in the first instance, to settle some pretty basic questions, such as the following. Does your problem concern (a) an injury you have suffered, (b) some money you are owed, (c) a product or service with which you are unhappy, or (d) a problem arising from a contract? Is your problem with (a) an individual, (b) a business, (c) a public body? When did the problem occur? Where did the problem arise? At first sight, this may seem like quite simplistic stuff (for example, the third question ignores distinctions between when a cause of action might have accrued and when the person came to have knowledge of the problem) but that would be too lawyerly a way of looking at it.

Somehow, we need to get from the plastic bag full of 'evidence' to a more coherent and structured rendition of the problem. In the late 1980s, in developing the Latent Damage System, Phillip Capper and I compiled a detailed methodology for designing and building such systems.[7] We have the technology today to help court users, with no human assistance, to identify whether, on the face of it, they have a legal problem, the nature of that problem, the possible remedies, and the options available to them for the resolution of their difficulties (for example, a court, tribunal, or ombudsman). The groundwork has been put in place. It is time to put the thinking into action, as the developers of the Civil Resolution Tribunal in British Columbia have done, in developing their Solution Explorer.[8]

Similar techniques can also be used in developing the legal guidance systems, as has also been done in British Columbia. In well-understood, relatively self-contained areas of law, it is possible to build diagnostic systems—users are asked a series of questions and legal answers can be generated, with explanations of their lines of reasoning. For instance, the Latent Damage System (discussed more fully in Chapter 26) answered the question, 'when can my action no longer be raised because it is time barred?' Despite my enthusiasm, however, I know from the painful experience of developing that expert systems are time-consuming and difficult to develop; much more so than most commentators and reformers allow. We cannot expect a full suite of diagnostic guidance systems to be available in the short term. The challenge, pragmatically, is to identify the most recurrent legal problems and start with these. It will be the work of many years to have in place a range of systems that can guide on most everyday legal problems.

Meanwhile, there are many less sophisticated tools that can guide court users, whether in assessing their grievances or considering the merits of their cases. Easy-to-use, menu-driven systems allow users to make simple selections and, again based on a cruder kind of decision tree, to help whittle away irrelevances and arrive at conclusions that will be broader brush than expert systems but illuminating nonetheless. Again, this technique is well-established and indeed better road-tested than expert systems. In the UK, the service known as Resolver (also see Chapter 9) which has had more than 2.7 million users, employs this kind of straightforward interactive, largely menu-driven dialogue.[9]

More basic still are straightforward legal websites that help users roam around and grasp broad sets of legal issues.[10]. However, the current range and combination of available legal websites (private, public, and voluntary) can confuse users—they overlap and duplicate, they are inconsistent in style and tone, and it is hard for non-lawyers (and most lawyers) to determine whether given materials are accurate and up to date. To overcome these shortcomings, the trend in legally oriented websites is to move beyond providing broad information to offering more focused guidance. This can be done using, for example, basic checklists and flowcharts, guided visual pathways, and moving from blocks of text to the use of animations and cartoons to bring complex issues to life. Here, as elsewhere, the contribution of design thinking should be considerable.

Another online resource that may be invaluable for self-represented litigants will be online communities, social networks of a sort that enable users to come together and share their experiences of engaging with the legal and courts systems. Participants might ask others whether they have faced problems like theirs. Given the success of similar systems in health care, most notably PatientsLikeMe[11] with more than 600,000 members, we have reason to think that these communities, especially if well moderated, could be of great help and comfort.

In the longer term, machine learning systems could also be of use on Tier 1 of the online court—for example, systems that could predict the likely outcome of given categories of dispute. However, I expect this technology to be of greater use on the second tier, as discussed in the following chapter and in Chapter 29.

Boundaries of Tier One

Some judges and lawyers will insist that if the various tools and facilities suggested above are offered on Tier One, then this is too great an extension of the courts. They will say that it is not for the courts to provide legal advice. One response to this is to suggest that the assistance outlined is general guidance rather than bespoke legal advice and so there is no problem. This looks like an admirable bit of fancy footwork, but I find it difficult in this context to draw a clear distinction, in terms of outcome, between bespoke human advice and detailed machine-based guidance especially when the systems are diagnostic.

In any event, I come at this from a different direction and ask, 'why not?'. Why not extend court service to provide concrete support for court users? Indeed one of the main elements of the online court is the 'extended court'—using technology precisely to widen the reach of the courts and help litigants unfamiliar with the law. Other than involving lawyers or voluntary legal advisers in helping parties classify and analyse their positions, which takes us back to square one (not enough humans to go round and the cost for small claims is disproportionate), the only other alternative I can see is indeed to harness the power of technology. One other option, of course, is to offer no help at all but this leads in one bound to grave inaccess to justice.

Online guidance embedded in online courts is a strong illustration of radical change. It is not a polished version of yesteryear's court service. It makes us uncomfortable because it is such a departure from the traditional conception of a court. But if we genuinely want to help self-represented litigants, why not help them comprehensively? It would be remarkable if we intentionally chose to develop systems that offered less help than we were able; for example, by limiting the help to plain text on websites, when diagnostic tools would be so much more useful. I recognize there may be constitutional issues here (see Chapter 23), but so long as this online guidance is offered as part of a wider court service and not as a service delivered directly by judges, I suggest this extension to courts is not just possible but highly desirable. The role of judges, who make independent and binding determinations, does not change. But a wider court service is in place, offering more help to court users.

Those who insist that online guidance, to a greater or lesser extent, is a service too far may place the dotted line in Figure 10.5 (see the previous chapter) much nearer the boundary with Tier 2. It will be recalled that Tier 1 of the online court sits at least in part on the 'dispute avoidance' layer of the architecture introduced in the previous chapter. In ordinary language, this means that some of the online tools to help parties assess their cases will be provided by the state, while others will be made available beyond the public court system by voluntary providers, private sector businesses, students and scholars, law firms, and alternative providers. The great opportunity here is for the state to collaborate with these others in ensuring that a rich body of resources is available to Tier 1 users. It will not help if there is too definitive a boundary between the state's systems and the rest. From the users' point of view, it will be best if they can move seamlessly into Tier 1 after receiving guidance from beyond the court system. On this view, we need a collaborative shared space in which non-state based providers can contribute tools and facilities that act as front-ends to the court system itself. This space is depicted in Figure 11.1, as a zone between two dotted lines.

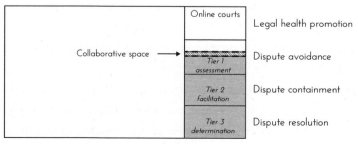

Figure 11.1 The collaborative space

This zone is of paramount importance. This is where, for example, pro bono online services of law firms will be positioned, alongside the websites of advice centres. This is how we give these non-state services teeth. Instead of hovering, rather disconnected, on the web, they will now interface directly with the online court. I accept there will be challenges in defining the precise relationship between the services in the zone and Tier 1. At a minimum, it could be a set of application programming interfaces (APIs) to ensure compatibility between services within and beyond the online court. More ambitiously, these services could in some way be certified by the online court. In any event, the challenge is to galvanize the community of non-state providers, profit-making and non-profit alike, to build online guidance systems that can prepare non-lawyers for their use of online courts.

A digression

For the sake of completeness, there is one nagging issue that I am keen to acknowledge and analyse even though it lies beyond the scope of online courts as specified in the previous chapter. The issue is that any court system, whether traditional or online, can only be brought into play when a person *recognizes* that he or she has a potentially justiciable problem. Innumerable sound claims no doubt never come before the courts because individuals have no earthly clue that they have legal entitlements that might well be upheld and enforced.

In Chapter 6, I argue that a justice system worthy of its name is not one that just resolves, contains, and avoids disputes effectively, but is also a system that allows people to understand the entitlements that the law confers. In this way, the law empowers them.

It enables them to secure the benefits that the law affords. For example, it should enable them to know in advance, at least sometimes, when they have a possible claim with a realistic prospect of success. In *The Future of Law,* published in 1996, I wrote in this context about the paradox of traditional reactive service.[12] I had in mind lawyers, who say to their clients (unhelpfully), 'I wish you had come to me three weeks earlier with this problem'. The reason this is unconstructive is that if you are not a lawyer you tend not to know when you have a legal problem and are therefore in need of counsel. Which leads non-lawyers to point out that it appears you have to be a lawyer to know when you need a lawyer. Or, in the context of disputes, it appears you have to be a lawyer to know if and when you have a possible claim.

This paradox is a troubling one—unless there is some kind of blatant trigger, some obvious indication that legal help is required or that court action should be initiated (when, for example, something clearly goes very wrong in one's life), it may be difficult for most non-lawyers to identify not just *that* they should take action, but *when* they should take action. This process of recognition, *effective* recognition, presupposes a knowledge of the law that most non-lawyers do not have. People who are not able to recognize that they have a possible claim are often excluded from the justice system. This is an instance of my fourth type of access to justice problem (Chapter 5).

It is beyond the remit of this book to suggest in detail how this paradox and dilemma might be resolved. But I believe that technology can help and I want to plant some thoughts. In the first instance, when there is a change in the law, why not use technology to notify people immediately? This would help tackle the problem that Jeremy Bentham so many years ago spoke about under the heading of 'promulgation'[13]—that, effectively, the state should have responsibility for making people aware when there are changes in the law or when new laws are passed that are relevant for all of us. Across the world, there are very few systems that do this, either state-provided or otherwise. Nor are there advanced systems to help people recognize when they should be turning to the state—to the public court service—to enforce their rights.

One approach here is the technique known as 'alerting'. This involves sending messages to people automatically, drawing their attention to new law or to common problems to which there are legal remedies. These messages could be personalized so that the updates and problems are ones that are likely to be relevant for individual recipients. These could be based on profiles that might be submitted to websites dedicated to providing this service, or connected to profiles as they appear on social networks. Looking further ahead, legal alerting may soon be based routinely on machine learning systems (see Chapter 26) which will be able to predict and anticipate when people have legal problems on the horizon and notify them when the law might afford them some benefit or advantage.

Another tack is to introduce legal content into online communities. For example, participants in communities on, say, health or finding employment, might find it useful to have legal guidance on related, relevant issues, and some indication of the common circumstances in which those who have health difficulties or have lost their jobs may have legal entitlements.

One further approach is that of 'embedding' triggers into the growing number of systems that people use in their social and working lives, so that when a user's circumstances give rise to a credible claim or entitlement, they would automatically be notified of this. We can easily imagine this the context of consumer protection law. Today, it is generally down to consumers to recognize when their rights may have been breached. Instead, by legislation or regulation, online service providers might be required, automatically and in some detail, to draw attention to the fact that a problem might be justiciable (although it would not be advisable to use that particular word).

It may be thought that this greater proactivity in nudging people towards the courts would be a retrograde step into a more litigious society. I respond to that charge in Chapter 22.

Chapter 12

Containing Disputes

The spirit of Tier 2 is that disputes are contained. This is instead of allowing them to escalate and fester as they so often do in the current system.

To recap. Self-represented court users with a potential claim enter the online court on Tier 1. Here they are given help in assessing whether they have justiciable grievances and are also offered some guidance on the merits of their cases. On the strength of this assistance, when they learn there is little prospect of success, some or many users will no doubt decide not to proceed. Those who do elect to take their cases further will proceed into Tier 2, where a form of 'facilitation' takes place. This is the beginning of a more formal interaction with the online court. Depending on the sophistication of the tools made available on Tier 1, or from beyond the online court (as discussed in the previous chapter), users will pass data from their Tier 1 interactions into this next tier. If advanced systems have been used, for example, then fairly structured case summaries will be introduced. If more basic systems have been relied upon, such as simple web sites, then completed questionnaires or case summaries will be brought forward into Tier 2.

Case officers

Case officers operate on Tier 2. Their principal job is to work with parties in settling disputes, where appropriate, without involving judges. When a case cannot be settled at this stage or when the case officer considers a dispute requires judicial attention, it will be passed to the online judge. In some cases, perhaps of considerable complexity or sensitivity, the case officer may consider, in consultation with a judge, that a dispute should be referred directly to the traditional court. The work of case officers will largely be conducted online, on the basis of materials passed to them from Tier 1 of the online court. On some occasions, it may be useful for case officers to speak with the parties by telephone conference call.

Crucially, Tier 2 service is not offered as an alternative to the public court system but as an integral part of it. It takes place before the formal commencement of an action which happens on Tier 3.

The work of the case officer is as a form of facilitator; an ADR practitioner of sorts. It is her or his responsibility, where possible, to contain disputes. This process can also be regarded as a second stage of triage (the first taking place on Tier 1). He or she will draw on a broad range of techniques, including negotiation, mediation, early neutral evaluation, negotiation, conciliation, and nudging, to help parties sort out their differences amicably. Sometimes the case officer may gently knock heads together, cajole a little, and call on common sense, a commodity often absent when humans fall into conflict. Generally, this facilitation will take place against the backdrop of the law but it will use different techniques from those employed by lawyers and judges. On occasion, though, if the case in law is all but unarguable or a particular decision from the judge is overwhelmingly likely, the case officer will draw this to the attention of the parties. Constitutional purists could challenge this, of course, but the orientation of Tier 2 is pragmatic and solutions-oriented.

I am again encouraged by statistics from the Financial Ombudsman Service (FOS, also see Chapter 9). Only 8 per cent or so of their 400,658 resolved claims in 2017/2018 were by the final decision of an ombudsman.[1] On my architecture, this would mean that around 92 per cent of the claims were resolved on the equivalent of Tier 2.

There has been a running debate in England and Wales about the necessary qualifications for case officers. One side argues that they should be lawyers. The other side argues the reverse. The former say that much of the work on Tier 2 requires legal knowledge and experience, and that court users will reasonably expect their main point of contact to be legally trained. The latter insist that case officers should not be offering legal advice and that the work on Tier 2 is primarily facilitation, akin to the skills needed as an ADR and ODR practitioner. I suspect different justice systems will settle this issue in different ways. My inclination is that, ideally, we should have hybrids in the role and resist the temptation to apply old categories to fit new concepts. We should want people schooled in law and also trained to contain disputes. It would make sense for case officers to specialize in particular problem areas, so they are familiar with the applicable law. On no condition, however, should they act as 'lite' judges. Nor should they be driven too strongly by traditional legal method. Too often, thinking like a lawyer is a barrier to ending a dispute. We should welcome new skills and mindsets into our online courts. In this spirit, the UK Tribunals are taking an enlightened approach—by the summer of 2019 they will have sixty facilitators, from legally qualified registrars to unqualified facilitators.

One of the most promising methods for case officers would be a variant of online negotiation or mediation. In the past, online negotiations and online mediations have been proposed and undertaken outside the court system as a form of electronic ADR. This has been favoured when face-to-face negotiation or mediation were difficult logistically, perhaps when the parties were located far apart or, given the size of a given dispute, it would have been too costly to gather in person. Using email exchanges and online discussion areas, for example, conflicts can now be resolved electronically by what is often termed 'e-negotiation' (directly between the parties) or 'e-mediation' (enabled online by an independent third party). In these different ways, parties to a dispute can settle their disagreements across the internet without convening in a meeting room or courtroom. The key difference with online courts, again, is that this form of assisted negotiation or mediation is offered as part of the court system itself. It is a core service on Tier 2.

Tools and techniques

In the first generation of most online courts, the facilitation process will be largely undertaken by human case officers, communicating electronically. But online courts should also incorporate tools which enable parties to try to settle their disputes without involving a third party. This was the original vision of pioneers in the field of ODR—that systems might replace human intermediaries and that the dispute resolution process itself, in one way or another, would be taken on by some form of technology. An early and much-quoted example of this was Cybersettle, a web-based system that was launched in 1998. It was claimed that the first version of Cybersettle handled over 200,000 claims with a combined value of more than $1.6 billion. Most of the cases were insurance or personal injury claims. It used a process, much vaunted by ODR experts, and still a dominant technique today, referred to as 'double-blind bidding'—online, a claimant and defendant each submit the lowest and highest settlement figures that are acceptable to them. They do not disclose the amounts but if the two ranges overlap, a settlement can be suggested by the system, the final figure often being a split down the middle. This type of automated negotiation is used when liability between parties is agreed but there is dispute over the amount due.

In the court system of England and Wales, the 'online civil money claims' system (a Tier 2 facility—see Chapter 16) already allows parties to make offers and respond to them. It is a simple and new tool but has helped settle 195 cases without the intervention of a judge or case officer. Recently, there was a successful illustration of a more advanced version of blind bidding, although the settlement took place outside the court system as a form of ODR (in the sense of electronic ADR) and not within the online court. The conflict was over unpaid fees and was being pursued in the court system. The parties were reported to have settled the dispute within an hour, using a tool known as SmartsettleONE.[2] Note that the proposal in this book is that such tools should be provided on Tier 2 as part of the public court service.

Looking ahead to the second generation of online courts, we can expect the use of such tools to be commonplace. We can also anticipate the deployment of much more advanced systems—for example, using game theory to help with complex negotiations, and machine learning to help parties predict the likely outcomes of their cases—see Chapter 25.

Is this court work?

Just as with online guidance and Tier 1 services, one question that immediately leaps forward is whether any kind of Tier 2 work is properly the province of a public court service.

If a public court service is conceived as an institution that exclusively employs judges to determine disputes then, by definition, a Tier 2 service will be beyond its remit. When they hear about this additional layer of activity, the instinctive reaction of many judges and lawyers is to regard Tier 2 as a useful form of ADR or ODR, that is, as a private sector offering that complements judicial work but, properly speaking, sits beyond the court system. But, to reiterate, that is not what this book advocates. On the contrary, Tier 2 is an integral part of the 'extended court'.

Again, as with Tier 1 services, some deeper probing is needed to understand the rationale here. If it is accepted, as I argue in Chapter 6, that a justice system worthy of its name should deliver dispute containment as well as dispute resolution, then providing Tier 2 services is a way of doing precisely this. Given also the various outcomes of courts that I identify in Chapter 4, if we have within our grasp a way of our courts directly helping users to dispose of their problems more proportionately, then why not broaden the remit of our courts accordingly? To leave this to private sector ADR/ODR, would be to miss the opportunity to deliver a more relevant and accessible court system, a public service to which all people could turn with greater confidence. As discussed, this could only serve to strengthen the rule of law.

I consider whether this is, *constitutionally* speaking, a proper function of the courts in Chapter 23. For now, there is another more prosaic objection. Our courts are already overworked and underfunded. Why would we give them more to do? I leave it to the report of the Civil Justice Council to respond to this:

> Paradoxically, at a time when saving costs is a government priority, we propose that the courts extend their scope—beyond dispute resolution to include both dispute containment and dispute avoidance. Our assumption is that better containment and avoidance of disputes will greatly reduce the number of disputes that need to be resolved by judges ... This could be the legal world's 'fluoride moment'—just as putting fluoride in the water in the 1950s radically reduced the need for dental work on tooth decay, then, similarly in law, appropriate investment in containment and avoidance should greatly reduce the number of cases coming before our courts.[3]

Prevention, in other words, should be better than cure and I continue to propose two online methods for this purpose: online facilitation to bring about dispute containment, and, as discussed in the previous chapter, online assessment to encourage dispute avoidance. As part of the court system, these services will reduce the need for the involvement of judges in many cases.

Chapter 13

Online Judging

The most controversial and, for some, the defining feature of the first generation of online courts is that judges hear arguments and evidence, come to their decisions, and then make these determinations known to the parties and to the world at large without setting foot in a physical courtroom. This comes about if parties are unable to dispose of their dispute on Tiers 1 or 2. They then progress to Tier 3, the home of 'online judging'.

In the first generation of online courts, online judging is undertaken by fully fledged, living and breathing human judges, whose decisions are every bit as authoritative as when they sit in physical courts. The underlying process becomes asynchronous rather than synchronous. Traditional court work is synchronous in the sense that the participants must gather (whether in a courtroom or virtual hearing) at the same appointed hour and the proceedings unfold in real time. It is a live performance. In contrast, online court activity is undertaken asynchronously, which means there is no need for everyone to be available at the same time. Like using email, participants can make their contributions whenever suits them. Diaries do not need to be aligned. And judges do not need to be sitting at their laptops when parties submit their documents. There is no suggestion, for the first generation of online courts, to stress again, that the decision-making processes of judges will be replaced by artificial intelligence (AI), although this is a future possibility that I consider in Chapter 27. Rather, online judging today involves traditional judges working in a very different environment. And although their decisions are not read out or handed down in an actual courtroom, they are as binding and enforceable as when they are.

Deciding cases without hearings

The first observation to make about judges working from papers alone is that this is neither new nor entirely unusual. It is common practice in many jurisdictions for routine procedural matters to be settled by telephone conference, and for interim, interlocutory, and intermediate determinations to be made by judges without venturing into physical courtrooms. This is also an everyday occurrence in the conduct of arbitrations. In the courts, paper determinations, as they are referred to in England and Wales, are also not unfamiliar—some final decisions today are made by judges without oral hearings. And there are good reasons to do so more often. Lower court judges often say that many of the cases that come before them could be decided fairly (substantively and procedurally) 'on the papers alone', without physical hearings, backed up perhaps by telephone conferencing (used in England and Wales since in the early 1990s). Indeed, many judges say that it does not make sense (it is disproportionate) for all cases to be heard in the traditional way.

And so, the big question is not, as many would imagine, whether online judging is possible at all. We know that it is. At its simplest, this could be a paper determination in response to documents that have been transmitted by email. The question is to what extent, consistent with the principles of justice laid out in Chapter 7, it is desirable for this innovation to be more widely embraced. Equally we should be asking how can we use the power of technology to deliver a service that is better than the conventional offering.

When we are thinking about the desirability of judicial work being conducted outside a courtroom, it is worth reminding ourselves that much of the serious thinking by judges on many cases has always been conducted far from the courtroom, whether in chambers, at home, in a taxi, or on a walk. It has never been claimed, so far as I know, that judges should only be permitted to think when they are in a physical hearing room.

Online judging in operation

There are two broad ways in which online judging can be introduced and conducted. The first is to transplant a simplified version of current processes and procedures into an online environment. In England and Wales, for example, this would involve online judging largely mirroring and to some extent replicating traditional judging—performing as impartial arbiters, judges would still receive arguments and evidence from both sides. Parties would lay out their cases in a prescribed order, in a structured form that strongly resembles traditional pleading, except that users of the online court would not have the opportunity to make oral arguments. The rules of the online court would be a simplified version of the traditional rules, although much of their complexity would be hidden by embedding them in the system. For most judges and barristers, this approach would be reassuringly familiar. It would be a streamlined version of an age-old set-up with which current judges would be immediately conversant.

The second approach to online judging, in the broadest of terms, is not to graft modern systems onto longstanding processes but to harness the power of technology in devising entirely new ways of delivering the *outcomes* that parties seek. The focus here, consistent with outcome-thinking as outlined in Chapter 4, is not to preserve the traditions and trappings for their own sake, but to design systems around the needs and wants of court users. At this stage in the evolution of online courts, there are few examples of entirely new approaches. But there is one in England and Wales that holds great promise and, I suspect, will be the first of many bold attempts to rethink the judicial process. I am referring to what are known as 'continuous online hearings'. Sir Ernest Ryder, the Senior President of Tribunals, explained the idea in 2016 in the following way:

> Change your view of litigation from an adversarial dispute to a problem to be solved. All participants ... are able to iterate and comment upon the basic case papers online, over a reasonable window of time, so that the issues in dispute can be clarified and explored. There is no need for all the parties to be together in a court or building at the same time. There is no single trial or hearing in the traditional sense ... We will have a single, digital hearing that is continuous over an extended period of time ... the judge will take an inquisitorial and problem-solving approach, guiding the parties to explain and understand their respective positions. Once concluded, this iterative approach may allow the judge to make a decision there and then, without the need for a physical hearing;[1]

Although designed and conceived for our tribunal system, I and others believe that a version of continuous online hearings could be used in low-value civil cases. I accept that this would require a new set of civil procedure rules and would represent a departure from the adversarial process. But, on the face of it, this could lead to a greatly simplified, less forbidding, and proportionate system that would be much easier for self-represented litigants to use.

Whichever approach is preferred—streamlined or radically changed—judges will doubtless be invited to work in different ways when deciding cases in online courts. New skills will therefore be needed, and these will call for judicial training. Some judges might baulk at the prospect of returning to the classroom, especially if the new working methods replace practices which they hold dear. However, like other high-powered individuals, from neurosurgeons to astronauts, judges will need to adapt to thrive in the 2020s and beyond.

In truth, the job description of online judges will differ significantly from that of traditional judges. In turn, this shift in profile may well lead to greater diversity in the judiciary. Judicial careers may soon be available to lawyers who might have aspired to the bench but previously have been excluded, because of physical disability, for instance, or when their only option has been home working because of childcare constraints.

I do not expect online judging to be accepted without resistance from the judicial and legal establishment. Some readers of the past few pages will already be worried about any weakening of the adversarial process or threats to open justice. These and other misgivings are addressed in the third of part of this book.

Avoiding appellate-court-itis

One objection to online judging that should be nipped in the bud is what I call, in Chapter 3, the argument from 'hard cases'—it might ask how a judge, working online, would handle a case like *Donoghue* v *Stevenson*? Instead of acknowledging that many everyday disputes might indeed be handled in online courts, critics focus immediately on the atypical, namely, those cases that for a variety of reasons stretch the finest judicial minds.[2]

In reality, though, the first generation of online courts will be devoted to the work of lower courts around the world, preserving traditional judicial service for highly complex and socially significant cases and for those in which the law is unclear or arguable. When a challenging or potentially-landmark case comes before the online court, the case officer or the judge will likely refer it immediately to the traditional system. Whether that case will evolve through the appeal system and become a towering binding precedent will then be down to the vagaries of the conventional court system, as discussed in Chapter 23.

I take comfort when thinking about the first generation of online courts and hard cases from the work of Judge Jerome Frank (an American Legal Realist). In his highly readable work, Frank criticizes his fellow jurists precisely for their preoccupation with the most celebrated cases. He talks of the 'upper-court myth' which assumes that superior courts are the heart of justice systems,[3] and accuses them of suffering from 'appellate-court-itis', an 'occupational disease to which upper-court judges are susceptible'.[4] This is an unhealthy fixation with the hardest of cases addressed in the upper courts. The problem with this, he says, is that these complex decisions are exceptional in legal systems. They offer little insight into the everyday operations of the great number of lower courts that in fact handle the lion's share of the workload of the system. If we want to understand the law in action, he argues that we should look to these lower courts. In my work with the judiciary of England and Wales, I often hear Frank's arguments echoed by District judges, who say to me, respectfully, that the top judges who make speeches and write reports about the court system have limited insight into the daily operations and realities of the administration of our busy lower courts.

In the same vein, when members of the senior judiciary greet the idea of online judging with a battalion of reasons why decisions

cannot be resolved by judges sitting remotely, they are often suffering from appellate-court-itis. They are trying to project online
judging onto their rarified work. Legal academics frequently do
the same. Like Frank, I say that we should never forget the cen-
trality of the grass roots work of our lower courts. More, when we
try to reform and improve our system, a good place to start is precisely the high volume, relatively low-value cases that are decided
in these lower courts. We should remember that this everyday work
consumes most of the resources of the court system.

More profound challenges are raised by the second generation
of online courts, in which the decisions of case officers and judges
might conceivably be taken on by machines. In that event, might a
Donoghue v *Stevenson* pass unnoticed through the online court, oblivious to deep issues of principle? There is a risk here but I can imagine the day when machine learning technology will help identify
those cases that raise difficult questions of law (see Chapter 23).
I have no doubt that deep issues of principle are missed *today*, when
people decide not to pursue their cases or when, in the flurry of
high-volume, low-value litigation, lawyers and lower court judges
overlook great points of law, in the name of pragmatism or proportionality, or perhaps because they miss the point.

What cases are suitable?

It does not follow, however, that all lower court cases are suitable for online resolution by judges. And those that are not will
be handled within the traditional system. In the original work of
the Civil Justice Council's advisory group (Chapter 9), we were
to a large extent constrained in our thinking by our terms of reference which invited us to look at the potential of online dispute

resolution techniques for low-value civil claims. For this purpose, 'low value' was stipulated as less than £25,000. I do not recall that too much thought was given to this limit. But that a ceiling was set at all was probably because the conduct of low-value cases was frequently criticized as incurring disproportionate expense. While this appeal to proportionate justice was no doubt well-intentioned, I fear it led to a common view that the value of a case set the line of demarcation between cases that were suitable for online treatment and those that were not.

Much more work needs to be done to identify the characteristics of cases that make them suitable for online judging. Other than the value of a case, other dimensions that are important include the complexity of the law and fact patterns, the volumes of documents involved, the sensitivity of the matters in dispute, the types of legal problem at issue, the extent to which a case turns on the credibility of witnesses, and the efficiency of current processes. I know of no systematic attempt so far to analyse and isolate the sorts of cases that would be most appropriate for online courts. I expect that our thinking on this will become more reliable when online courts are used widely. It will be important that we have sufficient opportunity and data to enhance our insight and develop good practices.

Will judges read?

When judges come to dispense justice from the kitchen table or even the bath, how will we be confident that they have actually read the arguments and evidence that have been submitted to them in electronic form? This question is often put to me in tones that suggest online judging has been delivered a knock-down blow. Notice, in the first place, that this is not a new concern. I have frequently heard disgruntled solicitors and barristers doubting whether judges sitting in bricks-and-mortar courtrooms have previously bothered to cast their eyes over their tightly framed papers.

This objection is really more of an indictment of judges than a shortcoming that can be attributed to the technology. It should be recalled that, according to my proposed architecture, the judges who are working online are fully qualified and appropriately selected individuals. If the suggestion is that judges would indolently cut corners or recklessly ignore papers, then this would constitute a remarkable dereliction of judicial duty, wherever they are sitting. It is reasonable to hope that a rigorous judicial appointment system will weed out such judicial miscreants.

If, however, the suggestion is that judges who work online might unwittingly skim rather than diligently scrutinize documents, then that is a different allegation. The premise here might be that if judges sit in public and, at least in principle, are open to observation and criticism, they are more likely to have read their papers scrupulously, lest they are caught on the hop in open court. My instinct is that, if we appoint good judges, then duty will prevail and those who sit at home will be as committed as those who work in the traditional way. But this belief will need to be tested empirically as online courts come to be used.

Meanwhile, there should be safeguards in place. The first is having a transparent system, open in the two senses I discuss in Chapter 19 (information and real-time transparency). Online courts may not be open to precisely the same scrutiny as traditional courts but we will have considerable visibility of their operations and results. Certainly, if the dialogues from *online continuous hearings* were publicly available, then I can imagine this would be as much if not more of an incentive to perform as well as when sitting in a physical court. It may also be that such dialogues could be subject to random-sample audits. Equally, court users could be interviewed and claims of judicial neglect could be pursued. Beyond the normal appeal processes (another safeguard), judges may not like the idea of being subject to this kind of performance review, but, as I have argued elsewhere and has now been widely recognized in the UK tribunal system, given that judges are accountable public servants, it is hard to find compelling reasons to exclude them entirely from any kind of ongoing assessment or appraisal.[5]

Chapter 14

Assisted Argument

Although it is not a defining purpose of online courts to exclude lawyers from the process of litigating, they are generally conceived as a service that can be used without formal legal representation. If we are to introduce an affordable public online dispute resolution system, it makes sense to relieve parties of the expense of lawyers. However, if lawyers are not advising, how can litigants set out their stalls and make their legal arguments on their own? In Chapter 11, I discuss tools and methods to help lay people organize and classify their cases (turning a grievance into a justiciable problem) and to analyse and reason (coming to a legal view). I turn now to another self-help task that lay people must take on as users of online courts, that of arguing and persuading—presenting a case to a judge on Tier 3 (and conceivably, in a less formal way, to case officers on Tier 2). Of all the challenges that arise in the design and development of the first generation of online courts, here is perhaps the most forbidding. How can non-lawyers with no legal experience be expected to argue and persuade when barristers spend a lifetime mastering this skill?

Before answering that question directly, we should pause to acknowledge that today's courts are already over-flowing with self-represented litigants who are expected to do precisely this. Indeed, the set of injustices (not least, substantive and distributive) that flow from the current system are one amongst many reasons that I and others are calling for radically new methods of handling disputes in the court system. It is because non-lawyers feel unable to represent themselves adequately or confidently that they often choose not to litigate in the first place or, if they decide to have a go, they end up feeling deeply disenchanted with the system.

New forms of interaction

At first glance, it is hard to imagine what technologies or systems might enable a lay person to argue and persuade like a lawyer. What kind of decision-support system could produce a compelling and robust legal argument? One pitfall here is to regard this challenge in terms of automating the work of today's lawyers or helping non-lawyers to communicate with online judges 'like' lawyers do in 2019. Consider instead the possibility of using 'online continuous hearings', as being pioneered by the Tribunals and discussed in Chapter 13. On this model, if imported into online courts in civil cases, the judge would lead much of the process. Self-represented litigants would not be asked to produce definitive and complete pleadings in advance. Instead, especially when there are limited Tier 1 and Tier 2 facilities, court users would be asked to set out their grievances in ordinary language, and the judge would invite further details to help shape the case. This more interventionist approach would in some ways resemble the investigatory or interrogatory processes of civil law jurisdictions. In many low-value civil disputes, good judges are able very quickly to get to the heart of the matter, to separate wheat from chaff, and to help pinpoint the key points of contention, whether of fact or law. In more advanced online courts, where there has been Tier 1 and Tier 2 assistance (see Chapters 11 and 12), case summaries or analysis will already be to

hand and have been passed through the system—perhaps a diagnostic from Tier 1 or a note from a case officer on Tier 2.

Argument and persuasion

Even if the online court in question is one that preserves the
traditional, adversarial process, outcome-thinking should also encourage us to take a different approach. Rather than wondering
how we might replicate lawyering and the production of legal arguments, we should focus instead on what outcomes are needed
and whether we might be able to achieve these in ways other than
by traditional legal argument and persuasion. The recipient in this
context is the judge. What information must be presented to judges
who are working online to enable them to deliver just decisions?
The law of evidence, the rules of procedure, knowledge of relevant
substantive law, experience of rhetoric and oral advocacy, along
with accumulated good practice—together, these lead to conventional argument and persuasion in the courtroom. But in their current form they are much too complex and esoteric to guide the
self-represented litigant.

Bear in mind, in early versions of online courts, that when cases
have fact patterns that are complex or contested, or when the law
is arguable, these actions will be directed by case officers or judges
to the traditional court. What we are focusing on, therefore, are
everyday cases which may seem hard for the self-represented litigant but are relatively routine for judges.[1] Recall also that some or-
ganization and analysis will already have been undertaken on Tier 1
and Tier 2, with results passed through. And bear in mind too that
the simplification of rules of procedure (Chapter 23) will certainly
help users to understand what is happening. Nonetheless, with or

without this assistance, court users on Tier 3 will in some way have to argue and persuade—make their cases to judges in a coherent and compelling way, by assembling evidence and formulating arguments. If lawyers or legal advice workers are not available to help in relatively straightforward cases, how might technology help?

Could artificial intelligence (AI) play a role here? I discuss AI at length in Chapter 26. For now, it should suffice to say that I have seen no fully operational systems that can automatically review evidential documents, distil the operative facts from these, and then formulate applicable legal arguments to a level that would help the envisaged court users. Since the late 1970s, academics working in the field of AI and law, especially on natural language processing, have valiantly tried to develop systems that can generate legal argument. But we are not there yet; not by a long way.

But there are a range of more basic tools that can help users structure and articulate their cases. In the first instance, there should be what I call 'just-in-time learning' facilities[2] *embedded* within the online court service. There should be e-learning systems to help introduce users, on a step-by-step basis, to central issues such as the difference between fact and law, and the structure and flow of sound legal reasoning. Using design thinking (Chapter 11), we should be able to produce punchy, intelligible, jargon-free introductions to using and arguing in online courts. We can also provide tools to help users compile lists of documents or to create timelines of events. They can download and study examples of past arguments to give a flavour of what works and what is expected.

We can go further and provide some form of 'legal argument generator' (for want of a better term) that does not depend on natural language processing. My premise in proposing this is that the current case load of low-value civil claims is dominated by a relatively small number of problem circumstances or fact patterns. I recall when Lord Bach chaired an advisory group on public legal

education, from 2008 to 2009, that eighteen life events were identified as consuming the lion's share of the work of the civil courts.[3]
My suggestion, bearing in mind that the first-generation online
court that I envisage here will not be used to resolve hard cases,
is that it should be possible for each life event (for example, 'I am
owed money' or 'I have been fired') to create a set of *argument-flows*
and *templates* that would capture the structure and content of the
standard arguments in each case. A court user would be asked to
select from menus that ask relatively straightforward questions and
to fill out forms online (in look and feel, again inspired by design
thinking). In this way, dialogues between the system and users will
help elicit the relevant details and structure these coherently. The
complexity will be baked into the system and hidden from self-
represented litigants, much as the complexity of machine code is
hidden from today's computer users. We know from Resolver, the
online service that helps with consumer complaints, how effective,
in this spirit, menu-driven systems can be.[4]

Based on users' responses and on the standard flows and templates,
these systems would be able to generate basic, soundly structured
legal arguments that reflect litigants' circumstances. They would use
basic rule-based expert systems technology (Chapter 26) like that
underpinning document automation software. I do not know of
any such systems in operation today but my research and development work in the 1980s suggests this is entirely feasible.

Nudging and judging

Although I think the facilities laid out above would take self-
represented litigants much further than they can go today in pro-
ducing structured and coherent legal arguments, I think it also

unavoidable, at this stage in the evolution of legal technology and online courts, that we also recalibrate the division of labour between judges and court users. We do not need immediately to take the more ambitious step of embracing online continuous hearings. Instead, we can maintain a fairly traditional adversarial process, but expect that judges in online courts will sometimes need to *nudge* parties—to prompt users in ways that will bring clarity to their arguments, to prod and probe when evidence is missing, and to explain when a point is being missed. Call it case management. Call it what you will. Judges who work online will need to be more proactive than when conducting traditional hearings.

Chapter 15

Law and Code

Online courts raise a whole host of thorny problems. In this chapter, I explore one of the trickiest, which is partly legal and partly technical. My aim is to contribute to an ongoing discussion about the nature of the *rules* that should underlie online courts and especially those that, for the convenience of users, are embedded within the systems. At the heart of this issue is the relationship between 'law' and what is often referred to as 'code' (very broadly speaking, software). The distinctions peppered across this chapter may seem arcane at first sight. But the issues involved are complex and require careful analysis. They should trouble not only policy-makers and legal theorists but all who are concerned about the integrity and provenance of online courts.

Background

Consider two broad classes of online *system* in law—those that seek to *advise* on the law (perhaps via some kind of diagnostic system or decision tree) and those that in some sense *execute* or apply the law (for example, by generating legal documents or by progressing a dispute resolution process like online form completion). The extended online court will have elements of both. In relation to systems that *advise* on the law, sometimes the law (including, for this purpose, legislation, statutory instruments, rules of procedure, and practice directions) can be directly translated into code. An early illustration of this was my doctoral work in the mid-1980s which involved a faithful representation of the Divorce (Scotland) Act 1976 into the formalism of a programming language.[1] Case law is harder to handle, of course, because the *ratio decidendi* of a case can rarely be formulated as some simple canonical rule, so that what is represented is necessarily a concise interpretation rather than a literal translation of the law. This was one of the main lessons from developing the Latent Damage System[2] (discussed further in Chapter 26). There is an alternative type of system that advises on the law—where the service contains, essentially, a summary or approximation of the law that is, in turn, represented as code. Many online legal services are of this sort. They provide informal guidance not unlike explanatory pamphlets on legal issues.

In relation to systems that *execute* the law, there are, broadly speaking, two types of underlying rule involved here—*explicit* rules and *embedded* rules. Each is a form of code. Explicit rules are those that users can read for themselves from the face of the system. Embedded rules are rules that the system follows but whose content is not immediately visible to users. Sometimes, explicit and embedded rules are *authoritative*, by which I mean they are derived (translated or interpreted) from the law. An example of an *authoritative explicit rule* would be an instruction to a user that he or she must respond within fourteen days to some request, where this is laid down somewhere in the law. An example of an *authoritative embedded rule* would be when users are limited in the number of characters their submission must be, when this is stipulated in some rule but that rule itself is not expressly articulated and visible from the face of the system.

Sometimes, however, explicit and embedded rules are *informal*—strictly, they have no legal provenance. An example of an *informal explicit rule* might be when an opening screen says that users must use a Windows-based PC, when this is not required by any law. An example of an *informal embedded rule* might be where there is a restriction in the number of characters that users can use when filling out an online form but this limitation is derived not from the law but has been set perhaps by a software engineer. Notice that if a law grants a body or individuals discretion to set such character limits, this is *authoritative* and not *informal*.

Many informal embedded rules are best described as 'routines'— I am referring here not to legal procedures but to large chunks of code that have no legal content and do not affect the legal rights and duties of users (for example, if that key is pressed, then a file will be sent to a printer).

In this context, the 'code is law' issue (a phrase taken from the work of Harvard's Professor Lawrence Lessig)[3] is that from the point of view of users, there is little practical difference between a restriction imposed by an authoritative rule as opposed to an informal rule or routine. In other words, the informal coding of a well-intentioned programmer (for example, 'we'll give the user 400 characters here; that feels ok') seems to be as binding on users as the fourteen-day rule above. Both restrictions might be said to affect users' ability, say, to present their case fully.

Issues

Should, then, the rules underpinning online courts be made explicit, and, if so, must there be an indication of whether they are authoritative or informal?

As a general principle, if an online court service is intended mainly for use by lay people, then as few rules as possible should be made explicit to the user. The system should hide complexity and so make navigation through the law or legal processes as intelligible as possible for the non-lawyer. If rules are baked into the system, then non-compliance is not an option. Most internet users will have had experience of completing a form online but of not being able to progress to the next page because the current page is incomplete or contains an error. They know there is a problem not because they have read rules on the subject but because the rules are embedded in the system.

However, as a matter of public policy (derived largely on principles of open justice), I can see that there are strong arguments in favour of enabling users (or lawyers) as well as members of the public to be able to determine easily whether any stated rules are authoritative or informal and, if the former, the sources of these rules. Users might want to know why, for example, a menu has a very limited set of options.

Another important question relates to the status of informal rules, whether explicit or embedded. Given, as noted, that this informal code can have the practical effect of law and so to some extent affects the rights and duties of users, great care is required in, crudely, 'making up bits of the system as we go along'. On one view, and I am inclined to this position—unless the rules are routines, that is, unless they are code that has no bearing on the rights and duties of users, then *all* rules should be authoritative. On this view, those who are designing and building the service—whether software developers, lawyers, policy-makers, or judges—should not (subject to what is said below) be empowered to make up the rules on the hoof, no matter how well-intentioned or well-informed they might be. Writing code and developing an online court service should be a rule-implementing and not a rule-creating process. I find it hard—jurisprudentially—not to arrive at this conclusion. Coding should not be law-making.

However, in practical terms, I can see that this is problematic. If coders are only permitted to implement rules that have already been drafted (other than routines), how would, say, an online court rules committee anticipate all the rules required of a projected on-line court, especially if the development is 'agile' (that is, undertaken iteratively and incrementally)? It is simply not feasible, in the early stages of evolution of online courts, to give a rules committee the job of being 'architects', that is, of essentially designing the entire system on paper and in advance. They will not be able to foresee all aspects of the development process; and this would also require an unrealistic and often unnecessary level of specificity in the rules.

The answer, in jurisprudential and practical terms, I think, should run something like this. (1) A rules committee should lay down general rules for the running of online courts that conform with an agreed high-level specification of the functionality of the system (agreed amongst politicians, policy-makers, and judges). (2) The committee should delegate rule-making/code-cutting re-sponsibility and discretion to a formally established smaller group that can work out the detail and proceed in an 'agile' way. (3) The rules and code that this group create would need to be formally articulated and made explicit, partly for public scrutiny and partly for a periodic, formal review by the main rules committee. (4) The committee and group should be encouraged to approach the task in the spirit of proportionality and resist the temptation to generate an over-complicated set of rules.

In this way, code is law but it is law whose creation has been for-mally sanctioned through some kind of delegated authority. This may seem heavy-handed but I do not think we can simply leave the rule-making and code-cutting to a group of developers and judges, no matter how senior and well-motivated. We cannot allow coding to become law-making.

Chapter 16

Case Studies

I have generally found that lawyers and judges are more easily persuaded by evidence than argument. For every argument, no matter how sophisticated, the competent lawyer can launch a credible counter-argument. Stronger evidence is harder to reject. Leaving the theory behind, then, what evidence is there to suggest that online courts are a social innovation that is worth pursuing?

As I write in early 2019, it is early days for online courts. We are at the foothills, with mountain ranges yet to climb. Extended courts are quite common but online judging (at scale) remains unusual. Nonetheless, the examples we do have are inspiring, compelling, and give a strong sense, I believe, of developments that are likely to unfold globally in the coming decade.

As I have done in the past in urging readers to contemplate transformation, I can do no better than quote William Gibson, who once said that 'the future has arrived; it's just not evenly distributed yet'.[1] In that spirit, my purpose in this chapter is to walk through some of the systems that are already up and running. These systems should confirm that the development of online courts is no pipe dream. I have tried to confine myself to live operational systems or concrete ongoing initiatives, rather than as-yet-unfulfilled aspiration or vision. For example, as I write this, there has been much media coverage of Estonia's apparent plans to settle small claims by 'robot judge'. Estonia may well be agile enough to deliver this in short order but even a glance behind the headlines reveals that this project is little more than an idea at this stage.[2]

England and Wales

The world's most ambitious court reform programme is currently being conducted in England and Wales. Costing more than £1 billion, it comprises more than fifty projects across all jurisdictions (criminal, civil, family, and tribunals). It is being driven by HM Courts & Tribunals Service (HMCTS), under the determined leadership of its Chief Executive, Susan Acland-Hood. HMCTS publishes full updates on their progress and it is clear from these that the vision is to build a greatly modernized system; indeed, to build the finest anywhere.[3] And technology lies at its core. The following selection of projects should give a taste of what is involved.

In crime, the various projects are underpinned by a system known as the 'Common Platform', which is being jointly developed by the police, the Crown Prosecution Service, and HMCTS. In large part, this is an attempt to achieve a longstanding objective of having end-to-end case management across the criminal process. A more specific illustration of technological innovation is the Single Justice Service, the idea of which is to allow defendants to plead guilty online in cases involving minor, non-imprisonable offences with no mitigating circumstances. The plea is then passed electronically to a magistrate for decision, using an automated case tracking system. This is already being used to handle around 500 fare evasion prosecutions each week.

In family, the aim is to use technology to make the entire family justice system simpler and more efficient. The online divorce project has attracted considerable attention. Its first phase has focused on applications for uncontested divorce, and was launched at the end of April 2018. Between then and mid–September, almost 14,000 online applications were received. Fewer than 1 per cent of these contained errors requiring re-submission. Since then, this figure has dropped to below 0.5 per cent. In the old paper-form system, the court required over 40 per cent of the applications to be corrected and re-submitted.

As for the tribunals, in many ways, they are leading the way in the reform.[4] They have introduced a system of online appeals to the Tax Tribunal; a similar facility for certain social security and child support appellants; and 'caseworkers' to carry out routine work previously undertaken by judges. Perhaps the most significant and strategic project in the reform of tribunals is the development of systems and processes to support 'online continuous hearings', as discussed in Chapter 13. This enables parties to engage in an investigatory online exchange with judges rather than a more adversarial, face-to-face interaction.

In civil, the current processes are particularly paper-intensive and so ripe for digitization. The most relevant project is known as 'online civil money claims'. Designed for claims under £10,000 and for self-represented litigants, this allows court users to resolve money claims in an online environment. The system supports both the issue and defence of a claim, it has a facility that allows without-prejudice orders to be offered and accepted, and it has been operational since late March 2018. So far, more than 25,000 claims have been issued, with 90 per cent of users either satisfied or extremely satisfied with the service. An advanced version of the system, largely for lawyers handling multiple claims, is under development.

The above, I stress, is but a sample of the projects, chosen because they align with the subject matter of this book. It is early days but central to the success so far has been the ongoing support and participation of the judiciary. (For those who understandably harbour concerns about the deliverability of public sector technology projects, I address these misgivings in Chapter 24.)

Civil Resolution Tribunal, BC

Currently, the world's best known and most advanced online public dispute resolution system is the Civil Resolution Tribunal (CRT), of British Columbia, Canada. Launched in mid-2016, it resolves small claims disputes under CAN$5,000, strata (condominium) disputes of any amount, and, most recently, motor vehicle accident and injury disputes up to CAN$50,000.[5] The CRT operates in four stages.[6] First, there is a tool to help users understand their legal positions, using a rule-based expert system called Solution Explorer (also see Chapters 11 and 26). This provides 'guided pathways' through the law. Next, there is an online negotiation facility that allows users to try and reach an agreement informally between themselves. Then, if negotiation does not work, a case manager is available to help facilitate an agreement which can be turned into an enforceable order. Finally, if settlement has not been reached, there is an adjudication process—a tribunal member can make a formal determination, akin to a court order. While the CRT service is very largely online, all CRT forms can be completed and submitted as paper forms, although I am told only 1–2 per cent of users choose to do so. Strictly, the CRT is an administrative tribunal, part of the public justice system with independent members, but not a court. One indication of its success is the recent expansion of its jurisdiction to cover motor vehicle claims.

In terms of the architecture proposed in Chapter 10, the CRT's first and fourth stages correspond to what I call Tier 1 and Tier 3. Their second and third stages are combined in my Tier 2. Perhaps the most innovative part of the CRT sits in their first stage—the Solution Explorer. This helps users diagnose their problems, and provides tools such as templates for letters to help users resolve problems on their own. It has certainly proven popular amongst users—the facility has been used around 60,000 times.

For the year 2019/2020, it is expected there will be thirty-nine tribunal members, with a caseload of around 10,000. The projections for the following year suggest a tripling of that caseload but with only a doubling of staff. In terms of current user satisfaction, 84 per cent are reported as likely to recommend the CRT to others.[7]

The success of the CRT, in my view, can in large part be attributed to the vision and energy of its Chair, Shannon Salter, and to the technological expertise of its main knowledge engineer, Darin Thompson. Without leadership and technical capability, online courts projects are unlikely to take hold.

Traffic Penalty Tribunal

The longest-standing online public dispute resolution system of which I am aware is the Traffic Penalty Appeal Tribunal (TPT), a body set up in 2000 to decide appeals against penalties issued for traffic contraventions in England and Wales (excluding London).[8] The TPT's thirty adjudicators (judicial office holders, appointed by the Lord Chancellor), with the support of fourteen administrative staff, decide around 25,000 cases each year. The TPT started its digital journey in 2006, under the inspiring leadership of Caroline Sheppard, with a system that enabled adjudicators to work remotely and submit their decisions electronically. A decade of innovations followed, culminating in 2016 with the launch of their

FOAM system (Fast Online Appeals Management) which brings the two parties together on a real-time basis, each able to present their cases for scrutiny by the other and by the adjudicator as well. Accessible via any internet-enabled device, including smartphones and tablets, appeals can be submitted and processed entirely online, while evidence—photos, videos, PDFs—can be uploaded and reviewed as the case progresses. The parties can communicate in various ways, including messaging and live chat. The adjudicators can communicate with the parties at any time, seeking clarification and providing updates. Once evidence and arguments have been submitted, the appellants can choose between having an 'e-decision', which involves a decision by the adjudicator without any kind of hearing; or they can ask for a telephone conference hearing with the adjudicator and a representative from the other side. Either way, the decision of the TPT is made available on the FOAM system.

Only 10 per cent or so of all decisions made by TPT adjudicators now involve a physical hearing. 11 per cent of cases close on the same day, just under 25 per cent are completed within a week, around 45 per cent in under a fortnight, and 70 per cent in four weeks or less. A survey of appellants in July 2018 found that 95 per cent of those who responded said they were 'very likely' or 'highly likely' to recommend FOAM to others.

China

In August 2017, I visited the West Lake Court in Hangzhou, claimed to be the most technologically sophisticated court in China. Professor Michael Fang, an ODR expert, was my translator and the main host was Judge Chen Liaomon, known as China's leading judicial protagonist of court technology. I was impressed with what I saw: a static robot in the reception area that offered online legal help for court users; on-site facilities for the e-filing of documents; dedicated virtual courtrooms; speaker-independent voice recognition (they no longer need stenographers); and a demonstration of China's first 'internet court', which resolves internet-related disputes concerning, for example, online loans, e-commerce (contractual and product liability issues), domain name disputes, and online copyright issues.[9] With 800 million internet users in China, the volume of related disputes has called for new methods. I am told that the court in Hangzhou has now handled more than 10,000 disputes, in roughly half the time of traditional hearings.

In 2018, two further internet courts were set up, in Beijing and Guangzhou. Most of the business of these courts is conducted online—filing of documents, submission of evidence (using blockchain to authenticate evidence), trial, and the handing down of decisions. As for the trial, this can involve virtual hearings and online judging. Pre-litigation mediation services are also offered— more than seventy external mediation organizations are accessible via a remote online mediation platform.

There are also AI tools to help draft claims and arguments, and to help parties assess possible litigation outcomes. Since my visit, the idea of the 'litigation-guiding' robot (an android) with a screen has also taken hold—in late 2017, a similar system was introduced in Beijing's First Intermediate People's Court and, reportedly, can answer more than 40,000 different legal questions and help court users understand their legal positions.[10]

Remarkable quantities of court-related data are also being gathered in China. The Supreme People's Court has built a platform that, in their words:

> has collected the information of over 94.25 million cases, over 46.30 million documents, 259 judicial research projects, over 24,000 pieces of judicial personnel information, and over 15.17 million

pieces of judicial administration information; automatically produced over 470,000 reports and statements, over 10 million pieces
of statistical data and over 100 million pieces of case information for
the courts nationwide.[11]

This use of 'big data', it is said, is to improve case handling and
support judicial reform.

Singapore

Court technologists around the world have followed developments
in Singapore carefully since 2000, when their courts first mandated
the use of e-filing of traditional documents for all civil cases. Lawyers
were given no choice. (If e-filing had been optional, experience
from most jurisdictions suggests that very few litigators would have
bothered to use the system.) In 2013, a new version went live. This
went beyond the automation of conventional process. Interactive
online forms ensured that filings were in accordance with court
rules and practice directions. Compliance was built in. Three
years later, in 2016, led by Chief Justice Sundaresh Menon (see
Chapter 24), a 'Courts of the Future' taskforce created an ambitious
plan that anticipated the use of AI and ODR. The following year,
an online system was then made available to support e-negotiation
between parties in their Small Claims Tribunals. Similar systems are
in place in their Community Disputes Resolution Tribunals and
Employment Claims Tribunals.

I know from conversations with their Chief Justice that Singapore
is committed to a more ambitious online system, initially for personal injuries claims arising from motor accidents. An 'outcome
simulator' is to provide guidance to potential claimants, prior to
commencement of proceedings, helping them decide on offers by
insurers, for example. If a writ is eventually filed in court, the State

Courts intend that parties use 'tech first' to reach amicable settlements. Parties will have the choice of participating in court-assisted dispute resolution sessions remotely and asynchronously. A similar approach to maintenance applications in matrimonial proceedings is to follow. It is anticipated that litigants will increasingly use these systems themselves without always engaging professional legal advisers.

Australia

Two Australian initiatives have caught my attention. The first is in New South Wales (NSW), where their online court is a forum that allows judges and lawyers to exchange messages about cases rather than attending a physical court room. The service is currently available in the NSW Supreme Court, Land and Environment Court, District Court, and Local Court, and is gradually being extended to other lists. The main purpose of this online court is to allow lawyers, and sometimes (but less often) self-represented litigants, to manage interlocutory or procedural matters. Users are able to make various requests and judges can make corresponding orders. Procedure in the online courts is governed by a series of protocols. In the Supreme and District Courts, the service is restricted to some uncontested civil law matters—the judge selects suitable cases and invites lawyers to participate. Typically, the issues before the online court concern orders about dates of hearings and deadlines for the filing of documents. In the Local Court, the online court is available for some preliminary committal matters; the defendant must be legally represented. The number of registrations to use the online court has risen from 901 in 2013 to over 100,000 in 2018.[12]

The second Australian case study is 'eCourtroom', an online court facility used by judges to help with the management and hearing of certain cases before the Federal Court of Australia or Federal Circuit Court of Australia. Eligible matters include *ex parte* applications in bankruptcy proceedings, applications for examination summonses, and the giving of directions and other orders in general federal law matters. The service is integrated with the electronic filing facility known as 'eLodgment'. A transcript facility, viewable by all parties and the public, offers a record of all messages posted by the judges and parties. [13] The eCourtroom protocol stresses that conducting a matter using the facility is the equivalent of conducting a case in a traditional courtroom. This means, for example, that it can only be used for issues requiring consideration and determination by a judge and that it should not be used for communications solely between the parties or their representatives, especially if these communications are confidential or sensitive.

United States

In late 2018, the National Center for State Courts in the US conducted a public opinion survey, part of which was devoted to the possibility of resolving cases online rather than in the courthouse. While it was not clear from the questions whether public online courts or private ODR was envisaged, there was considerable support for some types of cases (for example, traffic violations and consumer debt) but a clear disinclination in respect of others (such as child custody or divorce). Significantly, respondents in the under 50 age group were notably more sympathetic towards online resolution than the over 50s.[14]

Meanwhile, a service called Matterhorn has facilitated the resolution of more than 40,000 cases.[15] Matterhorn is an 'online dispute resolution platform' that was developed at the University
of Michigan Law School, successfully piloted in 2014 in two
Michigan district courts, and now operates in over forty courts
and at least eight states. The system was designed to make communication between courts and citizens more efficient. It is available on smartphones, twenty-four hours a day, allowing litigants to
communicate asynchronously with judges, court officials, prosecutors, police, and other parties. It supports a wide variety of cases
including small claims, family court compliance, civil infractions,
and lesser misdemeanours. Parties are notified of courts' decisions
via the Matterhorn platform. The service was conceived also to
improve the judicial process. In the words of the system's designers:

> If technology can alter or replace the outmoded exoskeleton origin-
> ally constructed to support the essential decision-making process,
> judges will have greater capacity to handle tougher cases, enabling
> them to better fulfill their core functions as judges.[16]

Importantly, one of these designers, James Prescott, a law professor at Michigan Law School, is subjecting the use of Matterhorn
to scholarly empirical study and assessing the broader economic
and social impact of online courts.[17]

One of the first online courts in the US can be found in Utah.
In late 2018, they launched a pilot for the great majority of small
claims under $11,000. This implements a vision set out at length in
a law review article by Justice Constandinos (Deno) Himonas of
the Utah Supreme Court. Premised on keeping courts 'relevant',
not least for the great number of unrepresented parties in Utah,
the fundamental building blocks are a communication platform
where parties can try to settle their disputes without the involvement of the court; and the involvement of facilitators, who can

answer basic legal questions, try to mediate a resolution, assist in drafting settlement agreements, and help build trial documents if the case cannot be resolved informally. When passed by the facilitator to the judge, the latter can decide if a live hearing is needed; if not, with the parties' consent, the case can be resolved online on the basis of the documents.[18] This online court is now referred to locally as the 'pajama court', and seems to have brought about a notable drop in defaults in small claims cases from 71 per cent under the old system down to 53 per cent in the online court.[19]

It is early days for the system in Utah, as it is for most of the systems discussed in this chapter. But initial indicators are positive—it is clearly technically possible to build first-generation, three-tier online courts that both increase access to public dispute resolution service and reduce the costs and inconvenience for all participants. However, there are various objections that can be levelled at these systems. I turn to these now.

PART III

The Case Against

Chapter 17

Objections

For people beyond the legal world, the story so far may seem uncontroversial—like other professions and industries, the world of law should surely embrace technology, especially if this will bring court systems that are more accessible, affordable, intelligible, and quicker. However, many lawyers and commentators have raised important objections to the idea of online courts. These come in many forms—legal, ethical, social, cultural, emotional, technical, operational, psychological—but generally suffer from two defects. First, in counselling perfection, they run the risk of discouraging any kind of positive change or reduction of injustice. Second, they fail to acknowledge that people do not actually want courts. They want the outcomes that courts bring. And if these outcomes can be secured in new ways that are less costly, better, speedier, or handier than today's courts, then court users will switch to the alternatives.

In the end, then, it will come as no surprise to be forewarned that I find the various concerns over online courts are greatly out-weighed by their evident benefits.

My main focus in this part of the book is on first-generation on-line courts. As a brief reminder, there are two aspects to this: online judging, which involves human judges deciding cases on an asynchronous basis; and the extended court, which guides users on law and process, and offers various forms of non-judicial settlement.

Some common objections

There is one common objection that I can dispatch summarily—the claim that the overriding objective of those who champion online courts is to save money. There are several variants of this contention. One is that politicians are much more interested in containing public spending than in increasing access to justice. Another is that all government departments are under pressure to reduce costs and in the justice arena this is best achieved, according to bean counters, by closing courts. Both of these allegations may well have some substance in some jurisdictions but I find that almost all lawyers and judges who advocate digital reform are driven much more by a desire to increase access to justice. For those of us who are galvanized by *reducing injustice* and improving court service, costs savings are a desirable outcome but they are not the motivating force. To persist in believing or declaring that the introduction of online courts is but a ploy to cut costs is to disregard the heartfelt and explicitly stated views of innumerable judges, lawyers, and commentators.

It is notable, incidentally, that for many lawyers who are understandably angry about cuts in public spending on legal aid, the simple answer to inaccessible courts seems to be to set that tap running again—for the state to return to paying for the work of many more lawyers. My instinct, having spent a lifetime in the legal world, is to be sympathetic to this position. But greater funding cannot be the complete answer because too often this would surely be to fund an inefficient, antiquated court system. If our current system for resolving disputes is disproportionately expensive, we should want a better system regardless of who is paying. We need to fix the leaks, not just replenish the tank. We have to find a way of widening access and reducing unmet legal need at a cost that makes sense relative to the value of any given case.

Another common set of objections that should not detain us too long are those that exhibit what I call 'irrational rejectionism'—the dogmatic dismissal of technologies of which the critic has no direct experience (see Chapter 3). I reiterate this here because it surely will not do, no matter how eminent the rejectionist, to dismiss the idea of online courts without seeing a few systems in action and spending some time immersed in the literature. I say this with some passion because I am assailed almost daily by articulate and forceful judges and lawyers who snub online courts without any evidence of their operation in practice nor their purpose in principle. This kind of rhetoric would be accepted neither in the courtroom nor in informed public discourse, and will not be admitted here either.

A further objection that should be addressed at the outset comes from opponents of online courts who observe that no compelling business case can be been made for their introduction. To any entrepreneur and to most business people, this is a bizarre contention. Until any business is up and running, it is never possible to confirm or otherwise that it is performing according to plan. In new markets, by definition, there is little advance evidence. Those of us who advocate online courts, like those who launch startups, believe we have identified a new market (unmet legal need) or a gap in the existing market (efficient state-based resolution), we draw on the experience of analogous ventures (like those that inspired the Civil Justice Council group—Chapter 9), we do the maths on the basis of reasonable assumptions (fewer costly buildings, faster disposal of cases, more efficient administration), we weigh up the risks (such as technological failure—Chapter 24), we put in place precautions (for instance, restricting ourselves to low-value cases), we think through the implications (this book) and we conclude, because the status quo is decreasingly tolerable, that this is an investment worth making, so long as we are rigorous in monitoring progress and making changes accordingly. Any business

person would recognize this logic, as will any imaginative politicians and senior judges responsible for strategic planning. There are
no guarantees. No certainties. Assumptions about the future have
to be made. But the upside appears to be sufficiently attractive that
it looks like a sound investment.

A final objection that can be met in a few words is that not all
cases are suitable for online courts. I am the first to agree with this.
By implication, this way of framing the objection concedes that
some cases are indeed suitable and that is my major contention.
Nonetheless, as I say explicitly in Chapter 13, a great deal more
thinking and analysis needs to be undertaken to pinpoint the characteristics of cases that make them ill-suited for online disposal.

Voltaire's Riposte

In Chapter 8, I discuss Voltaire's observation that 'the best is the
enemy of the good', suggesting that 'the best is the enemy of the
better' might have been a better formulation. I draw a distinction
between the transcendentalists who set their sights on some idealized concept of a just court service and the comparativists who
focus on improvement rather than perfection, on removing manifest injustices.

Calling it Voltaire's Riposte, I will draw on this line of argument
liberally as I consider the various objections that are commonly
levelled at online courts. There are two strands to Voltaire's Riposte.
The first reminds us that although online courts have drawbacks,
they will constitute an advance on the disproportionate system
used for many of today's lower-value disputes; and so, on balance,
are worth embracing despite their shortcomings. The second is in
many ways more significant because it focuses on the great social

problem of unmet legal need, on what I have been calling, since the mid–1990s, the 'latent legal market'.[1] I am referring here to those innumerable occasions in the lives of most people when they need and would benefit from legal help but, in the past, this assistance has not been available. It has been too costly, complicated, forbidding, time-consuming, and so forth. Simply put, online courts will provide a state-based mechanism for the management and resolution of disputes in many situations where today there is effectively none. More crudely put, something is better than nothing. I am not suggesting that anything is better than nothing; but that the something I am calling 'online courts' offer inexpensive, swift, intelligible resolution or disposal when today many legal entitlements go unenforced and often are not even recognized. And it is important that this public service is available not only to help those who are excluded today, but also, as stressed in Chapter 1, to build and maintain confidence in the authority of law and in the rule of law.

Do I think online courts will invariably do a better job in all cases than the Lord Chief Justice of England and Wales, sitting in Courtroom 4 of the Royal Courts of Justice on The Strand in London? Of course not. But the Lord Chief Justice is not available to sit on all cases. Nor would it be proportionate for him to be so. Most disputes do not require his level of experience and expertise. With this in mind, had Voltaire known about online courts, he would also surely have counselled that 'the best is the enemy of the proportionate'.

One response to the Voltaire Riposte concedes that our current court systems could be greatly improved and much wider in reach but denies that the only way to make these changes is by introducing online courts. We have significant, long-standing problems with our court systems but, it can be argued, we should not assume that online courts are the only or the best alternative. As a matter of logic, this line of thinking is unassailable. I cannot claim that the only way to provide a cheaper, quicker, and simpler public court service is through online courts. But I am suggesting that it is the most credible alternative on offer today. It is striking that most critics of online courts have no alternative narrative, no systematic proposals of their own for tackling the access to justice problem. It is not that they are laying out their own buffet of tempting options. The best most can offer, as just noted, is that the state should invest more in conventional legal service to improve access and, at the same time, that the administration of courts should be modernized and streamlined. I accept that we cannot leap from their lack of proposals to the conclusion that online courts are the definitive solution. But, consistent with the Voltaire Riposte, I can say that we have found a new way, that growing evidence suggests this new way would be better than the old set-up, and unless and until someone can indeed come up with a plausible alternative, I maintain we should work hard to introduce and road-test this innovation. I know of no principle of justice that requires us to ignore such an opportunity.

Gathering data from online courts

Another objection that can be addressed quite swiftly relates to the data that should be gathered in relation to the performance of online courts. A growing body of academics have been increasingly concerned that those who are designing online courts are not thinking enough about the data that will be needed to evaluate their performance. The reason that this objection can be addressed swiftly is that it is entirely sound. We must capture and analyse as much relevant information as we can about the outcomes and impact of live, operational online courts. We need data to support the advanced research programmes that should run in parallel to the roll-out of online courts in any jurisdiction. Academics are already working hard in putting together appropriate research agendas.[2] And it is vital that we do indeed monitor and evaluate the impact of online courts, so that adjustments and refinements to the systems can be made in light of positive or negative experience. It would be absurd to suppose that the first version of an online court would be the last word, and not just because new techniques and technologies will come to be available. Those who design and develop online courts should also seek relentlessly to track and assess users' experiences (they should build feedback facilities into the system). Sometimes this will lead to fine-tuning, but we must be open to the possibility of fundamental re-design or even abandonment of innovations if the systems are conducive to injustices (Chapters 7 and 8) and failing to increase access to justice (Chapter 6). (Looking a few years hence, the data gathered could also be invaluable when we have machine learning systems (Chapters 26 and 27) that will be able to learn and make predictions about court outcomes on the basis of that data.)

That said, users ought not always to have the final say. Two celebrated individuals, from quite different eras, hit the nail on the head here. It is said that Henry Ford was dismissive when once asked whether he was inspired in inventing mass manufacturing of cars by asking customers what they wanted. He responded that if he had asked customers what they wanted, they would have asked for faster horses. And so it is with courts, users, and lawyers, for that matter. When we ask them what changes they want, they tend to come up with 'faster horses', that is, an improved and streamlined version of what we have today. Most users give little detailed thought to the future or to change. They do not spend their time immersed in emerging technologies or pondering transformation. It is best to test new ideas out on them, rather than inviting their views in the early reaches of research and development.

Steve Jobs was the other notable individual who helps us here. As noted in Chapter 4, he suggested with characteristic diffidence that users do not know what they want until Apple shows them. It is not that users know what they want but sometimes do not know what they need. According to Jobs, users also have a limited view of what they want.

In truth, users often have insufficient data or insight to make reliable judgements about projected systems. They are more reliable when they report on how they found a system or process with which they have interacted. Even then, our studies need to be sophisticated to control for bias, conservatism, and irrational rejectionism. And when court users are not lawyers, we have to bear in mind that court service for them is, as economists would say, a 'credence good'. This means that they often do not know enough to be able to judge the technical value or quality of the service.

Some critics may believe that empirical research will reveal the entire enterprise of online courts to be misguided and lead to their abandonment. I think we have already seen enough early successes (see Chapter 16) to suggest that online courts, in some manifestation, will increase access to justice. Our challenge is to identify the limits of the technology and to ensure we are making the most of the facility. Above all, we should not make assumptions about the world yet to come. There is no evidence from the future.

Chapter 18

Economy-class Justice

One plausible and common concern about online courts, ventilated within and beyond the legal fraternity, is that these systems are, essentially, for people of limited means. They will provide them with a service that is inferior to traditional court service, and the 'proper' good old-fashioned courts will be retained only for those who are better off. Poorer people, in other words, will be confined to an economy-class service while the richer will continue to travel on a first-class ticket. On this view, although they may be conceived as a way of increasing access to justice, online courts will in fact perpetuate and widen the gap between socio-economic classes, between the haves and have-nots.

The formal argument

This objection, in part, is an argument about distributive justice—with the advent of online courts, the capacity to enforce one's entitlements is a benefit that, it is claimed, will be *more unevenly* spread around our communities. This objection is also a claim about that aspect of procedural justice known formal justice, that like cases should be treated alike—the state should handle similar disputes in broadly the same way, not discriminating according to the means of the parties or their willingness to pay.

Before we explore the extent to which justice is served or denied in the senses identified, a question, partly of policy and partly
legal, jumps out for prior attention. The assumption made in most
versions of this objection is that users of the court system will be
offered the *choice* between online or traditional handling of their
cases, just as passengers on planes are free to select which class
of ticket they wish to purchase (noting that this latter choice is
not entirely free because it is contained by people's means—as
the old saying goes, the Ritz is 'open' to all). However, many if
not most advocates of online courts take the policy view that, in
cases deemed suitable for their use (see Chapter 13), online courts
should, at least at the early stages of a claim, be mandatory and not
optional,[1] so long as the needs of the vulnerable and 'hard to reach'
are not prejudiced (see Chapter 21). There should be no choice for
the parties. The online court *is* the only court in certain types of
cases. I predict this will be standard practice in most jurisdictions
in years to come. In which event, the economy-class objection becomes irrelevant. There is only one class of travel, as procedural and
distributive justice requires.

Response

But let us assume, to give the objection its best airing, that a choice
between online and traditional disposal is indeed on offer to court
users. Does this necessarily give rise to injustice? The basis of this
objection, clearly, is that traditional service is superior to online
service, and that parties with the wherewithal would invariably
prefer to have their cases heard in a physical arena than in some
allegedly inferior online environment. If money were no object,
who would opt on a transatlantic flight for a spartan cabin in which

the food is plain, the leg room is limited, and the crew are grim, rather than enjoy a lavishly appointed pod with comfy flat bed, fine snacks and beverages, and agreeable cabin staff? By analogy, the argument runs, anyone with their wits about them, given the choice, would favour a physical over an online court.

Of course, the court/plane analogy, is not without its problems. Court services have deep constitutional significance (see Chapter 1) that transportation systems do not. For most people, involvement in court processes is very rare, whereas air travel has become unexceptional for many. There are many more options (mode of transport and carriers) for the traveller than the litigant. Nonetheless, there is some useful common ground here, not least what we might call the 'A to B' point. The fundamental outcome of travel, generally speaking, is to get from A to B. The class of travel does not affect the basics—a first-class tripper arrives at the same destination and no quicker than the economy-class traveller. Equally, if a plane crashes, the disaster affects all classes of passenger. Likewise, with court process, no sensible proponents of online courts are suggesting that the fundamental outcome (for example, a fair decision) would be different, depending on whether an online or physical forum is involved. There is an 'A to B' in justice too. Court users may have different destinations in mind—as said, some may seek a legal remedy, others an apology, yet others want simply to move on and put the conflict behind them. None of these basic outcomes should be excluded using online courts. On any acceptable conception of online judging, the substantive result, if a case progresses right through the online system, will be the same as or superior to that from a physical courtroom.

The real choice, then, is not between different outcomes or decisions but between the procedures, processes, trappings, and mode of dispute resolution. On this argument (which is different from an argument based on, say, open justice), the flat bed and complimentary beverages are the wood panelling and wigs of the traditional court—a richer experience, and finer surroundings. We can see immediately that some people might regard such a service as the real thing, while regarding the online court as a lesser option. But if the outcome is the same, are the proponents of traditional courts really suggesting that, metaphorically speaking, a cheap and cheerful service should not be available? Are they insisting that people who want to use court services should be compelled to use a more expensive service than is necessary and one which is unaffordable to most? To those who say, 'yes', I would say money is certainly an object and counter with the Voltaire Riposte.

I would go further. Consider the promise of an online court as a service that, crudely, is quicker, cheaper, more intelligible and less combative and forbidding than that of a traditional court—and more convenient too (no need, for example, to take a day or more off). On this account, many would regard the online option as the superior service. It is far from clear that the online service is the inferior offering. And it is the views of court users rather than lawyers and judges that are surely paramount here. The weakness of the argument facing legal professionals who lodge this objection to online courts is that it is an excessively lawyer-centric view. Lawyers are familiar with courts, they tend to enjoy the traditions they embody, and find it difficult to imagine justice administered differently. They suffer from what I call 'status quo' bias (Chapter 3). They may say in their defence that they are in fact objecting on behalf of the client community who may not fully understand the technicalities of the court system. But this would be too patronizing an argument to sustain. Non-lawyers may not be fully familiar with the operation of the courts but they are surely equipped to grasp whether a system is being held out, with evidence, to deliver the outcomes they seek at a cost they can manage. And, in the end, if we are serious about user-centricity, which is the mantra of most system designers and fundamental to design thinking, then we should agree with Aristotle that, '[t]he guest will judge better of a feast than the cook'.[2]

Recall too that we are designing court systems for the future, when the users will increasingly be much younger than the middle-aged opponents who dominate today's debate. Court users, for whom online service will be second nature, will surely be more likely to regard smooth and seamless online service as superior to arcane and frequently unintelligible court hearings. My suggestion, then, is that, if not for the current generations of lawyers, then certainly for tomorrow's clients, online courts will indeed be regarded as providing the first-class service. Unlike the Ritz, though, it will genuinely be open to the great majority of people.

Chapter 19

Transparency

Two related and often heartfelt objections to online courts should be disentangled. Both focus on the absence of a physical court-room. One is that online courts are insufficiently transparent and so an affront to open justice. The other doubts whether it is possible to have a fair trial if the participants do not congregate physically—the worry here is that online courts might deliver decisions that are unfair (a concern about substantive justice) and that the procedures themselves are not fair (which contravenes procedural justice). In this chapter, I address the question of transparency and, in the next, I discuss the fairness of trials that are conducted online.

Transparency and open justice

In Chapter 7, I identify open justice as one of seven principles of justice that we should expect our court systems to embody. For our system to deliver justice that is open, I suggest that the operation of the entire court system should be open to scrutiny, as should the conduct and outcomes of individual cases. Our courts are a pivotal public institution, in which great power vests. They should be visible, intelligible, and accountable. In turn, this scrutability should enhance trust and confidence in the court system and in the rule of law more widely. Justice must not simply be done, we often say.

It must also be seen to be done. Historically, this transparency has been secured or at least assumed by ensuring that the overwhelming majority of cases are public hearings, open to anyone, whether or not involved with the case. In this way too, there can be public vindication of those in whose favour decisions are made. We object when the workings of courts are opaque or shrouded in mystery and we challenge hearings when they are held in private or in secret.

As noted in Chapter 7, when we call for open justice and transparency of a court system generally, we ask for visibility over court processes, procedures, and operations; over data about the throughput and volumes of cases, their subject matter and value; about scheduling, outcomes, and costs to the public purse. In respect of particular cases, open justice and transparency require that the public should have access: to advance notice of hearings; to some kind of record of proceedings; to information about the parties and procedure involved, and the nature of the dispute; and to some details about case management decisions, the substance of the determination itself, and an explanation of the finding. We can gather these various aspects of transparency together and call them 'information transparency'.

Traditionally, it has also been expected, other than in exceptional circumstances, that all hearings should be held in a public forum. And we expect, subject to reporting restrictions, that the media should be free to report on proceedings. Justice, in this way, can be seen to be, and reported as being, done in individual cases and across the system. We might refer to this as 'real-time transparency', denoting that proceedings can be observed live.

In most advanced justice systems across the world, certainly those of democratic states, there is currently a low level of information transparency and a high level of real-time transparency. While court services have been slow or reluctant to share their data, the doors to most courtrooms have been open. On the face of it, the introduction of online courts might reverse this state of affairs. In a digital society, with widespread access to the internet, it should be relatively easy to offer public access to all the information noted above as well as to the data that will arise as a bi-product of the operation of online courts, all of which in turn can be read and analysed, not to mention scraped, mined, sliced, diced, aggregated, and repurposed.[1] But for cases that are resolved online, there is no physical court into which the public or the media might venture. Is this reduction in real-time transparency a sufficient threat to open justice that the whole online court endeavour is doomed? Is this loss of real-time transparency so elemental and egregious that it cannot be offset by the benefits that online courts can bring, not least this anticipated increase in information transparency?

I believe open justice does not represent an insurmountable hurdle to the introduction of online courts, and I support this position below, by appealing to competing principles of justice, by suggesting that real-time transparency is more limited today than is widely acknowledged, and that, in the final analysis, not enough transparency is lost in introducing online courts to justify impeding their introduction—overall, online courts should indeed be more transparent than conventional courts.

Competing principles of justice

Opponents of online courts might begin their argument by claiming that open justice is an overriding principle, so that there is nothing more to be said. Any breach of open justice is unacceptable. Full stop. However, we know that this is not so because, in cases involving, for example, national security or vulnerable witnesses, it is not unusual to hold hearings or parts of them in private.

This confirms that open justice is not an inviolable principle. We can and do find exceptions. Not only that, in those countries, like England and Wales, where we forbid the use of cameras in most courtrooms, we are consciously taking the decision not to maximize openness, in the belief, for example, that this might lead to over-dramatization of proceedings and, in consequence, the possibility of injustice or a perception of injustice.

This takes us back to my analysis in Chapter 7, where I explain that when we speak of justice in the context of our courts, we might have one or more of *seven* different conceptions of justice in mind, only one of which is 'open justice'. And these various conceptions of justice can pull in different directions. For instance, in the context of a low-value civil claim, it is often contrary to proportionate justice to have parties take time off work to appear in court and pay lawyers much more than the amount at issue. Because many people cannot afford lawyers and court fees, we also have the pervasive and more fundamental problem of distributive justice—legal and court services are social goods that are unevenly distributed across society and are available, generally, only to those of means. This is what is commonly meant when people speak of the access to justice problem.

Here is the nub. It is not self-evident that open justice (characterized by real-time transparency) should always prevail when other manifest injustices are in play. It is not self-evident that when a plumber has a modest money claim against a customer, or a tenant is requiring a landlord to fix the lock on the back door, that justice insists these issues can only be considered by judges in open court.

More formally, if online courts constitute a system that is substantively, procedurally, distributively, and proportionately just, there are compelling arguments to give some ground on open justice. To put this in more concrete terms, if we can have an online court for low-value disputes that delivers just results, whose procedures are fair and felt to be such by users, and the service in question is much more widely available to the community, then, consistent with justice and common sense, judges and participants should not always need physically to gather together in the one room if doing so would be disproportionate or might deter people from enforcing their rights in the first place. Our current system is too costly, complicated, and time-consuming as a sensible mechanism for resolving many low-value claims. If we are willing to sacrifice real-time transparency in some cases, online courts will allow us greatly to increase access to justice.

Today's limited transparency

In the spirit of comparativism rather than transcendentalism (see Chapter 8), we should also remind ourselves that what we have today, even in physical courts that are regarded as the epitome of open justice, is *limited real-time transparency*. We should not suppose that the traditional court system in live operation offers a sparklingly clear window onto the minds of judges.

To what extent does being in the same room as a decision-maker provide genuine insight into their reasoning processes? It would be bizarre to suppose that when we observe a judge who is actually wrestling with a thorny question of fact or law that their thought processes are somehow revealed in their entirety. We should surely not confuse external signs of some decision-making process (apparently listening, concentrating, deliberating) and really knowing what is going on in the judicial head. Although parties and lawyers might be reassured by facial expressions of judges (grave and contemplative, and perhaps therefore appearing fair), we cannot be sure what lies beneath. At the same time, we should treat with some caution the ostensible reasons given for decisions on the one hand and, on the other, the actual thought processes and biases, conscious and unconscious, that lead to any given judgment. A group of legal writers known as the American Legal Realists in the early to mid-twentieth century cast doubt on the assumption that judges are driven inexorably by logic from premise to conclusion as is manifested in our law reports. Joseph Hutcheson famously raised the possibility that judges are often driven less by the law than by their hunches. They intuit their decisions, and then fish about for findings of fact and for legal rules that can justify these conclusions.[2] Karl Llewellyn explained the same phenomenon in terms of *rationalization*, contrived after decisions are reached and 'intended to make the decision seem plausible, legally decent, legally right ... legally inevitable'.[3]

How far are we prepared to go in the name of open justice, I wonder, in understanding why and how judges come to their decisions? Although judges may sit in open court and deliver judgments that lay out their reasoning, we do not, for example, attach electrodes to judicial temples to monitor their brain activity as proceedings progress. Nor do we require judges to submit, say, to polygraph testing, to confirm that the words they have written reflect their actual states of mind, in so far as judges can fully identify and articulate their psychological processes. We would all agree, I hope, that such scrutiny of judicial brains and minds would be an affront to proportionate justice, as well as distastefully invasive. There are limits to what we will do in the name open justice. The question of this chapter is, where should we draw the line?

What is left to lose?

As a practical matter, we should ask ourselves what impact online courts will actually have on open justice? On the positive side, if the systems work as widely envisaged, they will massively increase 'information transparency'. Via the internet, the public will have access to much more data about cases, and so have a far clearer view of the workload and output of the courts than today, when much of the data itemized earlier never sees the light of day. Will this manifest increase in information transparency be sufficient to compensate for the reduction in 'real-time' transparency, that is, the loss of opportunity to observe proceedings in person (to the extent that we are able so to observe)? I believe that it will.

Note that if the hearings are 'online continuous hearings', as are currently being piloted in the UK Tribunal system (see Chapter 16), then it is possible that transcripts of the conversations amongst the judges and parties could be made publicly available. In my view, this would be a *more* transparent system than the conventional hearing. It would be different, of course, but open justice would be better served than today (remembering too that today there is 'no recording' in such disputes, other than the judges' notes).

If a hearing is not online and continuous, however, and is conducted in a more traditional adversarial spirit, what do we lose when cases are not resolved by judges in a public hearing but instead are decided by judges on an online basis? So long as many significant civil cases are still conducted publicly, I do not see that the justice system as a whole is thereby rendered less public. There will still be countless opportunities to see the system in action and, as noted, the operations and performance of tomorrow's courts will be greatly more visible than in the past. As for individual cases, so long as data about them is made available before, during, and after a case is decided, what is left to worry about? What more visibility should we want? In the end, the call for transparency and open justice can often be reduced to a call to fulfil the desire of some parties, often understandable, to be publicly vindicated and for their opponents to be publicly denounced. In short, once the common concerns are whittled away, the residual worry is that online courts will lead to litigants in low-value cases losing their day in court. Is this a price we are prepared to pay to eliminate the manifest injustices (distributive and proportionate) that inhere in our current system? If it is accepted that greatly increasing access to justice is more important than preserving a public forum for expiation for the privileged few who are today's court users, then the answer is surely an emphatic 'yes'.

As another practical matter, also consider the infrequency with which low-value claims are actually observed in the courtroom by independent observers. As for the media, reporting of court proceedings is clearly declining—more than half of England's local newspapers no longer have court reporters.[4] As for the general public, there appear to be no statistics on this. I hear from judges and officials in England and Wales, however, that the attendance rate is very low, bordering on negligible. The physics of traditional hearings are such that, realistically, only a very few uninvolved observers can and do attend these meetings. And when they do, much of what unfolds is not intelligible to them. A hearing, moreover, is but one element, albeit crucial, in the life cycle of a dispute. Observation at a hearing therefore offers insight into but part of the whole process.

On balance, then, it is strongly arguable that online courts are, in practice, more conducive to open justice than traditional, physical courtrooms.

Readers may somehow feel short-changed by the above analysis or may still harbour some residual nagging doubts. It may well be then that their concerns about losing some public hearings are rooted less in arguments about transparency and open justice and more in doubts about whether online courts can really provide *fair trials*. It is to that doubt that I now turn.

Chapter 20

A Fair Trial

Can an online court really deliver a fair trial? For many lawyers, this is a pivotal question. Sometimes it is posed as a legal inquiry, by reference to Article 6 of the European Convention on Human Rights (ECHR). But it can also be framed as a question about justice, asking whether the work of courts must be conducted on a face-to-face basis and whether an online court delivers fair outcomes. A related point of contention is over the 'majesty' of the courtroom and its possible loss when cases are settled without parties convening in a public space. I explore these questions in this chapter and conclude by looking beyond law to psychotherapy—this, to help us keep an open mind.

Article 6, ECHR

Article 6 § 1 of the ECHR concerns the right to a fair trial and reads as follows:

> In the determination of his civil rights and obligations or of any criminal charge against him, everyone is entitled to a fair and public hearing within a reasonable time by an independent and impartial tribunal established by law. Judgment shall be pronounced publicly ...[1]

In the context of online courts, this sentence and a half have become the subject of some considerable discussion in the ODR and online court communities. The crux is this. Is the process of online judging sufficiently 'public' to satisfy the requirements of Article 6? There are two ways to consider the implications of Article 6 for online courts. One is to determine what the law *is*—to interpret the words of the ECHR through detailed legal analysis, and consider related decisions by the European Court of Human Rights and of judges in jurisdictions that are signatories to the Convention. The other way is to make a claim for how the law *ought* to be interpreted. Consistent with the thrust of the book, the main aim of which is to make the case for online courts, I prefer the second. If only in outline, I want to show why, in terms of social policy and principles of justice, we should want the courts to interpret Article 6 in a manner that supports rather than rejects the idea of online courts.

My focus here again is on the 'online judging' of low-value civil disputes and so is narrower than Article 6, much of which concerns the trial of criminal offences (I do recognize that criminal cases present additional challenges—see Chapter 9). My focus is also on *first-generation* systems which involve human judges making decisions on the basis of evidence and argument submitted to them electronically. There is no physical hearing. In considering Article 6, therefore, if we simply and slavishly equate 'physical' with 'public', then we might as well pack up and go home, because online courts would, on this ground alone, be in contravention. A case before an online court is not held in a physical 'public hearing'; nor are its decisions 'pronounced publicly' from a courtroom. To take this line would be a very literal interpretation; too literal perhaps for continental European lawyers who tend not to be strict constructionists. In developing the law in this area, I would expect, in the European tradition, that the courts will look beyond the words to the spirit and purpose of Article 6. And so do I.

The text of Article 6, as quoted above, was drafted around seventy years ago, more than two decades or so before the internet was invented and four decades before the world wide web came into being. No-one other than a few science fiction writers had global communication, information-sharing, and social networking in mind when Article 6 was conceived. Our concept of 'public' has since evolved. When we offer online access to meetings, lectures, events, and indeed courts, we talk quite naturally about offering 'public access'. When we speak today of making information 'public', we invariably have the web in mind as the medium of choice. Can we therefore analogously and responsibly extend the 'public' of Article 6 to embrace online courts?

The case law and secondary literature on Article 6 is formidable. The official guide to Article 6 for civil trials, published by the European Court of Human Rights (although not binding on it), runs to eighty pages of notably small type with around 500 citations of what are said to be the leading judgments.[2] I know of no cases that have addressed online courts specifically, although alternative methods of dispute resolution have been addressed.[3]

The purpose of Article 6, according to the Guide, is to protect litigants, 'against the administration of justice in secret with no public scrutiny'.[4] As the case law on Article 6 develops over time and addresses online courts explicitly, it seems to me both necessary and consistent with its stated purpose, that there is a particular focus on three of the principles of justice identified in Chapter 7— procedural justice, open justice, and distributive justice.

Procedural justice is about fair process and so fair trials. According to my discussion in Chapter 7 there are four key components: like cases should be treated alike; parties should be given the opportunity to state their cases before a judge who has no personal interest in the dispute; judges should be impartial and work in a judicial system that is independent; and they should judge the cases and not the parties. Arguably, this view of procedural justice goes further than Article 6. In any event, I argue in this book that online courts, if introduced according to the architecture of Chapter 10, tick all four boxes. In some ways, in fact, online courts provide a more emphatic tick than conventional courts: for example, the parties, as discussed in the previous chapter, are to a greater extent 'blind' to the judges, and the workings of the courts are precisely designed for non-lawyers.

In relation to open justice, the thrust of Article 6 strongly echoes the arguments of the previous chapter regarding transparency. There is clearly a connection between open justice and the notion of a fair trial. No-one could sensibly contend, however, that transparency of itself will ensure that trials will be fair. But it might be claimed that a trial can only be fair if it is conducted in public. Yet this would surely be too bold an assertion. We can easily imagine a case in an online court that is conducted fairly (procedurally just) and delivers a fair decision (substantively just) and yet was not held in open court. Assuming the high degree of information transparency outlined in the previous chapter, it would be strange to say that because there was no real-time transparency, then the trial by that fact alone was not fair. This, again, would be to stipulate that open justice overrides all other principles of justice, a position rejected in the previous chapter.

Then there is the question of distributive justice. Article 6 states that 'everyone is entitled to a fair and public hearing'. This might be construed restrictively as a call for any hearings that there are to be fair *and* public. Consistent with the case law, however, a better interpretation is that this clause seeks, in the end, to bring about greater access to justice. Here we see the pervasive tension between distributive justice and open justice. If we really do want everyone, or at least many people, to have access to the courts, then it is hard, in practice, to envisage how our current 'public' system can be scaled to deliver a proportionate service.

It is clear from the guidance and cases that the requirement for a hearing to be public is not absolute. This was seized upon some time ago in relation to ADR:

> [S]ince ADR procedures are introduced by States in order to increase access to justice, States are permitted to compromise some of the rights held in Article 6 at first instance so long as the guarantees found therein are secured during the appellate stage. [5]

Accordingly, my argument to the guardians of Article 6—judges, academics, lawyers—is that we broaden our horizons and, in the interests of distributive and proportionate justice, revisit our common understanding of what it means for a court system to play 'public' host to fair trials. What surely matters above all else is that the decisions of our courts are fair, that the processes are fair and that participants feel that they are so, and that court service is available across the community at a proportionate cost.

Of course, we must have safeguards. For example, case officers and judges should be empowered to direct a case at any stage to a traditional hearing, when issues of open justice are of particular concern. And there should be appeals from online courts to traditional courts. Whether there should be an unfettered right of appeal and whether appeals should be on points of fact as well as law, I am not yet sure. Much depends on the throughput of the online courts, the types of cases deemed suitable for them, and the level of user satisfaction.

The human face of justice

Doubts will remain. Are we not losing some essential ingredient of the court system in deciding cases online? The instinct of many will be that there must be a loss, that the administration of justice is an intrinsically human business and best, or perhaps only, achieved when human beings come together in the same place. This argument was well made by Andrew Langdon QC in late 2016, in his inaugural speech as Chairman of the Bar of England and Wales:

> The humanity of physical presence is, I suggest, an important component in the delivery of justice ... Being in the physical presence of a witness or a jury or a defendant or a judge or your lawyers ... isn't that fundamental to our innate sense of how justice should be delivered? ... Justice has a human face, and it's not a face on a screen ... Many smaller cases benefit from getting everyone together in one place. The dynamic between the parties becomes evident; whether one side is unfairly dominating the other, whether one party is as well-heeled as the other.[6]

He rests his case. And it is a compelling case. But it is not compelling enough. There are, of course, a variety of claims tucked away there. Justice must be done in person. All participants must be able to look one another in the eyes. Claimants and victims need a face to face. The humanity of justice can only be achieved in a physical courtroom. Justice is personal. Physical presence is essential and levels the playing field.

What, then, is the nature of this heartfelt, 'innate', visceral view that justice (loosely conceived) must be administered in a physical courtroom? Is it an empirical claim, a legal argument, a constitutional tenet, or a philosophical precept? It is not obviously any of these. On what principles of justice does it therefore rest? Have I missed one? And if so, what is it? I have discussed this at length with lawyers and judges and, in the final analysis, the very strong sense that they and others have about justice being properly administered only in a physical courtroom is, it seems to me, an emotional and psychological claim, conditioned largely by past experience. This is not to question the sincerity or depth of feeling involved. Nor to deny the significance of emotion; after all, I identify this in Chapter 4 as a central aspect of outcome-thinking.

I have no doubt that critics of online courts believe with all their hearts that a move away from physical hearings is a gravely retrograde step. Barristers and judges have devoted much of their lives to one conception of dispute resolution. They find it hard to conceive that their work might be done in radically different ways and have become attached to the environment that has played host to their careers and prosperity. But this really is a claim of transcendant justice, preoccupied with identifying a form of 'perfect justice' rather than working out how we might overcome the manifest injustices of today's system. It is not wrong to hanker after a perfect or near-perfect institution, steeped in tradition and reflecting what feels like a primal sense of justice. But to allow this line of thinking to dominate would be to let form triumph over substance. Once again it would be to celebrate the ceremonial, vintage Rolls Royce rather than work towards ensuring transport for all.

There is one concrete claim in the earlier extract that merits separate attention—that when parties gather together in person, the playing field is levelled. All parties are somehow equalized before the judge in a way that is unlikely when proceedings are conducted online. Or so the argument runs. But a contrary line can be taken. When parties use online courts, the judges cannot see the colour of their skin, the cut of their cloth, or the size of their legal retinue. In the positive Aristotelian sense noted in Chapter 7, justice is reassuringly blind in online courts.[7]

In any event, what about the period before parties appear before the judge? That is when the inequalities are most often manifest.

That is when the 'well-heeled' can throw lawyers into the works to delay, evade, obfuscate, wear down, and in other ways capitalize on their financial advantage. Today's system does little to overcome this dominance in the pre-litigious stages. With online courts, it becomes easier to involve the public court system earlier, and so this bullying (for that is often what it is) can more easily be pre-empted.

Loss of majesty

Another concern that falls under the heading of 'fair trial' was raised by Lord Briggs in his interim report on the structure of civil courts, published in December 2015, when he stressed the importance of incorporating 'the majesty of the court' into online courts.[8] Since then, the point was made more forcefully by Andrew Langdon:

> Most of us—lawyers or not—instinctively understand the solemnity or as it is sometimes put, the 'majesty' of the law. The historic prominence of a court building in the municipal setting demonstrates that our ancestors understood it also. Whereas no-one wants court users to be overborne or intimidated, neither will it be helpful if respect for those who administer the law is diminished by the very fact that those who come before the court are only in the virtual presence, rather than the actual presence of judicial authority.[9]

The easy response to this is that many of our modern courts are far from majestic, certainly not the canteens of chrome and pale laminate that I describe in Chapter 5. Worse, consider again Hazel Genn's observations that our courts are in a 'sorry state' with some public areas that are 'run down and squalid' (Chapter 2). To celebrate our court buildings again runs the risk of lapsing into romantic transcendentalism.

However, the quotation above rightly reminds us that online courts should be designed in a way that captures and conveys the authority of conventional courts. The systems should somehow stimulate as much if not more confidence in and respect for the judiciary. Moreover, daily interactions with online courts should offer clear and frequent affirmation of the authority and the rule of law. While investing the online court with this weight and import may involve simulating in electronic form some of the symbols and icons of traditional courts, much new thinking is needed here— about the 'look and feel' of online court service. The services of talented designers should be engaged to infuse the values and prin- ciples of the justice system into the online environment. Again, de- sign thinking should play a central role not only in helping project and preserve the authority of law but also in clearly differentiating public online courts, in process and substance, from private ODR services that are steadily appearing on the web.

More generally, outcome-thinking invites us not to fixate on and even perpetuate the current characteristics of our court sys- tems such as 'majesty' but to give thought to what results or con- sequences we consider desirable. Is majesty an intrinsic good, important for its own sake, or do we value it because of the out- comes it secures? My sense is that it is not majesty in and of itself that is the fundamental value. Rather, we want to have a system that is authoritative, respected, and supportive of the principles of justice introduced in Chapter 7. We also want a system that is con- sidered relevant and not detached from the mainstream social and working lives of citizens. We want a system that celebrates the best of the remarkable online world that we have built and now inhabit.

The Voltaire Riposte, in this context, inclines us to ask whether we should prefer a majestic, rarely used, physical court system at the periphery of the lives of citizens, or an effective, popular, authoritative, relevant, and respected system that sits comfortably in contemporary life?

Returning to the question posed at the end of Chapter 4, are there features of our current court systems that are so intrinsically valuable or important that their replacement should be resisted even if a different approach can yield better outcomes? In the debate over majesty, are we really suggesting that we maintain our great halls of justice, *because of* their soaring spires, vaulted ceilings, burnished oak, and panelled walls adorned with forbidding crests? Or should our system have claims to authority because of the quality and impact of its endeavours rather than the trappings from the past?

Lessons from psychotherapy

When pondering challenges to our traditions and in seeking guidance or inspiration, I often encourage legal professionals to look beyond the law. In the context of fair trials, the field of psychotherapy can shine a light, although not perhaps in the way that readers might envisage. An analogy can be drawn between court service and psychotherapy in that many exponents and observers consider these both to be social and cultural phenomena that have personal interaction at their core. These are quintessentially human services that are surely best served by people coming together.

To challenge that view at least in psychotherapy, I commend to judges and lawyers the work of Irvin Yalom, emeritus professor of psychiatry at Stanford University, and a pioneer in psychotherapy. In his autobiography, *Becoming Myself,* Yalom recounts his initial reaction to the idea that *therapy* might be conducted on the phone:

How can one possibly do decent treatment without actually seeing the patient? Wouldn't the therapist miss all the nuances—the mingled glances, the facial expressions, the smiles, the nods, the handshakes at departure—so absolutely essential to the intimacy of the therapeutic relationship?[10]

As we have seen, doubting lawyers make a similar case. How can judges possibly come to their decisions without actually seeing the witnesses? In the words of Andrew Langdon:

Let me ask: how often during a case does a judge, able to absorb atmosphere, nuance and interaction at close quarters, suddenly gain an insight: push aside the pleadings, the pre-court assertions: the penny drops. Will that be as frequent—or as accurate a perception, in virtual reality?[11]

Not all lawyers and judges share these sentiments, however. Here is a contrary view, well put by Mr Justice MacKenna in 1973:

I question whether the respect given to our findings of fact based on the demeanour of the witnesses is always deserved. I doubt my own ability, and sometimes that of other judges, to discern from a witness's demeanour, or the tone of his voice, whether he is telling the truth. He speaks hesitantly. Is that the mark of a cautious man, whose statements are for that reason to be respected, or is he taking time to fabricate? Is the emphatic witness putting on an act to deceive me, or is he speaking from the fullness of his heart, knowing that he is right? Is he likely to be more truthful if he looks me straight in the face than if he casts his eyes on the ground perhaps from shyness or a natural timidity? For my part I rely on these considerations as little as I can help.[12]

Further doubt was cast on the reliability of oral evidence of witnesses by the then Mr Justice Leggatt in 2013, when he observed in the context of commercial litigation that:

the best approach for a judge to adopt in the trial of a commercial case is, in my view, to place little if any reliance at all on witnesses' recollections of what was said in meetings and conversations, and to base factual findings on inferences drawn from the documentary evidence and known or probable facts.[13]

This, once again, is support for the idea that some or much of a judge's deliberating (including fact-finding) can be done on the papers.

And, of course, the world has moved on, technologically speaking, so that all four of our commentators would likely be surprised at developments, as noted in Chapter 3, in the field of affective computing (systems that can detect and express human emotions). There are systems, for example, that can already determine more accurately than human beings whether a person is lying in a physical courtroom.[14] This is but one illustration from a set of technologies that will rapidly challenge the common assumption that humans are best placed to determine the emotional state or truthfulness of other humans and must gather face to face to do so.

Returning to our psychotherapist, Yalom now regards himself, in retrospect, as a 'prig'. He came to concede that long-distance therapy was feasible. Later, he used Skype and concluded that 'there is little difference in outcome between my live therapy and my video therapy', although not for all patients.[15] So it is with many judges who have presided over virtual hearings. More recently, Yalom went further:

> [W]hen I first heard about text therapy, in which therapists and clients communicate entirely by texting, I was once again repelled ... It seemed like a distortion, a dehumanization, a parody of the therapy process. I wanted nothing to do with it and moved back into my full prig mode.[16]

He was then introduced to Talkspace, the largest online text-therapy platform, which allows users to send and receive texts with a therapist for a monthly fee.[17] In 2014, more than 1,000 therapists were users. Interestingly, when the service was developed, supporting voice messaging as well as live video-conferencing, Yalom expected that patients would evolve from text through voice to video, to 'the real stuff'.[18] However, many patients preferred texting to voice and video. Although this was 'counterintuitive' to Yalom, it transpired that they 'felt safer with the anonymity of texting, and ... younger clients were extremely comfortable with texting' and though a therapist may not pick up a message for some hours, for the patient there 'is still a *sense* of immediate contact'.[19] I find the analogies here with asynchronous online courts to be striking.

Would that judges and lawyers were as open-minded as Yalom. Remarkably, this world authority on psychotherapy, in his eighty-fifth year, concludes that:

> in the right hands of well-trained therapists, the texting approach may offer a more personal encounter than face-to-face meetings with therapists who rigidly follow mechanized behavioural manuals.[20]

Is it fanciful to suppose that users might find online courts to be a more personal encounter than face-to-face hearings with judges and lawyers, following reams of rules of procedure? Firm distinctions can be drawn between court and therapeutic processes but I have heard innumerable lawyers say to me that online courts would be a distortion or dehumanization, or words in that spirit. Perhaps they need to observe online courts in action, much as Yalom was exposed to the technologies used in support of online therapy, and came to change his view.

Chapter 21

Digital Exclusion

A common objection to online courts is that their use will demand access to the internet and a level of computer literacy that many citizens do not have. The concern here is that if the only route to the court system and so to justice is via technology, then this will effectively exclude all those who do not use technology or cannot do so proficiently. Online courts, it is feared, will be a new obstacle to justice. On the face of it, this is a robust and important challenge. I argue in this chapter, however, that it is often overstated. If we unpack and analyse the various apprehensions here, it transpires that there is more noise than signal in this objection. However, there is clearly a case to answer and in offering my response to the question of digital exclusion, this leads me to raise some broader questions of exclusion which have largely been overlooked in the past.

Those who are digitally excluded can be taken to include 'those who lack access either to the internet or to a device, or the skills, ability, confidence or motivation to use it'.[1] Broadly speaking, I find that there are two groups of people who express concerns about digital exclusion—the open-minded and the closed-minded. The open-minded are genuinely curious and want some insight into who might be left out and to what extent. Or they have genuine misgivings about the likely take-up of the systems and want to know if some particular social grouping might be disadvantaged.

They do not have in mind the answer they would like when they ask the question.

The closed-minded, on the other hand, have come implacably to a view on the matter and no amount of evidence can shift their positions. They know the answer they want. Whatever their motivations, they are not keen on the idea of online courts and have fastened on digital exclusion as one of their knock-out reasons for rejecting or postponing the whole unfortunate business.

The statistics

Tellingly, in 2018, in the well-researched JUSTICE report on the subject, it is said of the UK that the 'scale of digital exclusion in the justice context specifically is unclear'.[2] The Ministry of Justice paints a more specific picture, quoting figures in a paper of September 2016 that suggest 30 per cent of the UK population are 'digital self-servers', 52 per cent can be 'digital with assistance', while 18 per cent are 'digitally excluded'. However, they take these statistics from a government paper that was published in 2013. Since then, internet usage levels have changed markedly, in large part because users have come to enjoy access via their smartphones. Whereas 78 per cent of the UK population said they used the internet in 2013,[3] if we fast-forward five years, according to the Office of National Statistics, 90 per cent of adults in the UK in 2018 were recent internet users.[4]

The levels of usage in age bands is instructive (figures rounded)— 16 to 44 (99 per cent), 45 to 54 (97 per cent), 55 to 64 (92 per cent), 65 to 74 (80 per cent), and 75 and above (44 per cent). Clearly and unsurprisingly, the lowest level of usage is amongst elderly, although we are seeing that figure increase steadily (largely as people from 65 to 74 join the over 75s and others pass away). The other sector of our communities who, disproportionately, are not internet users are adults in the DE socio-economic groups (people who are unemployed, semi-skilled, or unskilled workers), 22 per cent of whom are not online.[5]

This, however, is not the end of the story. First of all, we should remember that if we are thinking strategically about online courts, we should be projecting into the early to mid-2020s, when these systems will have been rolled out extensively. By then, if usage trends continue, there will be fewer people who are not connected. More importantly, as researchers at the Oxford Internet Institute found in their original studies, many apparently internet-excluded citizens can be described as proxy or secondary users.[6] This means that they are themselves not users but have others who sit in the driving seat on their behalf. These non-users are indirect bene-ficiaries of the internet. Some elderly people, for example, fall into this category—Grandpa may feel allergic to the web, but his granddaughter does his online shopping, books his cinema tickets, and renews his car tax on his behalf. If we take these proxy users into account (more than 40 per cent of non-users seem to have someone to use the internet on their behalf),[7] the percentage of adults in the UK who are excluded from accessing the internet falls to around 6 per cent.

While this statistic takes the wind from the sails of most critics, the 6 per cent is nonetheless an important minority of great social concern. These are our elderly citizens and our least well-off. Sometimes referred to as the 'hard to reach', they are amongst the most vulnerable[8] in society and are frequently deprived not only of legal support but also of health services, social services, and—to be honest—compassion from many of their fellow human beings. Distributive justice screams loudly for these individuals to have the support that enables them to understand and enforce their entitlements. If our court services should help anyone, it should surely be those who are unable to help themselves.

That said, any suggestion that we should slow down development of online courts because 6 per cent of the population is digitally excluded would surely be to overreact to the challenge. I would say this even if the 10 per cent statistic is preferred. Whether it is 6 per cent or 10 per cent, the great majority of citizens are now digitally empowered, directly or indirectly, and the level of take-up is only going in one direction. I do not agree, incidentally, with those who claim in the context of online courts, that self-represented litigants 'are likely to be more digitally excluded than the general popu-lation'[9] not least because, according to this book, self-represented litigants who use online courts in the future will in fact *be* the gen-eral population.

'Assisted digital'

One plausible approach to the digitally excluded might be to run the traditional paper-based physical court system in parallel, to keep it available for those who are unable to use the internet. Aside from the enormous inefficiency of this approach, this would make little sense because the 'hard to reach' are effectively excluded from the traditional system too.

The answer must surely be to offer some kind of practical help and support to those who are unable to use the online court services (I am less sympathetic to those who are able but unwilling). In other words, we should want *every adult* to be capable of being a proxy user. This should be the goal for all who care about digital exclusion.

The Ministry of Justice and Her Majesty's Courts and Tribunals Service in England and Wales are adopting a sensible approach in this spirit. They call it 'assisted digital'. To make sure their services 'can be used by everyone' they propose to help users through face-to-face assistance, a telephone service, and a web chat facility. They also talk about '[a]ccess to paper channels for those who require it', which means allowing people to complete paper forms which are sent to HMCTS who then convert them into digital format (two 'front doors' rather two parallel systems).[10] Practical help should also come from the voluntary sector and from lawyers who provide *pro bono* services. Indeed, there is good reason for much of this invaluable resource now to be allocated to its own version of 'assisted digital', to helping the hard to reach to become proxy users.

As for less confident users (as opposed to non-users), they should be greatly assisted by well-conceived online guidance (see Chapter 11), supportive case officers, and those judges who either 'nudge' (Chapter 13) or run online continuous hearings. Additionally, the JUSTICE report is right to say that 'thoughtful design and technology could minimize digital exclusion from online justice services'.[11] This, once again, is a call for design thinking (Chapter 11). I would add that the more support and service that is available on mobile devices, the better. I have been told for years that handheld devices, so long as their connection is maintained and paid for, now provide a lifeline for many who are otherwise hard to reach. In Uganda, the BarefootLaw initiative is ample confirmation of the way that mobile devices can significantly empower deprived human beings.[12] Worldwide, it is striking to note that 68 per cent of the world's population (more than five billion people) are mobile phone users and 39 per cent (almost three billion) access social media from their mobile devices. As for internet usage more generally, 53 per cent of human beings are now internet users (more than four billion people).[13]

In summary, I am less concerned about 'computer literacy' than most critics of online courts. I do, though, have a more general worry about literacy itself. There are many people, I fear, who are comfortable enough in navigating their mobile devices and laptops, but who lack the confidence, the verbal facility, the powers of expression, and the analytical skills to set out their stall with the clarity that they feel will be expected of robust legal argument. My hope is that the tools and methods described in Chapters 11 and 14 will be sufficient to help these users along but I am alive to the difficulties facing some court users who will have had little daily experience of using fairly formal and structured language.

Excluded today

To regain our equilibrium, it is worth once again invoking Voltaire's Riposte, the thrust of which, it will be recalled, is that we should be seeking improvement rather perfection in modernizing our court systems. This should urge us to remember those legions who are currently excluded today. One of the central premises of this book is that our court systems around the world, in both advanced and developing economies, are unaffordable and so inaccessible to the vast majority of people including, of course, the hard to reach. I would prefer that first of all and immediately we look after the most vulnerable in introducing online courts. I can anticipate a charge of injustice against an innovation that seems to be of least benefit to the least well off. But my realistic hope is that, in greatly increasing access to justice for others, aside from the evident benefits of doing so, this should release substantial resources, both public and voluntary, to devote to providing 'assisted digital' services.

Finally, it is striking that opponents of online courts who cite digital exclusion as a cause for grave concern rarely acknowledge the greater number of people who are effectively excluded from our traditional courtrooms today because of their physical or other disabilities. When working on the Civil Justice Council report on online dispute resolution, we received a submission, claiming that eight million people in England and Wales, because of their disabilities were unable to attend court or could only do so with great difficulty. In the UK, around 19 per cent of working adults have a limiting long-term illness, impairment, or disability,[14] for many of whom the use of an online court, appropriately and sensitively designed, would surely be more convenient and less traumatic than attending a traditional court.

7

Chapter 22

Encouraging Litigiousness

Are there not risks in making litigation too accessible and afford-able? In introducing online courts, are we not encouraging too much court activity and a culture that incites citizens to greater combat and acrimony? Could this lead to a society in which dispute resolution through online courts becomes a hobby for some, an obsession for others, and a new unsavoury business for yet others?

This is an important challenge but it is not a novel line of at-tack. Over the years, similar criticisms have been levelled when-ever there is the sense that people might be urged to contrive claims when no genuine loss or injury has been endured. Think of 'ambulance-chasing' litigators (who identify often-vulnerable people with inchoate grievances and work them into a frenzy of legal pursuit), third-party litigation providers (who fund legal ac-tions and receive substantial payback in the event of success), claims consultants (who leave voice messages with me on a daily basis), and contingency fee arrangements (under which lawyers enjoy a percentage of any damages awarded to their clients).

More litigious?

We might fear that online courts provide us with a short step into a society in which a civil action or dispute is not regarded as a route to compensation or restitution but is exploited as a steady source of income, 'a nice wee earner', as my fellow Scots might say; or as an 'asset class', as the investment community might speak of it.

I applaud greater access to dispute resolution but deplore people (citizens and lawyers alike) who game the system. I find it dispiriting, for instance, that otherwise law-abiding citizens stray entirely from the truth when concocting whiplash claims after car accidents, or overstate their losses when crafting their home insurance claims. I welcome all efforts to optimize dispute resolution processes but I share the nervousness of those who worry that the improved system might make it easier for the mendacious, vexatious, and the rapacious to pursue their own doubtful ends.

I want a justice system that enables citizens and organizations to assert their legal rights but I will join others in resisting the rise of a culture that is compensation-obsessed, unhealthily claims-conscious, excessively adversarial, combative, and litigious.

There is a balance to be struck here, but I am confident we are not striking it today, when the expense, delay, and upset of litigation are deterring people from seeking to enforce their entitlements. I start with the premise that any right properly conferred by the law should, in principle, be enforceable by the courts. This is fundamental to the rule of law (Chapter 1) and required by principles of both procedural and distributive justice. I cannot see what justification there can be for not allowing people to pursue legal claims for which there is a reasonable prospect of success. It may well be the case that when court service becomes more affordable, swifter, and usable without lawyers, that many more people will initiate many more claims. But if the new service is indeed enabling more people to assert their entitlements, then this should be welcomed as increasing access to justice and not decried as a shift towards litigiousness. To suggest otherwise would be to call intentionally for restricted access to legal and court services even when parties have credible, justiciable claims. This would be to conspire in a manifest injustice.

On the other hand, I can see that we would not want a system that would enable court users to launch the same claim repeatedly, nor one in which people wantonly pursue cases with very little prospect of success, nor indeed one which would tolerate the vindictive or obsessed to clog up the system with unmeritorious proceedings.

For this reason, I think it important that there should be appropriate incentives and disincentives in place that nudge citizens towards a proportionate use of online court services. We should borrow here not just from the experience of penalties and cost orders in our current system, but also some thinking from the world of economics, that should help us set prices for the use of online courts at a level that is affordable, equitable, and yet discourages the pursuit of unmeritorious claims. A concern here is that unless there is some form of means testing in place, some inequalities will arise, because the less well-off will be deterred by lower levels of online court fees more than the rich. We would not want people of modest means to be disincentivized the most. This would be a new form of inaccess to justice.

Less litigious?

Only time and empirical research will tell, but it is possible that the introduction of online courts might, in some walks of life, result in a shift in culture that will provide an important counter-balance to any increase in litigation. I am anticipating here, as discussed also in Chapter 9, that online courts might reduce the so-called 'inequality of arms' that often prevails amongst disputing parties. This occurs when one side is much better off than another, and thus more able to initiate and perpetuate court action, supported by small armies of legal counsel. Litigation can become a war of attrition, so that, for example, insurance companies can fund an extended litigation where an ordinary consumer might cave prematurely because of lack of resource; or a landlord might behave unreasonably, relatively safe in the assumption that the impoverished tenant is unlikely to be able to incur the cost of litigation. In contrast, as noted in Chapter 9, if inexpensive and quick public court services are in place, the insurance company will find it harder to prevaricate and the landlord may conduct himself more moderately. In these events, the possibility of greater litigiousness by those who were excluded in the past may lead to improved dispute avoidance and dispute containment. It will also be a victory for that aspect of proportionate justice that calls for dispute resolution to be less combative.

Chapter 23

A Jurisprudential Miscellany

Online courts give rise to a daunting array of jurisprudential concerns. By 'jurisprudential', I mean theoretical and philosophical questions that arise in relation to the law. In this chapter, I pick off a few issues that I regard as especially pressing. These relate to the separation of powers and the independence of the judiciary, the difference between adversarial and inquisitorial approaches to dispute resolution, litigants without representation, and the sustainability of the common law system. These are all supertanker topics in their own right that I cannot resolve here in full. But I offer initial answers that I hope will be useful. I conclude by identifying a new job for jurisprudence.

Separation of powers

To what extent are online courts an affront to the separation of powers doctrine, according to which, broadly speaking, the legislative, executive, and judicial functions of government should be independent of one another? The problem here might be with what I call the 'extended court' function which provides services that sit well beyond the traditional role of the courts in judicial decision-making. Tomorrow's courts, as conceived in this book, will also provide guidance on the entitlements of litigants, they will help users organize their arguments and evidence, and will offer early neutral evaluation or mediation facilities. One jurisprudential and constitutional concern with this might be that these additional non-judicial services somehow weaken the separation of powers and may prejudice the independence of the judiciary. The provision of concrete guidance to parties and the conduct of mediations, for example, stray well beyond the conventional province of the courts. The 'extended court' may be said to extend the courts much too far.

My response here is to draw a very firm distinction between what I propose we call the primary and secondary functions of online courts. The provision of authoritative, binding, impartial judicial decisions should and will remain the primary function of courts in the future, while the extended services will be a secondary provision. It is surely acceptable in principle and feasible in practice that this primary activity is kept entirely distinct from the other services, so that judges can maintain their independence and be seen to do so. In terms of the architecture proposed in Chapter 10, the primary *judicial* function is strictly confined to Tier 3 and the secondary *executive* function is tightly compartmentalized on Tiers 1 and 2. On this model, judges are in no way involved in the provision of services in the extended court (Tiers 1 and 2) and so independence and separation is thereby maintained.

In reality, though, the judiciary and the executive do work very closely in most jurisdictions. It is wrong to imagine the doctrine of the separation of powers means that the three organs of state are hermetically sealed and never in direct contact with one another. In England and Wales, HM Courts & Tribunals Service (HMCTS) is a government agency that is governed jointly by the executive and the judiciary through a unique partnership—with a Chief Executive who is jointly responsible, through an independently chaired Board on which senior judges sit, to both the Lord Chancellor and the Lord Chief Justice. Clearly, the judiciary works closely with HMCTS to deliver judicial services. In the words of Lord Thomas, the former Lord Chief Justice, 'the running of the courts is explicitly a formal partnership between the Executive and judiciary effected through the agency of Her Majesty's Courts and Tribunals Service'. He goes on to observe that, 'a very considerable amount of excellent work [is] being carried out under this partnership'.[1] My proposal is that the strict division of responsibilities introduced above would be a feasible extension of this partnership. It might then be objected that Tier 1 and Tier 2 services are beyond the scope of the executive. Certainly, these legal and quasi-legal services have not been offered in the past but there is no constitutional barrier to extending the service-delivery function of the executive in the manner described.

An alternative—which I do not support although it can be accommodated within my proposed architecture for online courts— is that services which are taken to constitute legal advice or guidance must sit above the dotted line in Figure 10.5. This means they would be not be delivered from within the public service, but instead be offered by others, perhaps by voluntary services and *pro bono* providers. But in taking this approach, we would no longer allow dispute avoidance to be a responsibility of the state. This would fly in the face of the wider concept of access to justice that I introduce in Chapter 6.

Adversarial versus inquisitorial

Many English lawyers and judges will be concerned that online judging, whether involving 'nudging' (Chapter 14) or online continuous hearings (Chapter 13), will entail a shift away from the adversarial system of dispute resolution that is characteristic of common law systems towards the inquisitorial (or investigatory) approach that predominates in civil jurisdictions. In an adversarial approach to civil proceedings (which has similarities with the criminal 'accusatorial' system), the judge acts as an independent arbiter. The process is conducted as a contest of opposing positions. This contrasts with the inquisitorial system which is a neutral attempt to find the truth. In an adversarial system, the parties marshal their arguments and evidence and, in written and oral pleadings, present these to the judge who has no role in preparing the case for either side. The judge in an adversarial system relatively rarely intervenes and so there is great reliance on lawyers. To level the playing field, when parties are self-represented, the judge may become more involved. In an inquisitorial system, by contrast, the court takes on an active, investigatory role, in order to determine the truth and to do so in the public interest. In the words of Jerome Frank, the adversarial system presupposes a 'fight theory' of trying cases, while the inquisitorial system assumes a 'truth theory'.[2]

Most legal systems have elements of both. The civil reforms in England of the mid-1990s, rooted in Lord Woolf's Access to Justice reports, are sometimes said to have diluted the adversarial process; in part by encouraging the courts to incline parties towards ADR; and, more relevantly, by calling upon judges to be more active in their 'case management'. When judges actively manage cases, it is no longer left entirely to the parties to determine, for example, how much time is needed for the preparation of their cases and how much time advocates might be given to present their arguments. That more active case management has been the cause of some consternation gives a hint of how passionately some lawyers and judges feel about their adversarial system. The inquisitorial system is often frowned upon by English and American lawyers, for not giving parties full freedom to set out their stalls and progress their cases as they see fit.

Do online courts genuinely present a threat to the adversarial system? Much depends on the design of the online court in question. The broad architecture sketched in Part II of this book allows the inclusion of an adversarial or an inquisitorial approach, or perhaps a hybrid of the two. There is nothing inherent in the concept of online courts that requires the abandonment of the adversarial system unless it is thought that it is only possible to be fully adversarial in a physical courtroom. Lord Devlin might be taken to have had this latter view when he claimed that the 'centrepiece of the adversary system is the oral trial', but he wrote these words well before the advent of the internet and still longer in advance of the invention of online courts.[3]

At the heart of the adversarial system is not the oral hearing but that the arguments are presented from both sides and that a judge sits impartially in deciding between competing accounts of fact and law. An online court can happily accommodate this mode of disputation and decision-making—parties set out their arguments through online argument and submission of evidence, while judges can sit as impartially at their dining room tables as they do in the courtroom. Likewise, the new simplified rules of court procedure, as recommended in this book and favoured by many others (most influentially, Lord Briggs),[4] can comfortably embody an adversarial process. An adversarial system does not require a massive body of barely intelligible rules.

It may be thought, however, that a case cannot be made with sufficient force and feeling in electronic argument and online submissions, and that it is only in the arena of the courtroom that advocates—in gladiatorial spirit—can persuade, cajole, and perorate most compellingly. It is only in person that a lawyer can put up the best fight for his or her client. It is only in the theatre of the courtroom that the judge can properly hear, observe, and digest the cases being made for parties.

Again, though, this praise for physical presence should not be seen as a generic defence of adversarial proceedings. Rather, it is a submission on behalf of an adversarial process underpinned by oral advocacy. In terms of justice, although not often expressed in these terms, the argument for oral adversarial pleading is a claim for one form of natural justice (a sub-species of procedural justice)—that each party should have an opportunity to plead his or her case. Proponents would say this requires not just any platform to set out one's arguments but a forum in which these arguments can be given their most compelling formulation, that is, an oral formulation. And this, in turn, it might be argued, is most likely to lead to a just (substantively fair) outcome.

There are, however, many counter-arguments. One is that the machinery of written pleadings, followed by oral advocacy contributes to a system whose costs are disproportionate in the overwhelming number of cases. This is not just an affront to proportionate justice. It also flies in the face of distributive justice, because it fuels a system that offers a superb service to those who can afford it but deprives most people of the opportunity to be heard at all. Judges and lawyers may rightly extol the virtues of oral hearings, but they rarely acknowledge that this mode of hearing is not scalable. It is unaffordable and disproportionate for many low-value claims.

A second response is that oral argument is often theatrically and excessively—again disproportionately—combative and unpleasant. This extends beyond the courtroom. The prospect of confrontational argument in court infests early pleadings and negotiations with the ethos of combat. Preparation for battle. When a disagreement is inchoate, this ethos can lead unhelpfully to the escalation of disputes from the outset. In low-value disputes, containment would often be in the real and common interest of the parties. Failure to contain can lead to proportionate injustice (when there is a level of belligerence that is out of step with the nature and scale of a claim).

A third counter-argument raises a doubt that niggles at the edge of the consciences of some lawyers. It is a strange system of justice that tolerates and often encourages the most expensive advocates to secure different answers on questions of legal entitlement than less experienced advocates or people representing themselves. This rightly perplexes people who are not lawyers. Surely the law is the law. How can it be, they might reasonably inquire, that the answer to a legal question depends on the price tags of the court lawyers involved? The uncomfortable reality, in many cases, is that if sufficient resources are deployed, arguments can be found for and against almost any point of law and, more specifically, the better the oral advocate, the better the chances of success. The price tags of the finest oral advocates suggest that courts may more likely be influenced disproportionately by persuasive oral argument than by written pleadings. This is the point of engaging these experts. The law as decided and applied in court, it transpires, is more malleable than is popularly supposed, which of itself opens the door to significant distributive injustice.

Fourth, it is significant that those who defend the adversarial process argue that its best expression is through oral argument. To claim, as is implicit, that legal persuasion and argument find their apotheosis in oral advocacy is probably false but lawyers' belief in the claim is itself revealing. Let me expand upon this. It is widely held by communication specialists that complex ideas are better explained with the support of visual aids than without. This has been known for years. A picture is indeed worth a thousand words. Public speaking supported by good visual aids (graphics, animations, videos) is generally easier to digest, more memorable, more digestible for lay observers, and speedier too (the same content can be presented in a shorter time). That two generations of court lawyers around the world have now largely ignored tools for the electronic presentation of evidence, despite its expressive power, suggests not just that lawyers are conservative. It also casts doubt on the claim that clients who are deprived of oral advocacy on their behalf are being deprived of the *best* expression of their case. In fact, lawyers already eschew better methods.

In any event, it is clear that the increasing use of online courts will mean a decline in the need for some (but not all) oral advocacy. But it is wrong to say that this necessarily involves the demise of the adversarial process and it is to go too far to say definitively that clients are thereby losing the *best* form of representation. What can be said is that this involves a substantial change and lawyers, like all professionals, are wary of change and defensive of their traditional methods.

Outcome-thinking leads us to worry far less about perpetuating old processes and methods than whether reforms will bring about better results. Are we willing to dilute or on some occasions surrender the adversarial process, if this enables us to deliver court services more widely, more quickly, at a lower cost, in a less combative way, and in a form that is intelligible to lay users? I can find no principle of justice that would require us to say 'no'. I accept that some cases are better suited to traditional oral hearing, when, for example, questions of credibility are better explored in person (at least for now). But for many low-value claims, I urge that our default service should be online. Once more, there is a lesson to be learned from the earlier modernization of the tribunals in the UK. When they were brought together in 2007, they were required to be flexible and informal in their processes and developed a specialist judge-led investigative methodology as a consequence.[5]

Above all in this connection, I again invite judges and lawyers to keep an open mind. Our adversarial system has evolved over many centuries, with its roots in cultures and communities which can be traced to the pre-print epoch. As we shift to a digital society, we should expect that some of our traditional methods of communicating in law might be subject to change.

We might therefore usefully look again at the arguments for a more inquisitorial system and ask whether the changes and opportunities brought by technology might now tilt in their favour. A move in this direction would to some extent change the judicial role, so that the judges in online courts will need, as Lord Briggs puts it, to 'be their own lawyers'.[6] That judges are ever not their own lawyers will be a revelation to many lay people. Surely judges know their law. In reality, many lower court judges are akin to general practitioners in medicine. They will have a considerable command of everyday legal issues but cannot be specialists in all areas. In hard cases, in adversarial judicial systems, the detailed authorities and arguments are put before judges by court lawyers. This is not how it works in inquisitorial systems, when judges themselves lead the way. Two observations can be made. The first is that, certainly in the near term, we expect hard cases to be diverted from online courts to traditional courtrooms. Second, it would make sense to have specialist judges working in online courts, those who can spot technical and complex issues swiftly and dispose of cases appropriately and confidently.

Lawyerless courts

Many advocates of online courts speak about reducing or eliminating the need for lawyers in low-value civil claims. A few are gleeful about this, tiresomely quoting Shakespeare along the way—'first thing, let's kill all the lawyers'. More often, though, lawyers are said simply to be too expensive. I know of no-one who sensibly contends that the overarching *purpose* of online courts is to dispense with lawyers. Over time, however, the widespread use of online courts is likely to reduce the number of court lawyers. That is the price we may need to pay, ironically, to make the law more accessible and affordable.

The countervailing narrative is that litigants need lawyers, they should be entitled to representation, they are disempowered without ready access to independent legal counsel, and that non-lawyers are invariably unable to understand the legal procedure and the substantive law that is applicable in their cases. The law is complex and lawyerless clients are at an enormous disadvantage. Lawyers are expert, trusted advisers, who put the interests of their clients ahead of all competing claims, it is their daily job to appear in courts, and so they go into battle far better equipped than any self-represented litigant.

There are many strands to disentangle here. Outcome-thinking reminds us, in the first instance, that there is nothing intrinsically valuable in having legal advisers. Having a lawyer to hand is not in and of itself of value. Rather, the great benefit lawyers bring is helping to attain some desirable outcome. Today's court lawyers are invaluable in helping clients identify and understand their legal position, guiding them through the mountainous procedure, and standing up in court on their behalf; although it is hard to justify a system that requires lawyers to navigate through avoidably im-penetrable court processes. Looking ahead, when there are systems that can advise on the law, if the procedure is simplified, there are no physical hearings, and there are case officers and judges to help court users along, there will be fewer opportunities for lawyers to add value, certainly in lower-value cases.

Lawyers who lament any drop in the demand for their services often seem to forget not only the great swathes of litigants in person who are lawyerless today but also the many citizens with justiciable claims who do not even make it to become self-represented because they feel excluded from the outset (because court service and legal assistance are regarded as unaffordable, inconvenient, too forbidding, and more). In a world in which most people are currently lawyerless, Voltaire's Riposte prompts us to celebrate that online courts will empower them, for the first time, to be able pursue their claims on their own.

However, there is an issue of sustainable justice here. If indeed the introduction of online courts diminishes the number of practising lawyers, we must be cautious that we leave ourselves with a sufficiency of lawyers to conduct the many and various tasks which for many years will not be replaced by new processes or taken on by machines. We should be wary of throwing the baby out with the bath water.

A different question that arises in the context of reducing the need for lawyers is whether or not online courts should expressly exclude the involvement of lawyers or whether the imperative here is to introduce new legal processes that are sufficiently simplified that lawyers are not in fact needed. Are we prohibiting lawyers or will they become redundant over time (alongside, it has to be said, all other professionals, who are going through similar ructions).[7] My own inclination is never to prohibit lawyers. Citizens should be at liberty, and are surely entitled, to secure their services. However, if discussions about online courts are dominated by their impact on lawyers, we are asking the wrong questions. What matters above all is just outcomes for court users who feel they have been treated fairly. And making sure that these outcomes are available to all and not a few. In the end, lawyers should survive and thrive not because their use is mandated but because they can bring value that no alternative people, processes, or systems can offer.

The common law system

Another concern under the heading of sustainable justice (Chapter 7) is that online courts will diminish the pipeline of cases that are the raw material of the common law. The same point has been made for many years by judges and academics in relation to ADR. I have often heard it argued, for example, that because many significant disputes in the field of construction law are being diverted out of the courts and into arbitration or mediation, then judges are not being given the opportunity to develop the law in this area in response to significant new circumstances. A sustainable common law system requires a sufficient throughput of cases that raise the latest and most challenging legal issues. While this objection is well made in respect of ADR, it is misdirected when levelled at first-generation online courts. First of all, following the architecture laid out in Chapter 10, the disputes are not in fact diverted out of the court system. Even those that are settled on Tier 2, and so without judges, are still within the extended court system which means that case officers will be given the opportunity to identify cases that are out of the ordinary and direct them accordingly either to an online judge or into the traditional system. Similarly, when hard cases come before judges who are working online, they will quickly recognize when these would be better addressed in the traditional system and allocate them accordingly.

Looking further ahead to the possibility of second-generation online courts, when cases might be assessed, settled, and even determined by machine rather human beings (see Chapters 26 and 27), here is an interesting question—how would the system 'know' if a particular case is one that raises, for instance, a challenging new question of law? In other words, how can a machine tell the difference between a clear case and a hard case? I do not yet have an answer to that question. In fact, it always troubled me in the 1980s that I did not have a response to a version of that question when it arose as I was writing my doctorate on AI and the law. More than thirty years on, I can now see a promising angle of inquiry into this problem that I would like to pursue in future research—using machine learning methods (see Chapter 26), it would be fascinating to take data sets of the law reports of cases that are widely acknowledged to be hard alongside sets of reports of cases that are accepted to be much clearer and see if algorithms might identify patterns, regularities, and correlations that would enable us to predict whether a new case is hard or clear. It is at least conceivable that such a system, if available in the online court, could allocate hard cases to the traditional court without any human analysis and intervention and could do so to a higher standard than case officers and judges (for more along these lines, see Chapters 26 and 27, on artificial intelligence).

Returning to the here and now, in the spirit once again of Voltaire's Riposte, we should always bear in mind when we worry about the sustainability of the common law system that what we have today is a rather peculiar and often arbitrary set-up. Non-lawyers are always surprised to hear that although the courts of England and Wales are generally bound by decisions of superior courts, fewer than 2 per cent of those judgments find their way into any form of law report. And whether cases that raise fundamental new points of legal principle reach the superior courts will depend on whether the parties decide to appeal rather than on the inherent significance of the point of law. And so, it is not that the common law system is faultless and online courts are the only blot on the horizon. At a time of rapid technological and societal change, when many hope (many technologists, for example) that the courts will be able to develop the law more rapidly than legislatures and regulatory bodies (legislating 'interstitially', as Oliver

Wendell Holmes put it),[8] our common law system itself must be modernized in any event. A promising development in this vein is the Financial Markets Test Case Scheme in England and Wales— when certain claims in the financial markets raise issues of general importance on which guidance is needed, this is a new procedure that enables a claim to be determined without the need for a cause of action between the parties to the proceedings.[9] We need many more innovations of this kind in our court system. (I would add, of course, that some claims under this scheme should surely be handled online, on the papers alone.)

A new job for jurisprudence

In this book, I provide an introduction to the topic of online courts. Much more thinking needs to be done, not only by policy-makers, judges, legal technologists, and litigators. Many of the most challenging issues that arise are philosophical in nature and call for the expertise of legal theorists, specialists in jurisprudence. Online courts raise fundamental questions of justice, authority, the role of judges, the rule of law, and many more issues that demand, at least in part, some theoretical (general, systematic, rigorous) attention.

Over the years, writers have identified 'new jobs' for jurisprudence.[10] In the 1980s, I identified another job for jurisprudence— as I put it then, '[b]ecause legal knowledge engineering [building AI systems in law] presupposes so profound a familiarity with the nature of law and legal reasoning, it is scarcely imaginable that such a mastery could be gained other than through immersion in jurisprudence'.[11] This was how you wrote when you were trying to secure a doctorate. But, in truth, my plea moved not a single needle. And nothing has changed since.

Today, bemused and exasperated, I look at the curricula for jurisprudence courses around the world and at leading jurisprudence textbooks, and there is scarcely a mention of the impact of digital technology on the judicial process. Indeed, in what is arguably the definitive introduction to the subject, *Lloyd's Introduction to Jurisprudence*, I see that the section on 'jurimetrics' has actually been removed in its entirety in the latest edition.[12] That section in an early edition[13] was one of my inspirations in 1981, when I started delving into the potential use of computers in the judicial process. Jurisprudence has gone backwards.

It is disappointing that jurisprudence courses around the world purport to expose students to the judicial process and yet ignore online courts, which are likely to bring the most fundamental reform to our judicial systems for centuries. It is equally regrettable that jurisprudents have ignored wider developments in technology and their profound impact, as Jamie Susskind shows in *Future Politics*,[14] on political concepts such as power, justice, democracy, and liberty. For centuries, these concepts have been central objects of study of legal philosophers. In most jurisprudence classrooms of today, however, they and the courts continue to be studied as though we are living in a print-based society.

Chapter 24

Public Sector Technology

One of the most compelling objections to the development and delivery of public online courts is precisely that the *state* needs to be involved in putting the systems in place. Governments around the world have a woeful track record of implementing technology projects. Case studies abound which tell of untold wastage, wanton incompetence, and scant supervision. We know that most major public IT projects fail. As a rule of thumb, technology professionals often say that only 15–20 per cent of large public sector technology projects are successful, that is, on time, within budget, with systems that do what was wanted and was expected.

Certainly, we know that most major court technology projects in England and Wales have run into grave problems. The current 'common platform' initiative, for example, is the fourth attempt in the last twenty-five years to integrate criminal justice systems. The original budget for Libra, the system for our magistrates' courts, was around £150 million and ended up costing about half a billion. Approximately £90 million was spent in failing to implement Lord Woolf's IT reforms in the 1990s. A later attempt at technology for the civil courts—electronic filing and document management (EFDM)—was conceived around 2004 and effectively abandoned in 2008 at a reported cost of tens of millions. The first (but thankfully not the final) effort to build systems for the Business and Property Courts, in Rolls Building, also ended in failure. I could go on.

Why projects fail

Over the years, I have pointed to the following causes of failed or abandoned technology projects in the justice system of England and Wales. The projects have generally been too large and not subdivided into manageable parts. The procurement and contract drafting processes have been weak. The timescales have often been unrealistic at the outset. The systems have been over-engineered and their scope increased mid-project. The Ministry of Justice and its predecessor departments have not been firm or decisive enough in managing external suppliers. The management of expectations of users has been poor. And there has been insufficient continuity of project management.

Hovering here like Banquo's ghost is the disaster movie of a project to build the California Case Management System. This was launched in 2001. The initial estimate of costs made in 2004 was $260 million, by 2010, this had risen to $1.9 billion, and the project was shelved in 2012.[1] In the inglorious end, it was deemed un-affordable and inadequately planned. This is a warning shot, a call for realism and humility, for online court projects around the world.

Critics have good reason, therefore, to be concerned about the poor track record of public sector technology projects. However, this is surely an argument for developing systems well rather than not at all. Technology projects are hard and rarely go without hitch.

As I write this chapter, in early 2019, the court system of England and Wales was affected by worrying system failures across the Ministry of Justice; this, in a legal system, where the world's most ambitious court technology programme is being pursued (see Chapter 16). It is worth noting, however, that the new public-facing systems, developed as part of the reform programme, worked throughout. In my view, this highlights the urgency of moving beyond current out-of-date administrative systems, beyond also the difficult transitional phase when old and new systems are working together, to an era when there is a full new suite of systems and more coherent governance in place. In England and Wales, the current programme leaders are more than alive to the challenges and the pitfalls.

In the Appendix, based on my experience of advising governments and judiciaries over the past twenty-five years, I briefly itemize the factors that I think are likely to be critical to the success of any public sector online court project. For now, I want to focus below on two major issues—not rushing and the need to pilot.

On not rushing

I welcome the recent news in England and Wales that the reform project is being extended. I have for long argued that the original time scales were too ambitious, driven by the idiosyncrasies of UK public sector spending rather than realism about the scale of the programme. The reform programme involves the most far-reaching changes to the court system in around 150 years. I do not think we should be rushing it.

Unrealistic timescales are one of the primary reasons for project failure. Insufficient time spent in the design of systems, for example, invariably leads to changes of direction in the middle of projects, which in turn brings delay or results in the delivery of systems that do not work as needed. Equally, time pressures often result in inadequate testing and training, which can then lead to systems that are faulty and to high levels of user dissatisfaction.

As a rule of thumb, I suggest that reformers and policy-makers should expect a full-scale court transformation programme to take around ten years. In the mid-1990s, I said the same of the Woolf technology reforms and at the time this was an unpopular view. Judges and politicians said that ten years was too long to wait. It is now almost twenty-five years since these unimplemented technology reforms were proposed. Hastily conceived systems in the late 1990s led to the delivery of no systems at all.

A related concern is that a likely consequence of moving too quickly is to miss the opportunity to think radically and imaginatively about new ways of working. The danger is that system designers default to automating and streamlining old ways of working because the thinking and planning behind large-scale transformation can be hugely time-consuming. Transformation should involve extensive co-operation amongst the designers, judges, and court users. This is a complex, iterative process and too often it is abandoned and replaced with systems that automate current practice and so deliver little more than 'mess for less'.

Consider some of the basic technology-related tasks involved in building online courts: (1) redesign of the underlying processes; (2) drafting of new rules of procedure; (3) piloting; (4) outline system specification; (5) consultation; (6) detailed specification; (7) procurement; (8) system development; (9) testing; (10) adjusting or rebuilding; (11) training; and (12) roll-out. I know that the favoured 'agile' methods of development may not follow this route linearly but these are the basic building blocks. Reflect now on how long much simpler systems take to design and put in place. Even if the funds and resources are available to accelerate development, there is no short-cut on some critical paths. A full-scale overhaul of a justice system deserves and requires extended thought and discussion. The ideas and arguments will need time to gestate; the proposals and changes need to be debated and digested.

The need to pilot

In our report for the Civil Justice Council, we recommended that online courts should be piloted in the first instance. This call for pilots was endorsed widely, from No. 10 Downing Street downwards, but was resisted in the early years. (Therein lies a tale.)

The benefits of piloting online courts are clear. It allows new systems to be tested in practice and then refined in light of feedback from users (facilities for gathering feedback should be built into the systems themselves). It enables judges to help identify the types of cases best suited to online handling. It is part of a controlled and measured way of introducing radical change.

There is also sound theoretical support for proceeding by piloting in low-value cases. As noted in the Introduction, it is generally accepted in the management and technology literature that so-called 'disruptive technologies' (those that fundamentally change the way that work is undertaken) are most successful when they start experimentally and modestly at the lower end of any given market. Through experience of daily operation, the systems are enhanced and gradually take on more challenging work. In time, they become the standard way of working. Bold attempts to replace the most complex and challenging work in revolutionary sweeps invariably do not succeed. As I say in Chapter 10, it is hard to change a wheel on a moving car. The solution to this dilemma, as noted, is to build a new car, run the old and the new in parallel, and, over time, transfer the passengers from old to new. This is how most major organizations around the world have successfully transformed themselves using technology. They have not grafted new systems onto their old ways of working. They have not stopped and built a vast new structure from scratch. They have started with modest first versions and grown incrementally.

My position on piloting is one aspect of a broader issue. I advise that new court systems should be developed and delivered in an incremental roll-out, in manageable lego-like modules, rather than as a 'big-bang' change. This is widely accepted as good practice in the world of technology, but time pressures often lead to this implementation principle being neglected. Ideally, I recommend the staged launch of a series of systems and changes, each bringing benefits in its own right. In support of this approach, some kind of 'road-map' is needed—not just an agreed vision of the final destination but a widely shared indication of the direction of travel and the various staging posts—the interim systems and benefits—along the way. Historically, most governments have been reluctant to commit to such maps. But it is vital. If we were driving to Glasgow from London, we would want to know which cities we should expect to go through (or bypass). Seeing a sign for Carlisle would be a good omen. Passing by Exeter would be a worry. But, if the project plan is opaque, judges and other interested parties will never know, as it were, if they are near Exeter or Carlisle. In some of the failed projects in the past, we have learned too late that we were in Sydney or had not left London at all.

Rather than thinking about introducing a new system in terms of specification and development, another way of describing the incremental approach is to liken this to constructing a platform onto which increasingly sophisticated systems and facilities can be layered. For most jurisdictions, the first version of any online court would probably be fairly crude, both technically and functionally. Judges, lawyers, and policy-makers should not look upon first versions as the final word.

As new technologies and techniques become available and operational experience builds, online courts can be refined and improved. The evolution of the services should be evidence-based. As stressed in Chapter 17, this calls for rigorous ongoing studies that evaluate the performance of online courts. This raises a worrying issue relating to data collection. In many jurisdictions, the availability of information about the workings and workload of the courts is lamentably low. There is an opportunity, in designing online courts to build in tools that capture all data flowing through the system, and to develop methods for analysing that data.

As a general rule, when off-the-shelf systems for online courts become available and perform most of the required functions, then I recommend that tailored versions of these are preferable to higher-risk bespoke developments. Certainly for pilots, there are compelling arguments in favour of conducting these initial experimental uses of online courts sooner rather than later; and deploying existing tools rather than waiting for systems to be developed from scratch. In absence of the availability of local off-the-shelf systems, it is also good practice to license systems that have been developed, tried, and tested in other jurisdictions.

In summary, then, start modestly by piloting, study the results through research, build incrementally and refine in light of experience, and do not proceed in one big bang—exercise some restraint.

Consider Singapore as a mini-case study. I was invited in late 2015 by the Chief Justice, Sundaresh Menon, to speak about the Civil Justice Council work on online courts and to follow this up with a presentation to senior judges by video conference. Not many months later, I received an email from the Chief Justice, letting me know, basically, that they were going to 'press ahead' and experiment. While most jurisdictions were disappearing down rabbit holes of speculative debate about the possible impact of online courts, others were ready to roll up their sleeves up, pilot, test, and deliver. It is tempting to say that Singapore is a much smaller jurisdiction and for that reason an easy environment in which to bring great change. But this is to neglect the difference in approach. In Singapore, they have an action-oriented, pragmatic, confident, pioneering, entrepreneurial, and energetic attitude. This is the spirit that will be needed, across the world, to kick-start online courts in the future.

PART IV

THE FUTURE

Chapter 25

Emerging Technologies

By 2030, and possibly much sooner, our courts around the world will have been transformed by technologies that have not yet been invented. I cannot of course prove this, but given the scale of the financial investment and human effort being directed at court technology and at artificial intelligence (AI), this seems to me a far more likely outcome than the moderate change that most lawyers and judges might project. Today, we are surely at the beginning of an inevitable technological transformation in our court and judicial services.

Although the substance of this book so far might appear radical to most lawyers, the use of online courts for low-value civil disputes is really but a modest opening gambit. As I suggest in Chapter 9, we can expect that extended courts and online judging will also be put into service, in most countries, in family, criminal, and administrative cases and, over time, in much higher value commercial disputes as well.

In this fourth and final part of the book, I go much further and predict wider developments for online courts. First, in this and the next two chapters, I explore various emerging technologies and consider their likely impact on online courts. Second, whatever technologies may be involved, the most ambitious use of online courts will be their deployment in increasing access to justice across the globe. That is the subject matter of the final chapter of the book.

In previous chapters, attention is confined to three principal environments for state-based dispute resolution—physical courtrooms,
virtual hearings, and online courts. However, a richer range of options is likely to be available before long. First of all, virtual hearings
will become increasingly lifelike as we take advantage of successive
generations of 'telepresence'. Next, our participation in physical and
virtual hearings will be enhanced by a technology known as 'augmented reality'. Thirdly, we should expect in due course a world
in which court service might be delivered in some form of virtual
reality (VR). This chapter explores this trinity of possibilities and
closes with some reflections on more advanced ODR.

Considering the future

I should issue a reminder about 'technological myopia'. This is the
term I introduce in Chapter 3 to refer to people's widespread inability to anticipate and imagine that tomorrow's systems will be
vastly more capable than those of today. Some lawyers and judges
will have used video conferencing for meetings or perhaps spent
a few minutes wearing a head-mounted display while playing
with their children's computer games. It is likely that they will not
have been using the latest technology. It is certain they have not
been using what I call 'as-yet-uninvented' systems. Indeed, even
when users enjoy, say, the very latest in video conferencing technology, it is again worth considering that what they have before
them is the worst that that technology is likely to be from here on
in. An upgrade will no doubt be waiting in the wings, greatly superior versions are being designed in the labs, the underlying techniques and technologies (bandwidth, compression, resolution, and
more) are being relentlessly improved upon, quite aside from these

game-changing as-yet-uninvented technologies that are bound to disrupt the market. My concern, as I try to take readers beyond the horizon, is that tomorrow's technologies are not dismissed on the basis of their current shortcomings. I ask yet again for an open mind.

Sometimes, however, an open mind need not be requested. Instead one finds one's mind opened involuntarily. In this spirit, in 1997, I caught a glimpse of the future. I had travelled with Lord Saville (at that time, a Lord of Appeal in Ordinary, a Law Lord, and the judge in England and Wales responsible for technology) to the research laboratories of British Telecom at Martlesham, in England. We were shown numerous prototypes that day but none struck us more forcefully than a demonstration of a revolutionary type of video conferencing system. It was a first attempt at an immersive system—we sat at a table that abutted a wall with a large screen, projected onto which were a group of people also sitting at a table. They were actually seated in a neighbouring room. But it looked and felt as though their table was an extension of ours, and that we were in fact gathered around one and the same table. The effect was remarkable; not the small puppet-like figure on the corner of a fuzzy monitor that we had come to know as video conferencing, but a life-size rendition of the other participants. We both concluded within minutes that we had seen the makings of a viable virtual alternative to the conventional court hearing. It would be many years before that facility would be commercially available. It would come to be widely known as telepresence.

Telepresence

Of all the jaw-dropping technology demonstrations I have attended over the years, including that defining visit to Martlesham, none opened my mouth (and mind) wider than my first view of Cisco's telepresence. I had been invited in 2006 to Cisco's offices in central London to 'meet' their General Counsel (GC) in California. I walked into the purpose-built room and saw BT's vision realized. Although he was sitting in an office over five thousand miles away, the GC appeared to me on a screen, as large as life. The sound was directional, the display was crystal clear, there was no latency (delay), and we sat together surrounded by matching chairs, tables, wall coverings, so that the impression was that we were (immersed) in the same room. It was wholly remarkable—high-quality video conferencing on steroids. When these systems are used, the mind joins the dots so that you feel you are physically in the same space as those to whom you are linked. Many years later, when using a later version of that system from London with a client in Hong Kong, the sense of meeting together was so strong that I unthinkingly offered the guy at the other end a cup of tea.

Over the years, I have taken various judges and policy-makers to witness telepresence in action. All have been greatly impressed but many told me that they have later struggled, as I have, to explain to others just how powerful this technology can be. Doubters will often say that a hearing by telepresence cannot be anything like being live and face-to-face. There is invariably some irrational rejectionism in this response, because few of those who speculate have actually experienced these systems. In truth, it can feel very like being in the same room. And that sense of colocation will only deepen with the emergence of new techniques, such as 3-dimensional holographic volumetric telepresence. A court appearance by holographic telepresence could become a regular occurrence in years to come, although, of course, a hearing that uses any form of telepresence is still a synchronous hearing.

Augmented reality

A different technology that has received much less attention by the legal fraternity is augmented reality (AR). Most science fiction movies of the last few years have this technology on full display, typically when a protagonist's view of the outside world is overlain by some data—the name of a passerby, the route to an assignation, the underlying structure of a building. The idea is that humans' perception of the real world is supplemented by machine-generated perceptual information, most usually in visual or auditory form (it can also be olfactory, but I leave others to tease out the implications of this for legal service). When executed effectively, the perception of the natural environment and the annotations merge into one and become a seamless experience. A variety of devices, some cooler than others, are used in support of AR—spectacles (better to call them 'smartglasses'), contact lenses, head-mounted displays, headset computers, and even virtual retinal displays. With these in or around your head, physical objects are digitally annotated in real time.

In providing additional information about the world around us, AR systems (also referred to as hybrid reality, computer-mediated reality, or mixed reality systems) are designed to enhance and supplement our perception of reality. Usually this is done by providing supplementary information but it can also mask aspects of the real world, hiding complexity or intensity.

I can envisage two broad uses of AR in the court system, but again for synchronous hearings rather than for online courts. Imagine litigants in traditional courtrooms, wearing some kind of unobtrusive hardware which might provide textual commentary on objects and people at whom the user is looking. Equally, through an earpiece this commentary and insight might be audible. 'This is the clerk of court. That is known as the bench.' I accept that the decorum (the 'majesty'—see Chapter 20) of the traditional court might be prejudiced by participants bearing ostentatious head-mounted displays but the court could issue guidance on what is seemly. A second use of AR would be in support of virtual hearings. Eye-tracking software could detect the people or objects on-screen that users are focusing upon and, again, offer explanations of whatever has attracted their attention. When the virtual hearing is of the kind that some participants are attending remotely, AR could superimpose images that would provide a clearer view of the court.

Some lawyers might find these ideas eccentric. But if court processes are to be rendered intelligible for lay people, we must broad-mindedly monitor emerging technologies and consider how they might improve the service experience. And bear in mind that younger users will be seasoned online game players and will have a very different view of what is normal and useful.

Court hearings in virtual reality

Whereas augmented reality changes users' perception of the world around them, virtual reality largely or entirely replaces that everyday environment with a wholly simulated one. The 'virtual' here is not the same as in 'virtual hearings' which essentially are video-enabled hearings, when all or some participants in a hearing attend by video link. Nor am I referring here to the use of VR as a form of electronic evidence. Lord Saville pioneered this in his Bloody Sunday Inquiry in a sobering reconstruction of some of the events of that day.[1] What I have in mind instead is a court hearing—again synchronous—that is actually conducted in a virtual environment. All participants would enter an alternative, online world and proceedings would be conducted there.

I am resisting any attempt to define VR. If the father of VR, Jaron Lanier, in his latest book, *Dawn of the New Everything: A Journey Through Virtual Reality*, can offer fifty-two different definitions of VR, I feel safe in keeping my description relatively high level (or low level, depending on your point of view). In the broadest of terms, though, mainstream VR involves putting on a purpose-built headset and becoming immersed in a computer-generated world, which might resemble the natural world (like flight simulation systems) or may be a world of fantasy (as with many games).

Two thoughts by way of warm-up. First, imagine a VR game, *Robo-Court* perhaps, where gamers could assume various roles in a court hearing and, subject to a set of rules, could participate in their own trials. The decisions could be crowdsourced by the user community. League tables would quickly emerge, celebrating, say, the prosecutors with the finest records. Second, imagine a simulated court environment, a training tool for lawyers and judges, which offers highly life-like exposure to countless permutations of cases and courtroom scenarios, perhaps using footage from real courtrooms. Users would be immersed in an environment that might look very like real-life courts. Neither of these two possibilities is improbable. The game might be fun; and if astronauts and surgeons can cut their teeth in simulators, there is scope for lawyers and judges to do similarly. But the potential for VR in the courts need not be restricted to gaming and training. It is conceivable that public hearings could actually take place in a VR environment. I can envisage a trial conducted in a fantastical environment, like a game, that bears no resemblance to reality. But I can more easily imagine cases being handled in life-like, simulated courtrooms, like the training environment, whose proceedings might follow conventional court rules or could be governed by simplified or improved processes. Why might we do this? Why was there ever a thriving community of Christians running an 'Anglican Cathedral' on Second Life, a virtual online world, with a weekly Bible-study class and daily worship services?[2] Human beings often find new ways to conduct old practices. I am not strongly advocating VR hearings of this sort. I am simply suggesting them as a possibility. Who knows, but some entrepreneurial start-up or especially innovative court administrator, or radical judge, might alight on a version of this idea and, after some design and development effort, it could take root. Recalling from Chapter 5 the etymological roots of 'court', from French, Latin, and Ancient Greek, referring to an enclosed space or yard, this could come to be regarded as a new safe online space where justice can be secured.

Recall too the conception of justice attributed to Aristotle in Chapter 7, which speaks of a blind form of judging, when judges are exposed to the case rather than the parties and the individual characteristics of the parties and their lawyers are obscured. Proponents of this conception of procedural justice might call for a VR court in which parties could appear not as faithful renditions of themselves but as avatars, masking their real identities and characteristics or leaving them indeterminable. The idea of being represented in VR by some kind of avatar may seem bizarre on first encounter. Surely this would conceal the real litigant, placing him or her at one remove from proceedings. But, in a different way, this is what lawyers currently are—a representation of their clients and their interests. They present cases in their own words and style and not in their clients'. Today's lawyers are avatars of a sort (although I accept that when clients themselves give evidence, the judge sees them as they are).

Advanced ODR

A word, finally, about emerging ODR techniques. Specialists in ODR have generally been delighted with the growing interest around the world in online courts, and have been particularly taken with the depth of the support in England and Wales from both the Government and the judiciary. However, the ODR purists are correct when they point out that, technologically speaking, what is currently being introduced, certainly the first generation, is a fairly primitive set-up. For the purposes of what is, essentially, electronic ADR, the ODR community has been discussing and designing much more advanced systems since the 1990s. While it is true that they have always been more ambitious than the pioneers of online courts, they cannot deny that building online techniques for a fairly generic state-based court system is a very different enterprise from running a private-sector start-up devoted, say, to one well-bounded type of dispute. Over time, as we progress to second-generation online courts, the more advanced systems that have been developed for private-sector ODR will no doubt be imported into the public systems.

Meanwhile, we can expect the ODR community to forge ahead in upgrading their systems and developing new applications. Some of the progress will be made by those engaged in ODR research— I would especially like to see more work on embedding models from game theory into systems that help bring about settlement.[3] I also anticipate that there will be much greater commercial exploitation of ODR in the coming years, bringing the most promising developments out of the lab and into the marketplace. Some of these systems will target the high-volume, low-value consumer complaints market, with a focus on online negotiation and mediation.[4] Others will look beyond the automation of ADR and use the reach and versatility of the internet to provide new ways of settling disagreements—for example, crowdsourcing both for the funding of claims[5] and to enable community voting on the outcomes of cases (and thus perhaps avoiding the bias of individual decision-makers).[6] Yet others will seek to provide more generic toolkits for resolving disputes online and not just low-value claims.[7]

In terms of the big picture, in their book, *Digital Justice*, Ethan Katsh and Orna Rabinovich-Einy, leading experts in the field, observe that ODR is:

> currently in the midst of a highly significant transition: from applications that focus on communication and convenience to software that employs algorithms ... [t]his may, at times, remove the need for a mediator ... or other dispute handler.[8]

In the language of Chapter 3, we are moving beyond the era of automating ADR to a time when we use technology fundamentally to transform services such as mediation and early neutral evaluation. The key enabling technology here will be artificial intelligence.

Chapter 26

Artificial Intelligence

In contemplating the second generation of online courts, it would be hard to ignore the recent upsurge of interest in artificial intelligence (AI) for lawyers and judges. Scarcely a week passes without news of 'an AI' or a 'robot lawyer' that is outperforming or poised to replace traditional human lawyers in some legal task or other. Most leading law firms in the UK, for instance, have signed licence arrangements with AI providers and are effusing optimistically about their investments. I am especially interested in these claims because I have a life-long interest in the field—from 1983 to 1986, I wrote my doctorate on AI and law at Oxford University and have been intrigued by all relevant developments since.

In a nutshell, though, I take the view that many of the current declarations from firms and providers exaggerate the likely short-term impact of AI (over the next few years). In mild exasperation, on 23 March 2017, I tweeted that:

> 'AI' has become a verb. 'We can AI that'. Often said by people who would struggle to distinguish between a neural network & a custard cream.

That said, I believe that most predictions about AI *understate* the likely influence of this technology on law in the long run (in, say, the 2030s and 2040s). Bill Gates once said, to paraphrase, that less happens in two years than we expect when it comes to technology,

but more happens in ten. So too with AI. I do not anticipate fundamental societal change in the next eighteen to twenty-four months.
However, I believe that the long-term effects are invariably misun-
derstood. As we venture deeper into the 2020s, I anticipate that the
impact of AI on our personal lives and on our social, political, and
economic institutions will become pervasive, transformational, and
irreversible. The law and courts will not be exempt.

Different conceptions of AI

It helps to be a little clearer about what AI is. I have always found
the term both helpful and unhelpful. The upside is that the concept itself often generates curiosity and excitement and, in turn, the
field frequently attracts first-rate entrepreneurs and technologists as
well as substantial investment. The downside is that the term is used
in many ways and is often wielded as no more than a rather blunt
marketing weapon or as part of an alerting headline or tweet.

There are two broad ways to define AI. The first is 'architectural',
in terms of the tools and techniques used. When I worked on AI
in the 1980s, the technological fashion was for rule-based systems
and logic programming. This was the first wave of AI that actually worked—systems that were explicitly programmed to undertake tasks by, essentially, following huge decision trees and flow
charts put together by human developers (more on which below).
Today, different methods, like 'supervised machine learning' and
'deep neural networks', are very popular. This is the second wave—
instead of following explicitly articulated rules, these systems 'learn'
from large bodies of past data. Ordinarily, however, technical terms
and concepts mean little to most non-specialists, for whom a
second type of definition—'functional'—is more useful. When we

speak about AI in functional terms, we are talking about what these systems actually do, what tasks they undertake. And, very generally, when many AI specialists and others refer today to AI, they are speaking of systems that perform tasks (for example, solving problems, writing music, recognizing emotions, laying bricks) that in the past we thought required the intelligence of human beings. This remains a loose characterization of AI but what is significant on this account, to repeat, is that machines are taking on more and more such tasks. And this seems to be what many lawyers and commentators have in mind currently when they speak of AI in law—systems that perform various types of legal work that historically required thinking, human lawyers. Some go further and speak of 'superintelligent' machines[1] which are AI systems that perform at a level that is well beyond the current capabilities of human lawyers. AI can thus be said to involve human and super-human performance.

The term, 'intelligence', for many observers, suggests perhaps that the latest systems are in some sense actually 'conscious'. In the philosophical jargon of AI, a system that is conscious would be an exhibit of what is known as 'strong AI'. This claim goes much further than I am prepared to travel at this stage. I do not discount the idea of conscious machines some years hence but they are not a focus here. Instead, my attention here is on 'weak AI'—functionally, these systems *seem* to be doing some of the work of lawyers but without the cognitive states enjoyed by humans, such as our self-awareness and emotional satisfaction.

Another distinction that is used in the world of artificial intelligence is between 'narrow AI' and 'artificial general intelligence' (AGI). The former are systems that perform clearly defined and limited tasks, often to the level of an expert or higher (in specific fields like law). AGI is much more challenging. This involves the development of general-purpose machines that can do everything or most things that intelligent humans can. We are many years away from this. Some indeed say this will never be achieved. I disagree ('never' is a long time). For now, it is interesting to note, paradoxically, that it is harder to develop machines that can undertake everyday tasks that in humans depend on their general knowledge, than systems that appear to be deeply expert in narrow fields.

In thinking about the long-term implications of AI, it is important to bear in mind, just as there seems to be no finishing line when it comes to technology generally, then the same goes for AI. The pace of change is accelerating. Every day, it seems, we hear of some new breakthrough. When discussing the future of AI today, all that most of us can do is extrapolate from what we already have. But we should acknowledge that it is likely if not probable that by, say, 2030, our lives will have been radically changed by systems that are not even conceivable today. Accordingly, we should not assume that the leading enabling techniques of today (for example, machine learning) will dominate for the foreseeable future. There will no doubt be a third wave of AI; and a fourth; and so on. Lawyers, judges, and policy-makers should be both humbled and open-minded about as-yet-uninvented technologies.

First wave of legal AI

My lifelong interest has been in developing computer systems that could solve legal problems and draft legal documents. I have found this work technically and philosophically fascinating, and have always hoped that it would be of practical significance too. When I started in the field of AI and law in the early 1980s, one approach was dominant. In building systems, we conducted an interview process known as 'knowledge acquisition'. This involved trying to extract the knowledge and reasoning processes from the heads of legal experts—'mining the jewels', as we used to say. We then codified the knowledge elicited in the form of complex decision trees, and dropped these into computer systems, providing flow charts around which non-expert users could roam. We called them 'rule-based expert systems'.[2] They asked users questions, and were able to provide legal answers and draft legal documents, often to a higher standard than human experts.

In 1988, I co-developed the world's first fully operational, commercial AI system in law (the Latent Damage System) with Phillip Capper.[3] The system advised on a corner of the law of limitation. It answered the question, 'when can a particular action no longer be raised because it is time barred?' In developing the system, Phillip and I created, essentially, a massive decision tree, with more than two million paths, representing all permutations of fact patterns and legal problems that we could imagine in this complex area of law. Phillip was the subject-matter expert, while I was the 'legal knowledge engineer' and, in crude terms, we reduced his interpretation of the relevant legislation and case law to a complex computer program—an explicit representation of his knowledge. The final system was delivered on 5.25 inch floppy discs (when discs actually were floppy). This was before the web was invented. The system reduced research time from hours to minutes. It offered a clear explanation of its lines of reasoning, and Phillip happily concedes to this day that the system outperformed him. But this first wave of AI systems were costly and time-consuming to build and maintain. And they held little appeal for law firms because they cut down the time taken to undertake legal work—not attractive in an era dominated by lavish and largely uncontested hourly billing.

Although sceptics are quick to claim that this first wave of AI had little impact, its underpinning techniques are still widely used today around the world—for instance, in online legal services offered by law firms and in document automation systems. More strikingly, the multi-billion-dollar tax compliance industry (personal and corporate tax) is largely built on this first wave of rule-based systems. Nonetheless, I accept that there are relatively few online legal problem-solvers like the Latent Damage System. The main reason these systems did not flourish, in my view, was that when the web was invented, most of us who were working on legal AI were seduced by the immediacy, the reach, the apparent simplicity, and the commerciality of this new medium. So we abandoned AI and began work on online legal services.

Breakthroughs in AI

Many of us gave little thought to AI for five years or so. Then the news broke in 1997 that Garry Kasparov, the world chess champion, had been beaten by a computer system, IBM's Deep Blue. In the 1980s, we thought this would never be possible. The only way we thought we could deliver AI was, as with the Latent Damage System, to compile a massive decision tree that represented human experts' apparent reasoning patterns. But leading experts—doctors and chess players, for example—insisted that, in the most challenging circumstances that faced them, their knowledge and experience could not be reduced to flow charts. Their best diagnoses or moves seemed to depend on some kind of ineffable, tacit knowledge—gut reaction or intuition—that could not be formalized in any program. This led us in the 1980s to conclude that there was a very clear division of labour between machines and humans. Machines were best suited to complex and routine work, but when the magic was needed—creativity and innovation—this was surely the unique territory of human beings. Most people still think this today. But this is a mistake. It was wrong in 1997 because we underestimated the exponential increase in the processing power of computers (see Chapter 3). By the time Deep Blue overcame Kasparov, this was a system that could explore around 330 million moves per second. Grandmasters can juggle about 110 moves in their heads at any one moment. Kasparov was not beaten by a system that played as he did. He was beaten largely by brute force processing.

IBM again made the news in another breakthrough in 2011. They had been working on a branch of AI that delivered systems that could answer questions (a QA system). And on a live broadcast of an American TV quiz show called 'Jeopardy!', their system, known as Watson, beat the two best-ever human contestants. This was a system that could, effectively, answer questions on any topic, more accurately and rapidly than any human being. The power of this system again was attributable to remarkable processing power; but it also had phenomenally large bodies of data to work on, as well as some explicitly represented knowledge. Although computer scientists may not agree, I think of Watson as a half-way house between the first wave of AI (rule-based systems as discussed above) and the second wave, which are dominated by 'machine learning'.

Whereas the first wave of AI systems had to be explicitly programmed by human beings, the second wave learned from large quantities of data. A useful way to understand the difference between the two waves is to think about how humans can learn foreign languages. At school, we learn explicitly articulated rules of grammar and large vocabularies of words. The alternative is to spend time in a foreign country, and absorb the language by living in its midst: within months, most people can speak passably with no formal understanding of grammar, nor any need to be immersed in large lists of words. They learn, essentially, from large bodies of data—everyday exposure to the spoken and written word. Learning language at school is like programming of the first wave, while picking up the language in the country of origin is akin to what we now call machine learning.[4]

AlphaGo is a leading example of a high-performing machine learning system. It was designed by Google DeepMind to play the game, Go, which has more possible moves than there are atoms in the universe. AI scientists had for long doubted that any AI system could play a respectable game of Go. And yet, in early 2016, AlphaGo beat the world's top Go player, Lee Sedol, by four games to one. Using 'deep neural networks', the system was trained by a mixture of 'supervised learning' (based on past games of human experts) and 'reinforcement learning'—basically, it played itself millions of times and thereby self-improved. (One of the most intriguing possibilities in legal technology is the use of reinforcement learning in developing systems in law; a great topic for a PhD.)

The thirty-seventh move in the second game of that 2016 AlphaGo contest is now the stuff of legend. No human being had thought of that move before. A leading AlphaGo player was said to describe it as 'beautiful' and that it brought a tear to his eye. In a human being, we would have characterized that move as 'creative' or 'innovative'. We may even have called it 'genius'. But it was none of these things. Its performance was based on massive processing power, operating on huge amounts of data, and on clever algorithms. Certainly, many of the games AlphaGo plays and the moves it makes are well beyond the contemplation of those who designed the system.

The AlphaGo story does not end there. Some observers insisted that although it was a remarkable system, at its core were the patterns of all the past *human* games. The claim here was that it could not perform as it did without having the original human insights to work on. Enter AlphaGo Zero in 2017. It was decided not to feed any past human games to this new version of the system. Instead, it was simply taught the rules of the game and left to figure out the best strategies and tactics on its own. AlphaGo Zero beat the original AlphaGo by 100 games to nil. This corroborated a hypothesis in *The Future of the Professions*—if our machines are becoming increasingly capable, then the relative contribution that humans will make in the workplace will diminish over time.[5]

Second wave of legal AI

Inspired by early successes beyond the law (in game playing and medicine, especially), machine learning has recently captured the imagination of the legal profession. Using a variety of algorithms, operating on large bodies of legal data, these systems can identify patterns, regularities, and correlations that human lawyers cannot when they use conventional methods.

Crucially, these systems are able to make a variety of remarkable *predictions*. In the world of litigation, when there are large bodies of documents to review, it is clear that, in terms of precision and recall, technology-assisted review (now being branded as a form of AI) can now outperform junior lawyers and paralegals. Using a form of 'supervised learning', these systems predict which documents expert lawyers would select as the most relevant. The predictions are based on those documents picked out previously by experts from a sample set. In corporate law, major due diligence exercises are benefiting from similar technology. From large data rooms, these systems are able to isolate, for instance, the contracts that appear to give rise to the most worrying risks and liabilities. And in the world of document automation, there are projects exploring the automated production of documents not on the classic rule-based model, but by using machine learning—systems that can predict, on the basis of past work product, what documents experts would draft.

The ODR and online court community have been most interested in machine learning systems that can predict the outcome of judicial decisions, often more accurately, it is claimed, than human lawyers. I return to this below and in the next chapter.

AI fallacy

Despite these advances, many professional and white-collar workers maintain that their work can *never* be replaced by machines. They argue that computers cannot think or feel and so cannot, for example, exercise judgement or be empathetic. This argument usually rests on what Daniel Susskind and I call the 'AI fallacy'—the view that the only way to get machines to outperform the best human lawyers will somehow be to copy the way that human lawyers work. The mistake here is not recognizing that the second wave of AI systems do not mimic or replicate human reasoning. Unimaginatively, this error takes an excessively human-centric view of AI. The point is widely appreciated when it comes to autonomous cars. No one seriously suggests that the best way to make progress in that field is to design and build robots that should sit in the driving seats of traditional cars, copying the way that humans drive. But that is the equivalent of imagining the robot in the courtroom, hospital, classroom, or office as a substitute for the professional.

Instead, our increasingly capable machines will take on the work of professionals by undertaking tasks in ways that are best suited to their unique capabilities and not ours. We saw this in 1997 when Deep Blue beat Garry Kasparov, and when AlphaGo beat Lee Sedol. They were outgunned by brute processing power and remarkable algorithms, operating on large bodies of data; and not by systems that sought to copy how these masters played. We will find the same in law.

AI and online courts

What is the likely impact of AI on judges, lawyers, and court officials? Generally, I assume the following line of argument (this is a simplification of the position laid out in *The Future of the Professions*). Leaving the term 'AI' to one side for now, it is clear that (a) our systems and machines are becoming increasingly capable; (b) they are taking on more and more tasks that were once the exclusive province of human beings; (c) although new tasks will doubtless arise in years to come; (d) machines are likely in time to take on many of these as well.[6] I have no reason to think this argument does not apply in the world of courts.

Many people respond that there are limits to what machines can do. They accept, as noted earlier, that systems can undertake 'routine' work but contend that there are many 'non-routine' tasks— creative and emotional ones, for instance—that only human beings can perform. They challenge (d) above and insist that when traditional jobs fade, new ones will always emerge, made up of those tasks that are beyond the reach of even the most capable machines. However, our extensive research into professional work does not support the view that the new tasks that emerge are and will be ones for which humans are better suited than machines.[7] It transpires that insistence that there are tasks that can never be undertaken by machines often rests on the 'AI fallacy'—the belief that the only way to develop machines that can perform at the level of human beings is to *copy* the way human beings work. The error here, to repeat, is to fail to notice that many contemporary AI systems operate not by copying human beings; instead, they function in quite different and *unhuman* ways.

When these unhuman systems of today are able to make predictions, identify relevant documents, answer questions, and handle emotions (see Chapter 3) at a higher standard than human beings, it is not just reasonable, it is vital that we ask whether, in decades to come, people or systems will be undertaking the wide variety of work that goes on in our courts today.

The brightest and the best human professionals are likely to last the longest—those human experts (judges and top-flight litigators) who handle tasks that cannot or should not be replaced by systems. However, there will not be a sufficiency of these tasks to keep masses of traditional court workers in employment. This is not an imminent threat. The 2020s will be a period of redeployment rather than unemployment—lawyers and judges will undertake different work and work differently, not least in online courts. But in the very long run, it is hard to avoid the conclusion that there will be much less work for today's court population to do.

As for online courts, it may be thought that there is little scope for AI for the first generation. However, the Civil Resolution Tribunal in British Columbia is already using rule-based expert systems for its Solution Explorer and Lord Briggs recommended the use of decision trees to help with the triage process that he proposes for the early version of online courts in England and Wales. In terms of the architecture introduced in Chapter 10, these diagnostic, first-wave legal AI systems sit on Tier 1 of online courts, both first and second generation. They can advise on what options are available to court users and on their specific legal rights and duties.

But the greatest potential for AI lies in the second generation of online courts, when, it will be recalled, the systems themselves rather than human beings will make many of the formal directions and decisions. On Tier 2 of online courts, where facilitation takes place, these systems will take on some of the work of case officers. One can easily imagine, for example, a machine learning system helping parties by predicting the likely outcome of their case were it to come before a human judge. This would perhaps be an AI approach to early neutral evaluation, based on statistical analysis of the past behaviour of the courts. We can also envisage a predictive tool that would identify, as suggested in Chapter 23, cases whose fact patterns suggest that traditional rather than online treatment would be preferable.

What about the work of online judges, on Tier 3? Can AI take on any of their work?

Chapter 27

The Computer Judge

Lurking in the shadows of this book and in all conversations about the future of online courts is the proposition that somehow, in years to come, judges might be replaced by machines.[1] Consider this rather lengthy quotation:

> Much to his horror (and mine) Joseph Weizenbaum, in his *Computer Power and Human Reason* tells of a discussion with A.I. pioneer John McCarthy, who had posed the question 'What do judges know that we cannot tell a computer?' McCarthy's answer was 'Nothing' and that the goal of building machines for making judicial decisions was perfectly in order ... A detailed study of this matter is sorely needed both to dispel the profusion of misconceptions and to assure the public that while computers will no doubt provide invaluable assistance to the judiciary in the future, it is neither possible now (or in the conceivable future) nor desirable ever (as long as we accept the values of Western liberal democracy) that computers assume the judicial function. In any event, computers cannot yet (if ever) satisfactorily recognise speech, understand natural language nor perceive images. Judges can. Computers have not yet been programmed to exhibit moral, religious, social, sexual and political preferences akin to those actually held by human beings. Nor have they been programmed to display the creativity, craftsmanship, individuality, innovation, inspiration, intuition, common-sense, and general interest in our world that we, as human beings, expect not only of one another as citizens but also of judges acting in their official role.[2]

What mutton-headed, technologically myopic luddite said this? I confess that these are my own words, as they appeared in 1986 in the *Modern Law Review*. Although this was comfortably more than thirty years ago, I can recall quite vividly what was going through my head (for want of a better term) when I wrote that passage. Today, I disagree with much that I said then. Emotionally, I no longer have any sense of horror in contemplating the possibility that judges might roundly be outperformed by machines. Technically, the passage of time has put me out of date. Computers often *can* (in some constrained circumstances) satisfactorily process speech and natural language. I also failed (along with most computer scientists) to predict that many of the remarkable advances in computing would come not through explicitly programming systems (whether, for example, to exhibit political preferences or creativity) but through machines 'learning' from vast sets of accumulated data. Morally, when I spoke of the values of western liberal democracy, I was reflecting the mood of the late twentieth century. As technology advances, it transpires, as Jamie Susskind explains in *Future Politics*, that our political conceptions change too. Liberal democracy in the twenty-first century may be significantly different from its ancestor.[3]

Machines and judges

The superficially straightforward challenge, 'can machines replace human judges?' conceals at least five questions. The first is whether it is *technically possible* for machines to replace judges. The second asks, even if it were technologically possible, would it be *morally acceptable* for machines to take on any judicial functions? The third inquires whether such systems would be *commercially viable*, that is, would their economic benefits outweigh their costs? Fourth, would this be *culturally sustainable*—could such systems be assimilated without rejection into court institutions dominated by age-old procedures with human judges at their core? Finally, there is a philosophical question. Is it *jurisprudentially coherent* to develop such systems? Is there anything specific about the structure and nature of judicial decision-making itself that places it, partly or entirely, beyond the scope of computation?

For the purposes of this chapter, my focus is on technical possibility and moral acceptability. I leave commercial viability to the market; pending evidence from first-generation courts, I defer for now the question of cultural sustainability; and I have addressed the jurisprudential question elsewhere.[4]

Technical feasibility

Students and scholars who begin to explore the *technical* question of whether machines can take on the work of judges will immediately find the literature, both academic and popular, littered with a basic confusion. Commentators fail to draw a distinction between systems that seek to copy the way that judges work on the one hand and, on the other, systems that deliver the outcomes we expect of judges but do so in unhuman ways. I fell into this trap myself in 1986, when I spoke of 'the creativity, craftsmanship, individuality, innovation, inspiration, intuition, common-sense' that I said were central to the work of judges. Others make the same mistake when they follow this line of reasoning: (1) judges *think* when they are doing their work, (2) machines cannot think, and so (3) machines cannot do the work of judges. Logicians and rhetoricians will recognize this as a version of the 'fallacy of the undistributed middle'. I call it the 'AI fallacy' (see Chapter 26). The error here is to assume that the only way for machines to do the work of human beings is for them somehow to mimic or copy the way that humans go about their business. In contrast, outcome-thinking (Chapter 4) urges us to focus not on *how* humans do what they do, but on the outputs and benefits they bring. In the context of AI, this inclines us to consider whether machines can deliver decisions at the standard of human judges or higher, not by replicating the way that judges think and reason but by using their own distinctive capabilities (brute processing power, vast amount of data, remarkable algorithms).

This leads me to suggest that there are really three different technical questions here. The first is, can a machine think, work, emote, create, reason, and feel like a human judge? The answer to this today is a resounding 'no'. Neurophysiologically and neurospsychologically, only a flesh-and-blood human being can function as a human judge does. This is true by definition. Unless and until we can build biological replicas of human beings—molecular reproductions or whole brain emulations—this may always be so. Even if we could, atom-by-atom, reconstruct a human judge, it is not clear, incidentally, that what would result would be a human judge. Philosophers and psychologists have argued over this one for decades.[5]

The second question is whether the outcome of the judicial method—very crudely, *decisions with reasons*—can be delivered by machines. For more than thirty years, the AI and law community has sought to answer this question by developing systems that can seek to analyse fact patterns, identify applicable law, and generate legal arguments. My own work on rule-based expert systems, as discussed in the previous chapter, was an early effort in this direction. Despite a great deal of hard work in this community, we are many years from having systems that, other than in very confined areas of law, can generate decisions with reasons. I am not dismissing the possibility out of hand, however. In the world of AI, there will be countless advances that will take us well beyond machine learning, the dominant AI technique of the moment. In this era of increasingly capable machines, then, it is not outrageous to expect at some stage, whether twenty or 100 years from now, that systems will outperform judges at their own game, delivering reasoned judgments with explanations that will look and feel like the finest of human judgments but sourced through AI rather than judicial 'wetware'.

The third question is whether it is possible to develop systems that deliver the social and economic *outcomes* we expect of judges and courts but do so in unhuman ways. My answer here is much more positive and takes us back to machine learning and the prediction of court decisions.

Prediction machines

Let me rewind almost four decades. In the middle of the front cover of my undergraduate dissertation, which I began in 1981 and submitted in 1982 at the University of Glasgow, I placed the following quotation for what I felt was dramatic effect:

> The day should come ... when you will be able to feed a set of facts to a machine that has cases, rules of law, and reasoning rules stored in it, and in which the machine can then lay out for you, step by step, the reasoning process by which you may be able to arrive at a conclusion. You can study it and then decide whether the machine is right or wrong. In some cases, the machine may not tell you exactly what the conclusion may be, but may say there is a probability that such-and-such is correct, and this probability is 90%.[6]

These were words spoken by Reed Lawlor in October 1960 at the First National Law and Electronics Conference, held in Lake Arrowhead, California. Lawlor at the time was the chairman of the Special Committee on Electronic Data Retrieval of the American Bar Association. (Is it not remarkable that there was such a committee almost sixty years ago?) I included this extract precisely because I felt most law professors and lawyers would think its message entirely ludicrous. Many members of today's legal profession, I fear, would still regard his words as outlandish. But, in truth, Lawlor's day has now come.

There is currently great investment, of time and money, in the field that is devoted to developing systems that seek to predict the behaviour of courts. In the academic world, I commend the work of Daniel Katz.[7] There are also numerous start-ups that are working hard to market fully operational systems. One of these, Lex Machina, is a useful place to start in thinking about the impact of these systems. Developed at Stanford University and acquired by LexisNexis in 2015, this service has been said to be able to predict the probability of success in patent litigation in the US more accurately than human patent lawyers. Notably, the system knows no law. The data that underpins its predictions are not law reports. (Contrast here a system developed at UCL in the UK whose raw data is reported decisions of the European Court of Human Rights).[8] Rather, Lex Machina draws on data *about* over 100,000 past cases—features such as the names of the judges, the law firms and the lawyers, the nature and value of the claims, and so forth. It transpires that, with enough such data points to hand, computational statistics can outperform the legal method in predicting the behaviour of the courts. Systematic approaches to predicting judicial decisions are not a new phenomenon; lawyers and psychologists in the mid-twentieth century (known as 'judicial behaviouralists') worked hard at this too.[9] But machine learning seems to be delivering much more promising results.

Reflecting on such systems at the launch of *The Future of the Professions*,[10] Lord Neuberger, then President of the UK Supreme Court, wondered aloud whether judges might be needed in the future if their decisions could be predicted so accurately. He was half-joking but this example takes us back to outcome-thinking (Chapter 4) and the perennial confusion between the hole in the wall (what the customer wants) and the power drill (the best available means of satisfying that want). Consider the question that all CEOs will ask when there is a dispute coming over their horizon. Invariably, they will want to know, 'what are our chances of winning?' Lawyers interpret this as a legal question. But that is power-drill thinking. Lawyers look at the world through legal spectacles. Or, as the organizational psychologist, Abraham Maslow once said, 'I suppose it is tempting, if the only tool you have is a hammer, to treat every problem as if it were a nail'.[11] The CEO does not ask for legal research and legal argument. The hole in the wall, the outcome, for the CEO here is some kind of probability. And if machines can demonstrably predict the results of disputes more reliably (and more cheaply and conveniently) than lawyers, then for this kind of task we can expect that the market will turn to systems rather than humans.

A judge or lawyer might well observe that these prediction machines are not engaging in legal reasoning or coming to legal decisions. From the point of view of Tier 1 and Tier 2 of on-line courts, this is surely fine. On these tiers, we are not wanting judicial determinations. Court users are wanting tools that can help them decide whether or not to proceed, settle, or walk away. Systems that can predict their chances of success would surely be invaluable.

Some realism

Some legal philosophers might go further and make the bolder suggestion that, in a way, predicting the law is actually what lawyers do. The strongest authority for this proposition would be Oliver Wendell Holmes who once famously observed that:

> The prophecies of what the courts will do in fact, and nothing more pretentious, are what I mean by law.[12]

This statement has been widely cited and discussed. As a practical insight into the law in action, it is one that I have found echoed in conversations with leading commercial barristers in London. When we discuss how they respond to clients who understandably want to know their chances of winning, they tell me that even if a case looks open-and-shut, they rarely predict a greater than 70 per cent likelihood of success. In part, they are being cautious but, more significantly, they tell me that there are many factors, often imponderables, that can determine the outcome of a case and that these extend beyond the black-letter law. Here lies a very exciting possibility—that prediction systems based on machine-learning, drawing on huge bodies of data *about* cases, much of which is unrelated to substantive law, can precisely take account of the so-called extra-legal imponderables. An extreme illustration of an imponderable in action came from the Israeli courts, a study of which showed a substantial difference in the outcomes of parole hearings, depending on whether they were heard before or after lunch.[13] This brings to mind the theory of 'digestive jurisprudence', according to which judges' decisions are determined by what they have had for breakfast.

Holmes belonged to a school of legal theorists known as the American Legal Realists. One group within that school came to be known as the 'rule skeptics'.[14] They argued that the legal rules in legislation and case law—the 'pseudo rules', 'accepted rules', 'paper rules', or 'verbally formulated rules'—were of limited use for lawyers who were trying to predict the outcomes of judicial decisions. To help clients, lawyers had instead to divine the 'latent rules' or 'real rules' which they claimed were discoverable from patterns in judicial behaviour. Karl Llewellyn, the pre-eminent rule sceptic claimed that these real rules would be better called 'the practices of the courts',[15] for he suggested that the law was 'what ... officials do about disputes'.[16] A similar line of thinking can be traced in sociological jurisprudence, where we also find suggestions that there is more to the law than what we find in print on paper. Eugene Ehrlich invited us to look beyond the 'norms for decision' (for example, legislation) to the 'living law', by which he meant the social rules that are actually followed by citizens in society,[17] while Roscoe Pound drew a firm distinction between the 'law in books' and the 'law in action'.[18] The American Legal Realists and sociological jurisprudents had no way of knowing that machine learning techniques would in due course provide the tools for identifying the patterns in judicial and social behaviour to which they refer.

But this is not simply theory. Prediction is central to daily legal practice. When lawyers are trying to determine what their clients' legal rights and duties might be at any given moment, especially in harder cases, they often think and talk in terms of what judges would decide if the issues came before them. When lawyers say that they cannot imagine the court accepting X, or that it would be hard for any judge to support Y, or again that they are confident than any panel would decide Z, they are expressing the content of the law in predictive terms. There are at least three dimensions to this. First, in the end what really matters in law is how a given legal issue would be authoritatively settled. The second is that in advising clients, lawyers really do engage in a form of predictive reasoning. They should therefore be intensely interested in the context of online courts in any systems that can predict judicial behaviour more accurately than they can. Indeed it is conceivable in the future that they would be regarded as negligent for not using such systems, just as doctors might be if they fail to call for or scrutinize MRI scans in support of their diagnoses.[19] Third, we can reasonably ask whether judges themselves might find it useful to use these predictive tools before they come to their decisions.

Predictions as determinations

By far the most controversial use of predictive techniques, however, would be in substituting prediction machines for judges. On this approach, prediction is not used a type of ODR, nor as a form of facilitation on the second tier, but as a tool by which a fully authoritative and binding court decision is made. For most lawyers and judges, this is at best barely conceivable and, at worst, a fundamental affront to justice. It is only human judges, surely, who can make binding court decisions.

Of course, decisions of the courts have only been made by judges in the past. But does this bind us for all time? Can we not conceive that a finding, with all the force and enforceability of a traditional decision, might be made by a machine? Consider outcome-thinking again. Recall my suggestion in Chapter 4, that patients do not want neurosurgeons; they want health. Likewise, litigants may not want judicial decisions; on one view, they want a binding decision by an institution we call a court. Or they might want peace of mind, or to be rid of a problem, or simply to have a problem resolved one way or another. The outcomes that litigants seek might be achieved using methods other than human judges in courtrooms even though, historically, there has never been a credible alternative. But we can, in principle, imagine a machine generating findings that, by law, are deemed authoritative. It could be enshrined in the rules of court, for example, that if the system predicts a court finding in favour of the claimant with a probability factor greater than, say, 95 per cent, then that finding becomes the official determination of the court. This may be thought to be undesirable or unlikely, but it is certainly a possibility.

Consider once more the backlog in the courts of Brazil of more than 100 million cases. I note again that there really is no chance whatsoever of that caseload ever being disposed of by judges and lawyers in traditional courtrooms. In the interests of moving on, in the spirit of a rough and ready decision, it is surely possible that some litigants involved in low-value disputes (especially young litigants, for whom online problem-solving is increasingly popular) might say that such a system of the sort I describe is preferable to the gridlocked traditional court. More formally, they might claim that such a system promotes proportionate justice (quick, inexpensive, easy to use, not combative, and so commensurate with the problem at hand); and that it also promotes distributive justice (because access to a state-based dispute resolution service would thereby be offered to many rather than a few in society). They might also claim that procedural justice has been delivered too—they understand the process and its limitations, they have documents or data lodged in support of their cases, and they are happy to stand by past decisions (as embodied in the data). Moreover, they could benefit from enforceable justice (Chapter 7), in that the machine-generated determination would be as binding on parties as a conventional judicial decision; enforcement and payment might even be built in, using some form of blockchain technology.

But there are problems here, two of which derive from different conceptions of justice. One is that such a system would fail to deliver open justice. The problem here is not just that there is no public courtroom in which the administration of justice can be observed at first hand, which is the essence of the objection addressed in Chapter 19. Worse, there is no human judge involved at all, and so, for instance, no written judgments to analyse, nor biographies to scrutinize. Worse yet, most machine learning systems are opaque. Unlike the first wave of legal AI, whose expert systems could explain their lines of reasoning, machine learning systems may well arrive at conclusions or perform tasks at a high level but they are unable to explain or justify their 'black box' behaviour. In individual cases, how can we countenance systems that are so patently lacking in transparency? More generally, what do we do if we are not able to assess the operational effectiveness of algorithms and data that might come to sit at the heart of our court system?[20]

Another problem is that acceptance of decisions based on such prediction machines might lead to substantively unfair outcomes, because they might be based on data or algorithms that suffer from bias. If past decisions are rooted in bias or prejudice, then the data that expresses these decisions is contaminated, and decisions (high probability predictions) derived from that data will perpetuate the inequities. Equally, the original algorithms themselves, written by software engineers, may reflect and propagate their personal biases, even if these predispositions are unconscious. In other words, the bias in these systems could again lead to substantive injustice.

These two objections, rooted in open justice and substantive justice, highlight two of the main shortcomings with machine learning systems generally—they are not transparent and the data and software on which they rely can be tainted. There is a burgeoning literature on these subjects[21] and countless initiatives and research centres now dedicated to these subjects. A few weeks after I submit the manuscript for this book, the Law Society of England and Wales will be publishing the report of its Technology and Law Policy Commission that has been investigating 'algorithms in the justice system'. I have also been invited by the Lord Chief Justice to chair his advisory group on AI. This is made up of senior judges and AI/law experts. I have little doubt we will at some stage examine the questions of transparency and bias.

I would need another few chapters to address these issues fully. Sadly, some of the responses in the popular literature have been superficial, even if well intentioned. For example, it is not at all clear, either technically or philosophically, what is meant when it is proposed, as many people suggest, that we should 'build ethics into AI'. Nor is it obvious what is meant when people demand that software engineers should 'program' their machine learning systems to provide intelligible explanations. This is to misunderstand the difference between the inductive processes that underlie machine learning and the deductive form of argument that we expect when we ask for an explanation.[22] I understand the hope that there might be quick technical fixes for the shortcomings of AI but they will require many years of work, in my estimation.[23]

In the context of online courts, there is one issue that can be addressed. It is a sub-set of the concern over bias. I have in mind a common reaction to the idea of using predictive systems instead of decision-making by judges. The reaction is that because these systems are based on relatively fixed bodies of past data, they would ossify the law and leave no room for growth or creativity. They would perpetuate positions embedded in the data and eliminate the scope for discretion or the development of new judicial thinking.

Critics are right to be wary of biases in past data but are often naïve in thinking that the systems crudely reproduce past decisions. With vast numbers of data points and different weightings effectively attached to each, machine learning algorithms may well generate output that appears creative and fresh (reflect again on AlphaGo—Chapter 26). It always amuses me in this connection when antagonists dismissively go on to say that the problem with these systems is that they are greatly constrained by only being able to operate on past data. I often challenge this and ask about the data upon which human beings rely—are they gifted with data from the future? Past data and experience are all we can have, except that machines have access to bodies of data that can be many of orders of magnitude larger than those available or analysable by humans. Besides, as long as hard cases are still being settled by machines, these bodies of data will be regularly refreshed.

In any event, I must reach again here for Voltaire's Riposte and mention once more Brazil's backlog of 100 million cases. I am told many of these are routine and low value. Even on the most negative analysis, would it not be better in most cases to have these disposed of by opaque predictive systems that would faithfully issue decisions consistent with judges of the past, along with any bias, rather than leave parties waiting for the human judicial decision that will never come?

Moral boundaries

Debates about the desirability of AI replacing judges often degenerate into arguments over what might or might not be technically possible. To get to the heart of the matter, I find it better to assume for the moral debate that machines can indeed fully replace judges; that there are no technical constraints. What would we then think?

There are some human tasks and activities, it might be said, that are so important to the human condition that we would never be comfortable in allocating them to AI and autonomous machines. In medicine, for example, most people today believe, I would guess, that the decision to turn off a life-support system and then to flick the switch itself should not be entrusted to a machine without a human in the loop. This is perhaps one illustration of a moral boundary beyond which our systems should not be permitted to roam. Sometimes, the moral buck should not stop at a robot. It is right and necessary, the argument would run, that a human being should take responsibility for such life-and-death decisions. Similarly, in the context of warfare, there are many who feel strongly opposed to autonomous weapons, to the notion that people might be killed by high-performing systems without the express authority of someone in command.

In this spirit, there are also some, perhaps many, who would say that decision-making by judges sits beyond a moral boundary. If the liberty, health, or wealth of citizens is to be reduced by the state, a fellow human being should be responsible for that kind of decision. This might be a visceral instinct. It might be rooted in some deeper philosophical position, relating, for example, to 'respect for persons'. It might be based on the view that all judges must be capable of showing compassion and mercy, neither of which can be simulated by machine (note that this view commits the AI fallacy, disregards outcome-thinking, and neglects the possibility that judges who show compassion or mercy today may do so unevenly, driven perhaps by unconscious bias). Or it might derive from some fondness for tradition, a belief that what has worked well enough in the past is right for that reason alone. In any event, we can expect that many will argue that computer judges would not be a good thing. Some may insist that machines should under no condition take on any judicial tasks. Others might concede that it makes sense to put in place such systems for very minor disputes. Indeed they could argue that we are morally obliged to do so if justice would otherwise be denied.

In public debate and social policy-making, these moral objections will need to be balanced against anticipated benefits such as everyday notions of affordability, convenience, speed, as well as weightier principles of justice, not least distributive justice.

My personal opinions on this issue are of no greater value than anyone else's. But I have a number of observations which might help readers. The first is that my own view has changed on this topic, as I say at the start of the chapter. I was genuinely horrified in the mid-1980s at the idea of a computer judge. I am not now. It may be that I have been in the field so long that I look at the world through AI-tinted glasses, but I think not. Having seen manifest injustice first hand, I now recognize that difficult moral issues invariably require a choice between two or more undesirable states of affairs. I can see the moral objections to the computer judge, but they can, in principle, be outweighed on my moral calculus by the manifest injustice of having no recourse whatever to the state for the resolution of legal problems.

The relativist point, made in Chapter 7, is worth reiterating. We should expect that views on the computer judge may not just change over time; they are likely also to vary from place to place. Again, it is probable that our grandchildren will have different views from ours. This might be because their ideas of right and wrong may diverge from ours but, more likely, they will live in an age when it will be commonplace for machines to be unarguably superior to humans in many walks of life. In that context, they might think it morally unacceptable to insist that humans undertake vital work when machines can do a better job. As ever, then, we need to keep an open mind, remembering too that the moral high ground is not necessarily held by those who prefer the *status quo*. In its conservatism, my generation runs the risk of being guilty of sins of omission, of failure to make changes.

Chapter 28
The Global Challenge

I invite readers, in arriving at your verdict on the desirability of online courts, not to focus on their current shortcomings but instead to consider whether their introduction would represent an improvement over our traditional court systems. In terms of the concepts introduced in the first part of this book, we should first ask whether online courts, for suitable cases, offer greater access to justice than today's courts. The answer here is surely very clear—online judging, as outlined in this book, will be a much more affordable way of resolving disputes authoritatively, while the extended court facilities will help users assess and contain their disputes in ways that are simply not possible today.

We should also ask which system, today's or tomorrow's (as outlined here), better promotes the seven principles of justice advanced in this book; and which better overcomes the injustices to which our current courts give rise. In relation to substantive justice (the fairness of decisions made), procedural justice (the fairness of the process), enforceable justice (the extent to which decisions are backed by the state), and sustainable justice (whether courts are sufficiently resourced), I conclude that there will be little difference in these respects between online and traditional courts in coming years. I also expect little difference in the outcomes (the practical results and the emotional effects) from the two types of courts.

The most striking differences between the old and new systems relate to distributive justice and proportionate justice. While traditional courts, by and large, are accessible to very few people and even then only at disproportionate expense and effort, online courts are being designed and developed precisely to overcome these injustices. If their promise is fulfilled, and the early case studies give us strong reason to be optimistic, then the social good that is public dispute resolution will be much more widely distributed across society. And this good will be accessible at a cost, within timescales, and in a spirit that is notably more proportionate to the value and scale of low-value disputes than when the machinery of conventional courts is brought to bear.

With regard to open justice, the initial and instinctive view, that this can be achieved to a much greater extent in traditional courts than in online courts, does not withstand scrutiny. Traditional courts (public hearings) offer greater 'real-time transparency' but much less 'information transparency' than online courts. In practice, though, there are very few observers of, and little rationale for observing, the kinds of minor cases for which online courts are currently being developed. I am convinced, on balance, that online courts can offer *greater* overall transparency than traditional public hearings. Accordingly, it seems to me that the benefits of online courts, for appropriate cases, far outweigh their shortcomings.

Even if readers remain unconvinced of this conclusion in respect of their own countries, I believe there are overwhelming arguments in favour of introducing online courts in nations where access to justice is limited and the rule of law does not prevail. In this final chapter, I address this global challenge.

International context

In September 2015, at a meeting in New York to mark the seventieth anniversary of the United Nations (UN), member states adopted a

'2030 Agenda for Sustainable Development'. This was described as a 'shared blueprint for peace and prosperity for people and the planet, now and into the future'. Central to this blueprint are '17 Sustainable Development Goals (SDGs), which are an urgent call for action by all countries—developed and developing—in a global partnership'.[1] The sixteenth of these (SDG 16) expressly refers to access to justice. Its purpose is to: promote peace and inclusive societies for sustainable development, provide access to justice for all and build effective, accountable and inclusive institutions at all levels.[2]

Sadly, however, progress towards this goal has been slow. In 2018, it was reported that:

> [m]any regions of the world continue to suffer untold horrors as a result of armed conflict or other forms of violence that occur within societies and at the domestic level. Advances in promoting the rule of law and access to justice are uneven.[3]

This diagnosis is supported by the statistics laid out in Chapter 2. The Organisation for Economic Co-operation and Development (OECD) say that only 46 per cent of the world's population lives under the protection of the law.[4] Each year, one billion people are in need of 'basic justice care' but in 'many countries, close to 30% of problem-owners do not even take action'.[5] As for legal aid, of 106 countries reviewed, it was found that around one-third 'have not yet enacted specific legislation on legal aid' and that the 'demand for legal aid for civil cases is largely unmet in most countries'.[6] At the same time, in some countries, their courts have enormous backlogs—for example, 100 million cases in Brazil, and 30 million in India.

We are all too familiar with the 'untold horrors' and, as the UN euphemistically puts it, the 'uneven' advances in promoting the rule of law and access to justice—iniquitous laws, disregard for human rights, arbitrary law-making, biased judges, corrupt officials, citizens' inability to understand their entitlements, unaffordable or too complex systems for enforcing rights, massive delay and backlog in courts, oppression of minorities, de facto criminal rulers, opacity of process, courts that are too slow and unaffordable, violence and armed conflict, legal rights decided upon by non-judicial public officials, laws neither published nor intelligible, unfair procedures, and disregard for international law. Tragically, this lawlessness is rife globally.

The internet

What can be done? One promising line of attack on some aspects of this lawlessness would be to harness the remarkable reach of the internet. As noted in Chapter 2, more people are now active users of the internet (53 per cent) than have access to justice (46 per cent). And that 53 per cent will rise steadily over the next few years. This provides us, globally, with a platform to offer some support to those who currently have no realistic access to justice nor protection under the law. One key here is to move greatly beyond the well-intentioned websites that many regard as the answer, to the introduction, as extensively as we can manage, of online courts.

To understand how and why online courts might succeed where legal websites have had modest impact, we need to look back. Over the last decade, there has been an explosion of websites designed to help people cope with the law. These have been made available in many countries, largely by charities, educational bodies, activists, students, and by law firms too on a *pro bono* basis. Many of these projects are impressive, devoted to educating the public on legal issues, helping citizens to understand their rights and duties, guiding them on complex legislation and regulation, alerting users to relevant changes in the law, explaining options for dispute resolution, walking through court procedure, and more. Often, though, these services are, essentially, conventional booklets that have been put online. Sometimes their language has been too legalistic and, in consequence, too forbidding. Others have been better conceived— interactive, with animations and graphics, and built using design-thinking methods, so that they have been made available with the needs of everyday users uppermost in mind.

So what is the problem? If growing numbers of people are online and good systems are increasingly available, surely sound progress is being made. I am afraid the combined current offerings them-selves are not sufficient. In the first instance, this online provision of legal issues has been piecemeal. Particular problem areas may be addressed but the coverage in most countries is neither systematic nor complete. Nor is it clear to the non-expert what resources are available and which are reliable. Typically, users will search rather haphazardly for some words on Google that are thought to cap-ture their problems. They will then be confronted by a bewildering range of sites. Rarely will they be provided by recognizable brands.

The nub

However, even if online resources were comprehensive, intuitive to use, and reassuringly branded, the reality, as noted in Chapter 9, is that there is an enormous gulf between knowing one's rights and being able to enforce them. And this chasm has been the space in which the corrupt and the unsavoury have been able to pursue their own nefarious goals with impunity. It has also been the space in which well-resourced organizations have been able to avoid in-dividual citizens who have justiciable claims.

Here is the nub of it. Knowing the law without the capacity to apply and enforce one's rights, as noted in Chapter 9, is like receiving a medical diagnosis but with no medical or surgical care available thereafter. The most elegant and well-researched legal solution is of little value unless the rights it identifies can be translated into action—as some kind of remedy or other satisfactory outcome.

Let me restate the vision I set out in Chapter 9. Online courts can bridge the gulf between people knowing the law and being able to enforce their entitlements. They can provide people not only with guidance on their legal rights but also with the institutional traction that historically has only been achievable through the deployment of lawyers. In two ways, then, online courts will create a bridge, a connection, between legal understanding and remedy. First, they will empower those with rights that might otherwise go unrealized, giving the self-represented some of the heft of a client with a lawyer. Second, the existence of online courts that put remedies at the fingertips of all will incentivize duty bearers actually to fulfil their obligations. The availability of swift, affordable, and understandable court service, underpinned by mechanisms for enforcement will surely change the behaviour of those who might otherwise be inclined to disregard the law. The playing field can be levelled, and inequalities removed—between wealthy and less well-off parties, between those who are represented and those who are not, between those who have always had the courts at their disposal and those who have felt alienated.

Unlike websites, the use of online courts carries the authority of law, underpinned by the coercive power of the state. Online courts deliver 'enforceable justice' (Chapter 7).

This matters

To reiterate what I say in the Introduction, I believe that all human beings—regardless of their capabilities, status, wealth, and wherever they live and work—deserve and should be accorded equal respect and dignity. I regard this as a global entitlement for all citizens, an end itself, whether or not it leads to a more harmonious, prosperous, or happier life for all. And this right to respect and dignity, I insist, should be enshrined in and enforceable by the law. It is a tragedy beyond words that 54 per cent of our fellow human beings are deprived of the protections, entitlements, and benefits that the law can and should afford.

A global effort

I conclude that we now need a global effort, dedicated to introducing online courts to countries that have great backlogs in their traditional court systems or severe access-to-justice problems. These countries could be invited to commit (by accord, protocol, memorandum of understanding, or the like) to the introduction and provision of online courts.

Satisfying all seven principles of justice laid out in Chapter 7, I am envisioning a world where more countries would thereby have transparent and sufficiently resourced court systems, that are backed by the state, are appropriately balanced, are accessible to all and that deliver fair decisions, while underpinned by procedures that are fair and perceived by users to be so. The broad social objective would be to increase access to justice, at least in three senses laid out in Chapter 6—to improve dispute resolution, dispute containment, and dispute resolution.

However, we can do more than simply invite nation states to sign up to the introduction of online courts. We should be able to develop and make available a *standard, adaptable, global platform for online courts*, supporting both the online judging and extended court functions introduced in this book. The platform, made available in open-source spirit, could come pre-populated with a set of embedded procedures that could be tailored to suit individual jurisdictions. A standard set of tools for users would be included in the suite, including apps that provide access via mobile devices and standard user interfaces that have been already been road-tested.

When I meet lawyers and policy-makers from developing nations who are anxious to know more about the British legal systems and have plans to put in place structures like ours, I now caution them against doing so. Why transplant a set of nineteenth-century institutions? Instead they might consider leapfrogging so-called advanced jurisdictions and directly introduce online courts. They would certainly find it a lot easier. Historically, regimes that have committed to the rule of law and aspired to the rapid introduction of a new or radically upgraded independent judicial system have faced various forbidding challenges—drafting rules of procedure, constructing appropriate buildings, engaging the legal profession, and recruiting impartial judges who are suitably trained. These challenges could to some extent be bypassed if a standard online court platform were put in place instead. With modest tailoring of existing operational systems, a facility for self-represented litigants that offered online judging could be up and running within months. With regard to building a judicial capability, to kick-start the system, pending the full assembly of an appropriate local judiciary, judges from around the world could be appointed to sit remotely and decide cases, with modest training in high-volume, low-value, relatively straightforward issues. There is already precedent for this as retired English judges today have been engaged to sit in a variety of countries beyond the UK. It would take longer to build the various facilities that make up the extended court—these again might be provided not by the state in the first instance but by charitable, educational, and voluntary services.

I do not for a moment imagine that the introduction of online courts would somehow encourage dictators and despots to change their ways. Nor do I expect they would have much effect on organized criminals. However, online courts might to some extent fortify those who are struggling to bring the rule of law to their countries and communities. They could be transparent on a global basis, which would mean open justice on a larger scale than is possible today. The activities of more courts around the world could be open to scrutiny. In some jurisdictions, this might increase the level of the account-ability of their justice systems. This transparency of itself might lead to better practice. Regimes that have little regard for the rule of law can more easily ride roughshod over the rights of citizens when they can do so beyond any public glare. However, few regimes publicly flaunt their lawlessness. Even the most pernicious pay lip service to the rule of law. When light can be shone directly and publicly on the way in which they administer justice, we might expect that their compliance with the rule of law and their promotion of access to justice will increase. This might fall under the heading of their doing the right thing for the wrong reason, but it would be a start. Improvement is better than perfection; comparatavism rather than transcendentalism; Voltaire's Riposte.

I accept this is a highly ambitious agenda and that all manner of cultural, technical, legal, and political obstacles stand in our way. But we should surely be able to find the resolve and the funds to design and build a standard global platform for the resolution of low-value civil claims in online courts. If the platform came to be used even in a small number of countries, it might change the lives of many. My early investigations in this direction, in a dozen or so jurisdic-tions, have been received positively. It is certainly worth a try. For those who care deeply about increasing access to justice, for court technologists, for judges and lawyers who are serious about change, for politicians who want to make a difference, and for human be-ings who care about peace and overcoming the suffering of others, this platform could well be our legacy.

APPENDIX
Checklist of Critical Success Factors

Over the years, I have evolved a list of factors that I believe are critical for the successful introduction of court technology. The list, as laid out below, was informed in large part by problems of the past.

Leadership

1. Support from the top – from leading politicians, judges, and officials.
2. Clear vision – of what the justice system *and* the technology will look like.
3. Robust governance – sufficiently senior individuals overseeing the work.
4. Ongoing review of critical path – too important to be left to managers.

Strategy

5. Modular development – an incremental transformation; not a 'big bang'.
6. Unifying process, procedure, terminology across all the justice system, in so far as possible.
7. Not 'mess for less' – innovating through technology, not just automating old ways.
8. Deploying technologies from the 2020s and not from the 2010s (or earlier).

Expertise and skills

9. Technical – deep design and technology skills.
10. Process analysis – deep *legal* process analysis talent.
11. Project management – experienced, credentialed managers.
12. Procurement – seasoned officers with successful track record.

13. Contracting – senior (not junior) officials supported by first rate lawyers.
14. Continuity of staff – humans should be expected still to be around in the 2020s.

Users

15. Involvement – users should be consulted (but do not always know best).
16. Judges – their wholehearted support is needed (but do not always know best).
17. Expectation management of users – over-hyping should be resisted.
18. Self-represented litigants – must not be forgotten as a principal user group.

Specification

19. Sensible – a system for mainstream users and not for technology specialists.
20. Over-engineering – to be avoided at all costs.
21. Realism – time scales should not be overly optimistic.

Procurement

22. Pragmatic – rather than purist (e.g., a manageable number of providers).
23. Legal /contractual – early and ongoing involvement of external lawyers.

Project management

24. Firm management of suppliers – crucial for delivery on time and on budget.
25. Scope creep – to be avoided at all costs (even if requests from judges).
26. Bad news – must be conveyed to leaders early (an all-important 'risk register' should be maintained)
27. English – jargon must be avoided; clear communication is key.

Technology

28. Emerging systems – likely to be wide use of telepresence and of AI.
29. Internet-based – court systems must be designed for a digital society.
30. Profession – progress must not be held back by conservative lawyers.

NOTES

Introduction

1. Cited in Thomas Kuhn, *The Structure of Scientific Revolutions* (1996), p. 151.
2. *The Future of Law* (1996).
3. See Richard Susskind and Daniel Susskind, *The Future of the Professions* (2015).
4. Quotation from welcoming speech at the First International Forum on Online Courts, held in London in December 2018. See Richard Susskind, 'Making the Case for Online Courts' (2018).
5. See https://www.oecd.org/gov/delivering-access-to-justice-for-all.pdf (accessed 26 April 2019).
6. See http://data.worldjusticeproject.org/ (accessed 26 April 2019) where Brazil is ranked 58 out of 126 countries in the WJP Rule of Law Index.
7. See Clayton Christensen, *The Innovator's Dilemma* (1997).
8. Most notably, Joshua Rozenberg at 'The Online Court: Will IT Work?' (2019), and Roger Smith at https://law-tech-a2j.org/author/rogersmith/ (accessed 26 April 2019).

Chapter 1

1. Lord Bingham, *The Rule of Law* (2010), p. vii.
2. I have relied particularly on Lord Bingham, *The Rule of Law* (2010); Hans Kelsen, *General Theory of Law and State* (1945); Herbert Hart, *The Concept of Law* (2012); Lon Fuller, *The Morality of Law* (1969); and Richard Posner, *How Judges Think* (2008). I have also been helped by the insights of the World Justice Project, https://worldjusticeproject.org/our-work/wjp-rule-law-index/wjp-rule-law-index-2017%E2%80%932018 (accessed 26 April 2019).

3. Hazel Genn, *Judging Civil Justice* (2010), pp. 115–16. Original emphasis.

4. Ibid., p. 117. Original emphasis.

5. Ronald Dworkin, *Law's Empire* (1986), p. 229.

6. For an important related discussion of the consequences for law of various 'truisms' about human beings and 'human nature', see Herbert Hart, *The Concept of Law* (2012) pp. 192–200.

7. Aristotle, *Nicomachean Ethics* (1999), Book VIII, Ch. 1, 120.

8. Hart, *The Concept of Law* (2012), pp. 125–6.

Chapter 2

1. See https://www.oecd.org/gov/delivering-access-to-justice-for-all.pdf (accessed 26 April 2019): '4 billion people around the world live outside the protection of the law'. This in 2016, when the world population was 7.4 billion.

2. See https://www.internetworldstats.com/stats4.htm (accessed 26 April 2019)

3. HiiL, *Understanding Justice Needs: The Elephant in the Courtroom* (2018), pp. 6 and 30.

4. United Nations Global Study of Legal Aid (2016), pp. 2–3, available at https://www.unodc.org/documents/justice-and-prison-reform/LegalAid/Global_Study_on_Legal_Aid_-_FINAL.pdf (accessed 26 April 2019).

5. See, e.g., TheCityUK's report, 'Legal Excellence, Internationally Renowned: UK Legal Services 2018', available at https://www.thecityuk.com/research/legal-excellence-internationally-renowned-uk-legal-services-2018/ (accessed 26 April 2019).

6. Hazel Genn, *Judging Civil Justice* (2010), p. 51

7. Ministry of Justice, 'Post-Implementation Review of the Legal Aid, Sentencing and Punishment of Offenders Act 2012 (LASPO)' (February 2019), available at https://assets.publishing.service.gov.uk/government/uploads/system/uploads/attachment_data/file/777038/post-implementation-review-of-part-1-of-laspo.pdf (accessed 26 April 2019).

8. Lord Bach, *Right to Justice: the Final Report of the Bach Commission* (September 2017), p. 12, available at http://www.fabians.org.uk/wp-content/uploads/2017/09/Bach-Commission_Right-to-Justice-Report-WEB.pdf (accessed 26 April 2019).

9. Ethan Katsh and Orna Rabinovich-Einy, *Digital Justice: Technology and the Internet of Conflict* (2017), p. 67.
10. See https://www.statista.com/topics/2333/e-commerce-in-the-united-kingdom/ (accessed 26 April 2019).
11. See Richard Susskind, *The Future of Law* (1996), Ch. 1.

Chapter 3

1. In previous books, I have called this 'innovation' but that term is now so widely over-used that I have jettisoned it, at least for now. See, e.g., Richard Susskind, *The End of Lawyers?* (2008); Richard Susskind, *Tomorrow's Lawyers* (2017); and Richard Susskind and Daniel Susskind, *The Future of the Professions* (2015).
2. The classic book on disruption (another over-used term) is Clayton Christensen, *The Innovator's Dilemma* (1997).
3. See Richard Susskind and Daniel Susskind, *The Future of the Professions* (2015), Ch. 4.
4. See ibid.
5. Ray Kurzweil, *The Singularity is Near* (2005), p. 127.
6. Daniel Susskind, *A World Without Work* (2020), Ch. 5.
7. Marco Iansiti and Karim Lakhani, 'The Truth about Blockchain' (2017), p. 118.
8. See Jamie Susskind, *Future Politics* (2018), p. 43.
9. https://www.sermo.com and https://www.patientslikeme.com (accessed 26 April 2019).
10. https://www.linuxfoundation.org (accessed 26 April 2019).
11. Robert Gordon, *The Rise and Fall of American Growth* (2016), Ch. 17.
12. Ray Kurzweil, *The Singularity is Near* (2005), p. 9.
13. Richard Susskind, *The Future of Law* (1996), pp. 91–6.
14. Ibid., pp. 285–92.
15. See Richard Susskind and Daniel Susskind, *The Future of the Professions* (2015).

Chapter 4

1. Since first writing and thinking about outcome-thinking, I read Seth Godin, *This is Marketing* (2018), which led to me include the emotional dimension. Chapter 3 of his book is especially useful.

2. See Hazel Genn, 'Online Courts and the Future of Justice' (2017), p. 8.
3. Adam Smith, *An Inquiry into the Nature and Causes of the Wealth of Nations* (1998), Book IV Ch.VIII, 49.
4. Cited in Daniel Susskind, *A World Without Work* (2020), Ch. 6.

Chapter 5

1. Judith Resnik and Dennis Curtis, *Representing Justice* (2011).
2. See, e.g., Penelope Gibbs, 'Defendants on Video—Conveyor Belt Justice or a Revolution in Access' (October 2017).
3. Oliver Wendell Holmes, in *Southern Pacific Company v Jensen*, 244 U.S. 205, 222 (1917) (he was referring to the common law).
4. On asynchronous process, see Ayelet Sela, 'Streamlining Justice: How Online Courts Can Resolve the Challenges of Pro Se Litigation' (2016), p. 360.
5. Decomposition in legal services is discussed more fully in Richard Susskind, *The End of Lawyers?* (2008), pp. 42–52 and Richard Susskind, *Tomorrow's Lawyers* (2017), pp. 32–42.

Chapter 6

1. Franz Kafka, *A Country Doctor* (1997), pp.29–33 and Franz Kafka, *The Trial* (1983), pp. 235–43.
2. Lord Woolf, *Access to Justice—Interim Report* (1995) and Lord Woolf, *Access to Justice—Final Report* (1996).
3. See Richard Susskind, *The End of Lawyers?* (2008), Ch. 7.
4. Quoted by Jerome Frank, 'Some Reflections on Judge Learned Hand' (1957), p. 675.
5. Herbert Hart, *The Concept of Law* (2012), Ch.V.

Chapter 7

1. Plato, *The Republic* (2007), p. 8.
2. Lord Devlin, *The Judge* (1981), p. 84. Original emphasis.
3. This takes us into a longstanding discussion in the field of jurisprudence, between 'legal positivists', who will generally argue there is no necessary connection between the law and morality, and 'natural lawyers' who argue that for any law to be valid it must have some minimum moral

content. See Herbert Hart, 'Positivism and the Separation of Law and Morals' (1958).

4. For an accessible introduction to ethics and meta-ethics, see John Mackie, *Ethics* (1990).

5. Richard Posner, *How Judges Think* (2008), p. 88.

6. For a richer analysis of procedural justice, distinguishing between 'perfect procedural justice', 'imperfect procedural justice', and 'pure procedural justice', see John Rawls, *A Theory of Justice*, (1972), Ch. II, Section 14. The current approach most closely resembles Rawls's conception of 'pure procedural justice'.

7. Tom Tyler, 'Court Review: Volume 44, Issue 1/2—Procedural Justice and the Courts' (2007).

8. Michael Sandel, *Justice* (2009), p. 19.

9. There is some overlap in this book with proportionate justice as discussed in John Sorabji, *English Civil Justice after the Woolf and Jackson Reforms* (2014), pp. 136–7.

Chapter 8

1. Tom Campbell, *Justice* (2001), p. 3. Original emphasis.

2. Lord Devlin, *The Judge* (1981), p. 3.

3. Amartya Sen, *The Idea of Justice* (2009), pp. 5–7. Emphasis added.

Chapter 9

1. Civil Justice Council, *Online Dispute Resolution for Low Value Civil Claims* (2015). As well as this report, our group set up a website with related materials at https://www.judiciary.uk/reviews/online-dispute-resolution/ (accessed 26 April 2019).

2. Civil Justice Council, *Online Dispute Resolution for Low Value Civil Claims* (2015), p. 5.

3. See Colin Rule, 'Designing a Global Online Dispute Resolution System: Lessons Learned from eBay' (2017).

4. Civil Justice Council, *Online Dispute Resolution for Low Value Civil Claims* (2015), p. 8.

5. Richard Susskind, 'Online Disputes: Is it Time to End the 'Day in Court'?' (26 February 2015).

6. JUSTICE, *Delivering Justice in an Age of Austerity* (2015).

7. Michael Gove, 'What does a one nation justice policy look like?' (23 June 2015), available at https://www.gov.uk/government/speeches/what-does-a-one-nation-justice-policy-look-like (accessed 26 April 2019).

8. Lord Thomas, 'Judicial Leadership' (22 June 2015).

9. HM Treasury, *Spending Review and Autumn Statement* (25 November 2015), available at https://www.gov.uk/government/publications/spending-review-and-autumn-statement-2015-documents (accessed 26 April 2019).

10. Lord Briggs, *Civil Courts Structure Review: Interim Report* (2015).

11. Lord Briggs, *Civil Courts Structure Review: Final Report* (2016).

12. Lord Chancellor et al., 'Transforming our Justice System' (2016).

13. On family work, see Sir James Munby, 'The Family Bar in a Digital World' (2018). On tribunal work, see Sir Ernest Ryder, 'Modernisation of Access to Justice in Times of Austerity' (2016).

14. See Lord Denning, 'Law and Life in our Time' (1967), p. 354.

15. See Richard Susskind, 'Lawyers and Coders Hack Away Dead Wood for Digital Courts' (2017).

16. See Richard Susskind, 'Making the Case for Online Courts' (2018).

17. Richard Susskind, *The Future of Law* (1996).

18. See, e.g., The Engine Room, 'Technology for Legal Empowerment: A Global Review' (2019), and https://justiceinnovation.law.stanford.edu/ (accessed 26 April 2019).

Chapter 10

1. Legal Services Act 2007.

2. In the Civil Justice Council report, we used the term 'resolution' in respect of Tier 3 decision-making. I now prefer 'determination' to 'resolution' because 'resolution' can be confused with ADR and ODR. More, 'resolution' is also used to refer to the fourth layer of the access to justice model. See Civil Justice Council, *Online Dispute Resolution for Low Value Civil Claims* (2015).

Chapter 11

1. Lord Briggs, *Civil Courts Structure Review: Final Report* (2016), pp. 49–50.

2. I am indebted to Roger Smith who introduced me in this context to the phrase, 'turning a mess into a problem.'

3. Tim Brown and Roger Martin, 'Design for Action' (2015).

4. See https://justiceinnovation.law.stanford.edu (accessed 26 April 2019). Also very useful in this connection but not written from a design thinking perspective, is JUSTICE, *Understanding Courts* (2019).

5. See Ayelet Sela, 'Streamlining Justice: How Online Courts Can Resolve the Challenges of Pro Se Litigation' (2016).

6. Atul Gawande, *The Checklist Manifesto* (2007).

7. See Phillip Capper and Richard Susskind, *Latent Damage Law—The Expert System* (1988).

8. Darin Thompson, 'Creating New Pathways to Justice Using Simple Artificial Intelligence and Online Dispute Resolution' (2015).

9. See https://www.resolver.co.uk (accessed 26 April 2019).

10. See, e.g., the following systems in the UK—https://www.advicenow. co.uk, https://www.citizensadvice.org.uk/, and https://england. shelter.org.uk/ (accessed 26 April 2019).

11. https://www.patientslikeme.com (accessed 26 April 2019).

12. Richard Susskind, *The Future of Law* (1996), pp. 23–7.

13. Jeremy Bentham, *Of Laws in General* (1970), p. 71.

Chapter 12

1. See https://www.financial-ombudsman.org.uk/publications/annual-review-2018/PDF/data-in-more-depth.pdf, p. 59 (accessed 26 April 2019).

2. See Graham Ross, 'First case in the Online Court to be Resolved by Algorithm' (2019).

3. Civil Justice Council, *Online Dispute Resolution for Low Value Civil Claims* (2015), p. 18.

Chapter 13

1. Sir Ernest Ryder, 'The Modernisation of Access to Justice in Times of Austerity' (2016).

2. Richard Susskind, *Expert Systems in Law* (1987), pp. 245–51.

3. Jerome Frank, *Courts on Trial* (1949), pp. 221–4.

4. Jerome Frank, 'Cardozo and the Upper Court Myth' (1948), p. 386.

5. Richard Susskind, 'Management and Judges' (2003).

Chapter 14

1. What constitutes a hard case and what constitutes a clear case is itself quite a hard question. See Richard Susskind, *Expert Systems in Law* (1987), pp. 245–51.
2. For example, in Richard Susskind, *Tomorrow's Lawyers* (2017), pp. 47–8.
3. Sadly, that research seems to have been lost in the mists of time but I well recall the number, '18'.
4. https://www.resolver.co.uk (accessed 27 April 2019).

Chapter 15

1. An updated version of my doctorate was published as Richard Susskind, *Expert Systems in Law* (1987).
2. Phillip Capper and Richard Susskind, *Latent Damage Law—The Expert System* (1988).
3. Lawrence Lessig, *Code Version 2.0* (2006). For further elaborations on Lessig's work on 'code', see Jamie Susskind, *Future Politics* (2018), Ch. 5.

Chapter 16

1. I have used this quotation from Gibson in three earlier books. See, e.g., Richard Susskind, *The End of Lawyers?* (2008), p. 145.
2. Eril Niller, 'Can AI be a Fair Judge in Court? Estonia Thinks So' (2019).
3. See, e.g., HMCTS, 'Reform Update' (Autumn 2018)—https://assets. publishing.service.gov.uk/government/uploads/system/uploads/ attachment_data/file/772549/Reform_Update_issue_2_September_ 2018.pdf.
4. See Senior President of Tribunals, 'The Modernisation of Tribunals— Innovation Plan for 2019/2020' (2019), available at https://www. judiciary.uk/wp-content/uploads/2019/04/InnovationPlanFor2019- 20Copy.pdf (accessed 27 April 2019).
5. https://civilresolutionbc.ca (accessed 27 April 2019).
6. Shannon Salter, 'Online Dispute Resolution and Justice System Integration: British Columbia's Civil Resolution Tribunal' (2017).

7. https://civilresolutionbc.ca/wp-content/uploads/2019/03/Technical-Briefing-March-29-2019.pdf (accessed 27 April 2019).

8. https://www.trafficpenaltytribunal.gov.uk/ (accessed 27 April 2019). Also see John Aitken, 'Lessons from a Trailblazer Model' (Autumn 2016).

9. https://www.netcourt.gov.cn/portal/main/en/index.htm (accessed 27 April 2019).

10. Xuhui Fang, 'Recent Development of Internet Courts in China' (2018).

11. The Supreme People's Court of the People's Republic of China, 'Court Reform in China', White Paper, (14 March 2017)—http://english.court.gov.cn/2017-03/14/content_28552928.htm (accessed 27 April 2019).

12. http://www.courts.justice.nsw.gov.au/Pages/cats/catscorporate_online_services/onlinecourt.aspx (accessed 27 April 2019).

13. http://www.fedcourt.gov.au/online-services/ecourtroom (accessed 27 April 2019).

14. https://www.ncsc.org/2018survey (accessed 27 April 2019).

15. https://www.getmatterhorn.com (accessed 27 April 2019).

16. Maximillian Bulinski and J.J. Prescott, 'Designing Legal Experiences: Online Communication and Resolution in Courts' (2019).

17. See, e.g., Avital Mentovich et al., 'Is Judicial Bias Inevitable? Courts, Technology, and the Future of Impartiality' (2019).

18. See Deno Himonas, 'Utah's Online Dispute Resolution Program' (2018).

19. https://www.govtech.com/civic/SXSW-2019-Utah-Pajama-Court-and-Resolving-Cases-Online.html?AMP&__twitter_impression=true (accessed 27 April 2019).

Chapter 17

1. Richard Susskind, *The Future of Law* (1996), p. 27.

2. See, e.g., Hazel Genn, 'Online Courts and the Future of Justice' (2017) and Natalie Byrom, 'Developing the Detail: Evaluating the Impact of Court Reform in England and Wales on Access to Justice' (2019).

Chapter 18

1. See Lord Briggs, *Civil Courts Structure Review: Interim Report* (2015), p. 84.
2. Aristotle, *Politics*, Part XI, available at http://classics.mit.edu/Aristotle/politics.3.three.html (accessed 27 April 2019).

Chapter 19

1. See, e.g., the data published by the Civil Resolution Tribunal at https://civilresolutionbc.ca (accessed 27 April 2019).
2. Joseph Hutcheson, 'Judgment Intuitive: The Function of the Hunch in Judicial Decision' (1929).
3. Karl Llewellyn, 'Some Realism about Realism: Responding to Dean Pound' (1931).
4. See Sue Prince, '"Fine Words Butter No Parsnips": Can the Principle of Open Justice Survive the Introduction of the Online Court?' (2019), p. 118.

Chapter 20

1. Convention for the Protection of Human Rights and Fundamental Freedoms Rome, 4.XI.1950, available at https://www.echr.coe.int/Documents/Convention_ENG.pdf%23page=9 (accessed 27 April 2019).
2. European Court of Human Rights, *Guide on Article 6 of the European Convention on Human Rights: Right to a Fair Trial (civil limb)* (2018), available at https://www.echr.coe.int/Documents/Guide_Art_6_ENG.pdf (accessed 27 April 2019).
3. Susan Schiavetta, 'The Relationship Between e-ADR and Article 6 of the European Convention of Human Rights pursuant to the Case Law of the European Court of Human Rights' (2004).
4. European Court of Human Rights, *Guide on Article 6 of the European Convention on Human Rights: Right to a Fair Trial (civil limb)* (2018), p. 72.
5. Susan Schiavetta, 'The Relationship Between e-ADR and Article 6 of the European Convention of Human Rights pursuant to the Case Law of the European Court of Human Rights' (2004), Section 5.
6. Andrew Langdon, 'Inaugural Address' (2016).

7. For a compelling discussion of this point, see Mentovich et al., 'Is Judicial Bias Inevitable? Courts, Technology, and the Future of Impartiality' (2019).

8. Lord Briggs, *Civil Courts Structure Review: Interim Report* (2015), p. 4.

9. Andrew Langdon, 'Inaugural Address' (2016).

10. Irvin Yalom, *Becoming Myself* (2017), p. 305.

11. Andrew Langdon, 'Inaugural Address' (2016).

12. Quoted by Lord Devlin, *The Judge* (1981), p. 63.

13. *Gestmin SGPS SA v Credit Suisse (UK) Limited* [2013] EWHC 3560 (Comm), para. 22.

14. See Daniel Susskind, *A World Without Work* (2020), Ch. 5.

15. Irvin Yalom, *Becoming Myself* (2017), p. 306.

16. Ibid.

17. https://www.talkspace.com (accessed 27 April 2019).

18. Irvin Yalom, *Becoming Myself* (2017), p. 307.

19. Ibid., p. 308. Original emphasis.

20. Ibid., p. 309.

Chapter 21

1. JUSTICE, *Preventing Digital Exclusion from Online Justice* (2018), p. 4.

2. Ibid., p. 9.

3. William Dutton and Grant Blank, *Cultures of the Internet: The Internet in Britain*, Oxford Internet Study 2013 Report (2013).

4. https://www.ons.gov.uk/businessindustryandtrade/itandinternetindustry/bulletins/internetusers/2018 (accessed 27 April 2019).

5. See Ofcom, 'Adults' Media Use and Attitudes Report' (25 April 2018), p. 201, available at https://www.ofcom.org.uk/__data/assets/pdf_file/0011/113222/Adults-Media-Use-and-Attitudes-Report-2018.pdf (accessed 27 April 2019).

6. On proxy users and levels of internet usage, see William Dutton and Grant Blank, *Cultures of the Internet: The Internet in Britain*, Oxford Internet Study 2013 (2013).

7. See Ofcom, 'Adults' Media Use and Attitudes Report' (25 April 2018), p. 201, available at https://www.ofcom.org.uk/__data/assets/pdf_file/0011/113222/Adults-Media-Use-and-Attitudes-Report-2018.pdf (accessed 27 April 2019).

8. For a helpful discussion of vulnerability, see Natalie Byrom, 'Developing the Detail: Evaluating the Impact of Court Reform in England and Wales on Access to Justice' (2019), pp. 9–12.

9. JUSTICE, *Preventing Digital Exclusion from Online Justice* (2018), p. 9.

10. Ministry of Justice, 'Transforming Our Justice System: Summary of Reforms and Consultation' (September 2016), presented to Parliament by the Lord Chancellor and Secretary of State for Justice, pp. 13–14, available at https://consult.justice.gov.uk/digital-communications/transforming-our-courts-and-tribunals/supporting_documents/consultationpaper.pdf (accessed 27 April 2019).

11. JUSTICE, *Preventing Digital Exclusion from Online Justice* (2018), p. 75.

12. https://barefootlaw.org/ (accessed 27 April 2019).

13. https://wearesocial.com/us/blog/2018/01/global-digital-report-2018 (accessed 27 April 2019).

14. https://www.scope.org.uk/media/disability-facts-figures (accessed 27 April 2019).

Chapter 23

1. Lord Thomas, 'The Judiciary within the State—The Relationship between the Branches of the State' (2017), p. 25.

2. Jerome Frank, *Courts on Trial* (1949), p. 102.

3. Lord Devlin, *The Judge* (1981), p. 54.

4. Described as 'a self-standing set of rules designed from the outset to be understood by litigants without lawyers'. See Lord Briggs, *Civil Courts Structure Review: Interim Report* (2015), p. 79.

5. I am grateful to Sir Ernest Ryder for this point. I was a member of the review team, chaired by Sir Andrew Leggatt, whose report proposed greater flexibility and informality in the work of tribunals. This is a fine example of proposed reforms that gave rise to concrete change. See 'Tribunals for Users' (March 2001)—https://webarchive.nationalarchives.gov.uk/+/http://www.tribunals-review.org.uk/leggatthtm/leg-00.htm (accessed 27 April 2019).

6. Lord Briggs, *Civil Courts Structure Review: Interim Report* (2015), p. 78.

7. See Richard Susskind and Daniel Susskind, *The Future of the Professions* (2015).

8. *Southern Pacific Co v Jensen* (1917) 244 US 205, 221.

9. See Practice Direction 51M, Financial Markets Test Case Scheme, available at https://www.justice.gov.uk/courts/procedure-rules/civil/rules/part51/practice-direction-51m-financial-markets-test-case-scheme (accessed 27 April 2019).
10. Cyril Harvey, 'A Job for Jurisprudence' (1944) and William Twining, 'Some Jobs for Jurisprudence' (1974), p. 149.
11. Richard Susskind, *Expert Systems in Law* (1987), p. 26.
12. Michael Freeman, *Lloyd's Introduction to Jurisprudence* (2014).
13. Lord Lloyd, *Introduction to Jurisprudence* (1979), pp. 468–72.
14. Jamie Susskind, *Future Politics* (2018).

Chapter 24

1. For a formal audit report of that system, see http://www.bsa.ca.gov/pdfs/reports/2010-102.pdf (accessed 27 April 2019).

Chapter 25

1. See Lord Saville, 'Information Technology and a Public Inquiry' (2003).
2. Richard Susskind and Daniel Susskind, *The Future of the Professions* (2015), p. 63.
3. Arno Lodder and John Zeleznikoff, 'Developing an Online Dispute Resolution Environment: Dialogue Tools and Negotiation Support Systems in a Three-Step Model' (2005).
4. For example, https://www.resolver.co.uk and https://www.youstice.com/en/ (accessed 27 April 2019).
5. For example, https://www.crowdjustice.com (accessed 27 April 2019).
6. For example, https://www.ujuj.com/ (accessed 27 April 2019).
7. For example, https://www.tylertech.com/products/modria (accessed 27 April 2019).
8. Ethan Katsh and Orna Rabinovich-Einy, *Digital Justice* (2017), p. 47.

Chapter 26

1. Nick Bostrom, *Superintelligence* (2014).
2. See Richard Susskind, *Expert Systems in Law* (1987).
3. Phillip Capper and Richard Susskind, *Latent Damage Law—The Expert System* (1988).

4. I have taken this example from Mike Lynch, at http://www.foundation. org.uk/Journal/pdf/fst_22_02.pdf (accessed 27 April 2019).

5. Richard Susskind and Daniel Susskind, *The Future of the Professions* (2015), Chs. 6 and 7.

6. For a definitive analysis of the impact of technology on the future of work, see Daniel Susskind, *A World Without Work* (2020).

7. See Richard Susskind and Daniel Susskind, *The Future of the Professions* (2015).

Chapter 27

1. For a provocative, recent discussion of this possibility, see Eugene Volokh, 'Chief Justice Robots' (2019).

2. See Richard Susskind, 'Detmold's Refutation of Positivism and the Computer Judge' (1986), p. 133.

3. Jamie Susskind, *Future Politics* (2018), Part IV.

4. See Richard Susskind, *Expert Systems in Law* (1987).

5. See, e.g., the Introduction to Douglas Hofstadter and Daniel Dennett, *The Mind's Eye* (1982).

6. Reed Lawlor and Herman Oliphant, 'Excerpts from Fact Content of Cases and Precedent' (1972), p. 245.

7. See, e.g., Daniel Katz, Michael Bommarito, and Josh Blackman, 'A General Approach for Predicting the Behavior of the Supreme Court of the United States' (16 January 2017).

8. Nikolaos Aletras et al., 'Predicting Judicial Decisions of the European Court of Human Rights: A Natural Language Processing Perspective' (2016).

9. See, e.g., Glendon Schubert, *The Judicial Mind Revisited* (1974).

10. Richard and Daniel Susskind, *The Future of the Professions* (2015).

11. Abraham Maslow, *The Psychology of Science* (1966), p. 15.

12. Oliver Wendell Holmes, 'The Path of Law' (1897), p. 4.

13. Cited by Daniel Kahneman, *Thinking, Fast and Slow* (2012), pp. 43–4.

14. See William Twining, *Karl Llewellyn and the Realist Movement* (1973) and Jerome Frank, *Courts on Trial* (1949).

15. Karl Llewellyn, *Jurisprudence: Realism in Theory and Practice* (1962), p. 21.

16. Karl Llewellyn, *The Bramble Bush: Our Law and its Study* (1969), p. 12.

17. Eugene Ehrlich, *Fundamental Principles of the Sociology of Law* (1975).

18. Roscoe Pound, 'Law in Books and Law in Action' (1910).

19. See Jamie Susskind, *Future Politics* (2018), pp. 108–10 and Anthony Casey and Anthony Niblett, 'The Death of Rules and Standards' (2017).

20. For a thorough presentation of the arguments against algorithmic decision-making, see Guido Noto La Diega, 'Against the Dehumanisation of Decision-Making—Algorithmic Decisions at the Crossroads of Intellectual Property, Data Protection, and Freedom of Information' (2018).

21. See, e.g., CEPEJ, 'European Ethical Charter on the Use of Artificial Intelligence in Judicial Systems and their Environment' (2018).

22. For a good discussion of explanations in AI, see Brent Mittelstadt et al., 'Explaining Explanations in AI' (2018).

23. For a nuanced assessment of these issues, I recommend Jamie Susskind, *Future Politics* (2018), Ch.16.

Chapter 28

1. https://sustainabledevelopment.un.org/?menu=1300 (accessed 23 April 2019).

2. https://sustainabledevelopment.un.org/sdg16 (accessed 23 April 2019).

3. Ibid.

4. https://www.oecd.org/gov/delivering-access-to-justice-for-all.pdf (accessed 26 April 2019).

5. HiiL, *Understanding Justice Needs: The Elephant in the Courtroom* (2018), pp. 6 and 30.

6. United Nations Development Programme, 'Global Study of Legal Aid' (2016), pp. 2–3, available at https://www.unodc.org/documents/justice-and-prison-reform/LegalAid/Global_Study_on_Legal_Aid_-_FINAL.pdf (accessed 23 April 2019).

FURTHER READING

There is a steadily growing literature on the subject of online courts. In the list that follows, I include the books and published articles cited in the main body of this work, along with a selection of other publications that I recommend to readers who want to explore the field further. I do not include references for all public reports and online services that are noted in the book—these can easily be found online, following the links in the endnotes.

Publications

Aitken, John, 'Lessons from a Trailblazer Model' (Autumn 2016), available at https://www.judiciary.uk/wp-content/uploads/2017/03/aitken-lessons-from-a-trailblazer-model-autumn-2016.pdf (accessed 27 April 2019).

Aletras Nikolaos, Dimitrios Tsarapatsanis, Daniel Preoțiuc-Pietro, and Vasileios Lampos, 'Predicting Judicial Decisions of the European Court Of Human Rights: A Natural Language Processing Perspective' (2016) *PeerJ Computer Science* 2: e93.

Aristotle, *Nicomachean Ethics*, 2nd edn, Irwin, T. (trans.) (Indianapolis: Hackett, 1999).

Baker, Stephen, *Final Jeopardy: Man vs. Machine and the Quest to Know Everything* (New York: Houghton Mifflin Harcourt, 2011).

Barnett, Jeremy and Philip Treleaven, 'Algorithmic Dispute Resolution—The Automation of Professional Dispute Resolution Using AI and Blockchain Technologies' (March 2018) *The Computer Journal* 61(3): 399.

Barton, Benjamin and Stephanos Bibas, *Rebooting Justice* (New York: Encounter, 2017).

Bentham, Jeremy, *Of Laws in General*, Hart, Herbert (ed.) (London: The Athlone Press, 1970).

Bingham, Lord, *The Rule of Law* (London: Penguin, 2010).

Bostrom, Nick, *Superintelligence* (Oxford: Oxford University Press, 2014).

Briggs, Lord, *Civil Courts Structure Review: Interim Report* (December 2015), available at https://www.judiciary.uk/wp-content/uploads/2016/01/CCSR-interim-report-dec-15-final-31.pdf (accessed 24 April 2019).

Briggs, Lord, *Civil Courts Structure Review: Final Report* (July 2016), available at https://www.judiciary.uk/wp-content/uploads/2016/07/civil-courts-structure-review-final-report-jul-16-final-1.pdf (accessed 24 April 2019).

Brown, Tim and Roger Martin, 'Design for Action' (September 2015) *Harvard Business Review* 56.

Bulinski, Maximillian and James Prescott, 'Designing Legal Experiences: Online Communication and Resolution in Courts', in Katz, Daniel, Michael J. Bommarito, and Ron Dolin, eds, *Legal Informatics* (Cambridge: Cambridge University Press, 2019, forthcoming).

Burnett, Lord, 'The Cutting Edge of Digital Reform' (3 December, 2018), Opening Address, First International Conference on Online Courts, available at https://www.judiciary.uk/wp-content/uploads/2018/12/speech-lcj-online-court.pdf (accessed 24 April 2019).

Byrom, Natalie, 'Developing the Detail: Evaluating the Impact of Court Reform in England and Wales on Access to Justice' (London: Legal Education Forum, 2019).

Campbell, Tom, *Justice*, 2nd edn (London: MacMillan, 2001).

Capper, Phillip and Richard Susskind, *Latent Damage Law—The Expert System* (London: Butterworths, 1988).

Casey, Anthony and Anthony Niblett, 'The Death of Rules and Standards' (2017) *Indiana Law Journal* 92(4): 1401.

CEPEJ, 'European Ethical Charter on the Use of Artificial Intelligence in Judicial Systems and their Environment' (2018), available at https://rm.coe.int/ethical-charter-en-for-publication-4-december-2018/16808f699c (accessed 24 April 2019).

Christensen, Clayton, *The Innovator's Dilemma* (Boston: Harvard Business School Press, 1997).

Citizens Advice, 'Responsive Justice' (November, 2015), available at https://www.citizensadvice.org.uk/Global/CitizensAdvice/Crime%20and%20Justice%20Publications/Responsivejustice.pdf (accessed 24 April 2019).

Civil Justice Council, Online Dispute Resolution Advisory Group, *Online Dispute Resolution for Low Value Civil Claims* (February 2015), available at https://www.judiciary.uk/wp-content/uploads/2015/02/Online-Dispute-Resolution-Final-Web-Version1.pdf (accessed 24 April 2019).

Denning, Lord, 'Law and Life in our Time', 1967 Turner Memorial Lecture (1967) *University of Tasmania Law Review* 2: 349.

Devlin, Lord, *The Judge* (Oxford: Oxford University Press, 1981).

Donoghue, Jane, 'The Rise of Digital Justice: Courtroom Technology, Public Participation and Access to Justice' (2017) *Modern Law Review* 80(6): 995.

Dutton, William and Grant Blank, *Cultures of the Internet: The Internet in Britain*, Oxford Internet Study 2013 (Oxford: Oxford Internet Institute, 2013).

Dworkin, Ronald, *Law's Empire* (London: Fontana, 1986).

Ehrlich, Eugene, *Fundamental Principles of the Sociology of Law*, reprint edn (New York: Arno Press, 1975).

Fang Xuhui, 'Recent Development of Internet Courts in China' (2018) *International Journal of Online Dispute Resolution* 5: 49.

Frank, Jerome, 'Cardozo and the Upper Court Myth' (1948) *Law and Contemporary Problems* 13: 386.

Frank, Jerome, *Courts on Trial* (Princeton: Princeton University Press, 1949).

Frank, Jerome, 'Some Reflections on Judge Learned Hand' (1957) *The University of Chicago Law* . 24: 666.

Freeman, Michael, *Lloyd's Introduction to Jurisprudence*, 9th edn (London: Sweet & Maxwell, 2014).

Fuller, Lon, *The Morality of Law* (New Haven: Yale University Press, 1969).

Gawande, Atul, *The Checklist Manifesto* (London: Profile Books, 2007).

Genn, Hazel, *Judging Civil Justice* (Cambridge: Cambridge University Press, 2010).

Genn, Hazel, *Paths to Justice* (Oxford: Hart Publishing, 1999).

Genn, Hazel, 'Online Courts and the Future of Justice' (16 October 2017), The Tenth Birkenhead Lecture, Gray's Inn, available at https://www.ucl.ac.uk/laws/sites/laws/files/birkenhead_lecture_2017_professor_dame_hazel_genn_final_version.pdf (accessed 24 April 2019).

Gibbs, Penelope, 'Defendants on Video—Conveyor Belt Justice or a Revolution in Access' (October 2017), available at http://www.transformjustice.org.uk/wp-content/uploads/2017/10/Disconnected-Thumbnail-2.pdf (accessed 24 April 2019).

Godin, Seth, *This is Marketing* (London: Penguin, 2018).

Gordon, Robert, *The Rise and Fall of American Growth* (Princeton: Princeton University Press, 2016).

Grossman, Maura and Gordon Cormack, 'Technology-Assisted Review in E-Discovery Can be More Effective and More Efficient Than Exhaustive Manual Review' (2011) *Richmond Journal of Law and Technology* XVII(3): 1.

Hart, Herbert, 'Positivism and the Separation of Law and Morals' (1958) *Harvard Law Review* 71(4): 593.

Hart, Herbert *The Concept of Law*, 3rd edn (Oxford: Oxford University Press, 2012).

Harvey, Cyril, 'A Job for Jurisprudence' (1944) *The Modern Law Review* 7: 42.

HiiL, *Understanding Justice Needs: The Elephant in the Courtroom* (The Hague: HiiL, 2018)

Himonas, Deno, 'Utah's Online Dispute Resolution Program' (2018) *Dickinson Law Review* 122: 875. HM Courts & Tribunals Service, 'Reform Update, Autumn 2018' available at https://assets.publishing.service.gov.uk/government/uploads/system/uploads/attachment_data/file/772549/Reform_Update_issue_2_September_2018.pdf (accessed 26 April 2019).

HM Treasury, *Spending Review and Autumn Statement* (25 November 2015), available at https://www.gov.uk/government/publications/spending-review-and-autumn-statement-2015-documents (accessed 26 April 2019)

Hofstadter, Douglas and Daniel Dennett, eds, *The Mind's Eye* (London: Penguin, 1982).

Holmes, Oliver, W., 'The Path of Law' (1897) *Harvard Law Review* 10: 457.

Hutcheson, Joseph, 'Judgment Intuitive: The Function of the Hunch in Judicial Decision' (April 1929) *Cornell Law Review* 14(3): 274.

Iansiti, Marco and Karim Lakhani, 'The Truth about Blockchain' (Jan–Feb, 2017) *Harvard Business Review* 118.

JUSTICE, *Delivering Justice in an Age of Austerity* (London: JUSTICE, 2015).

JUSTICE, *Preventing Digital Exclusion from Online Justice* (London: JUSTICE, 2018).

JUSTICE, *Understanding Courts* (London: JUSTICE, 2019).

Kafka, Franz, 'Before the Law', in *A Country Doctor* (Prague: Twisted Spoon Press, 1997).

Kafka, Franz, *The Trial* (Harmondsworth: Penguin, 1983).

Kahneman, Daniel, *Thinking, Fast and Slow* (London: Penguin, 2012).

Katsh, Ethan and Janet Rifkin, *Online Dispute Resolution* (San Francisco: Jossey-Bass, 2001).

Katsh, Ethan and Orna Rabinovich-Einy, *Digital Justice: Technology and the Internet of Conflict* (New York: Oxford University Press, 2017).

Katz, Daniel, Michael Bommarito, and Josh Blackman, 'A General Approach for Predicting the Behavior of the Supreme Court of the United States' (16 January 2017), available at https://ssrn.com/abstract=2463244 (accessed 24 April 2019).

Kelsen, Hans, *General Theory of Law and State* (New York: Russell & Russell, 1965).

Kuhn, Thomas, *The Structure of Scientific Revolutions*, 3rd edn (Chicago: University of Chicago Press, 1996).

Kurzweil, Ray, *The Singularity is Near* (New York: Viking, 2005).

Langdon, Andrew, 'Inaugural Address' (14 December 2016), Chairman of the Bar 2017, Middle Temple Hall, London, available at http://www.barristermagazine.com/inaugural-address-by-andrew-langdon-qc-chairman-of-the-bar-2017-delivered-in-middle-temple-hall-london-on-14-december-2016 (accessed 27 April 2019).

Lanier, Jaron, *Dawn of the New Everything: A Journey Through Virtual Reality* (London: Penguin, 2017).

Lawlor, Reed and Herman Oliphant, 'Excerpts from Fact Content of Cases and Precedent' (1972) *Jurimetrics Journal* 12: 245.

Lessig, Lawrence, *Code: Version 2.0* (New York: Basic Books, 2006).

Levitt, Ted., *Marketing Myopia* (Boston: Harvard Business School Publishing Corporation, 2008).

Llewellyn, Karl, *Jurisprudence: Realism in Theory and Practice* (London: University of Chicago Press, 1962).

Llewellyn, Karl, 'Some Realism about Realism: Responding to Dean Pound' (1931) *Harvard Law Review* 44(8): 1222.

Llewellyn, Karl, *The Bramble Bush: Our Law and its Study* (New York: Oceana, 1969).

Lloyd, Lord, *Introduction to Jurisprudence*, 4th edn (London: Stevens, 1979).

Lodder, Arno and John Zeleznikoff, 'Developing an Online Dispute Resolution Environment: Dialogue Tools and Negotiation Support Systems in a Three-Step Model' (Spring 2005) *Harvard Negotiation Law Review* 10: 287.

Lord Chancellor, the Lord Chief Justice, and the Senior President of Tribunals, 'Transforming Our Justice System' (September 2016), available at https://assets.publishing.service.gov.uk/government/uploads/system/uploads/attachment_data/file/553261/joint-vision-statement.pdf (accessed 24 April 2019).

Mackie, John, *Ethics* (London: Penguin 1990).

Maslow, Abraham, *The Psychology of Science* (Chapel Hill, NC: Maurice Bassett, 1966).

Mason, Stephen, '"Artificial Intelligence" Oh Really? And Why Judges and Lawyers are Central to the Way we Live Now—But they Don't Know it' (2017) *Computer and Telecommunications Law Review* 8: 213.

Mentovich, Avital, James Prescott, and Orna Rabinovich-Einy, 'Is Judicial Bias Inevitable? Courts, Technology, and the Future of Impartiality' (2019) *Alabama Law Review* 73 (forthcoming).

Ministry of Justice, *Virtual Court Pilot: Outcome Evaluation* (London: Ministry of Justice, 2010), available at http://www.justice.gov.uk/ (accessed 24 April 2019).

Mittelstadt, Brent, Chris Russell, and Sandra Wachter, 'Explaining Explanations in AI' (19 January 2019), FAT* 2019 Proceedings, available at https://arxiv.org/pdf/1811.01439.pdf (accessed 24 April 2019).

Munby, James, 'The Family Bar in a Digital World' (12 May 2018), Family Law Bar Association conference, available at https://www.judiciary.uk/wp-content/uploads/2018/05/2018-flba-cumberlan-lodge.pdf (accessed 26 April 2019).

Niller, Eril, 'Can AI be a Fair Judge in Court? Estonia Thinks So' (2019), available at https://www.wired.com/story/can-ai-be-fair-judge-court-estonia-thinks-so/ (accessed 27 April 2019).

Noto La Diega, Guido, 'Against the Dehumanisation of Decision-Making—Algorithmic Decisions at the Crossroads of Intellectual

Property, Data Protection, and Freedom of Information' (2018) *JIPITEC* 9: 3.

Plato, *The Republic*, 3rd edn (London: Penguin, 2007).

Posner, Richard, *How Judges Think* (London: Harvard University Press, 2008).

Pound, Roscoe, 'Law in Books and Law in Action' (1910) *American Law Review* 44: 12.

Prince, Sue, '"Fine Words Butter No Parsnips": Can the Principle of Open Justice Survive the Introduction of the Online Court?' (2019) *Civil Justice Quarterly* 38(1): 111.

Rabinovich-Einy, Orna and Ethan Katsh, 'The New New Courts' (2017) *American University Law Review* 7: 165.

Rawls, J., *A Theory of Justice* (Oxford: Oxford University Press, 1972).

Resnik, Judith and Dennis Curtis, *Representing Justice* (New Haven: Yale University Press, 2011).

Rossner, Meredith and Martha McCurdy, 'Implementing Video Hearings (Party-to-State): A Process Evaluation' (London: Ministry of Justice, 2018), available at http://www.lse.ac.uk/business-and-consultancy/consulting/assets/documents/implementing-video-hearings.pdf (accessed 24 April 2019).

Ross, Graham, 'First case in the Online Court To Be Resolved by Algorithm' (15 February 2019), available at https://www.themediationroom.com/single-post/2019/02/15/First-Case-in-The-Online-Court-To-Be-Resolved-by-Algorithm,

Rozenberg, Joshua, 'The Online Court: Will IT Work?' (2019), available at https://long-reads.thelegaleducationfoundation.org/ (accessed 26 April 2019).

Rule, Colin, 'Designing a Global Online Dispute Resolution System: Lessons Learned from eBay' (2017) *University of St. Thomas Law Journal* 13: 354.

Ryder, Ernest, 'The Modernisation of Access to Justice in Times of Austerity' (3 March 2016), 5th Annual Ryder Lecture: the University of Bolton, available at https://www.judiciary.uk/wp-content/uploads/2016/03/20160303-ryder-lecture2.pdf (accessed 24 April 2019).

Ryder, Ernest, 'What's Happening in Justice: A View from England & Wales' (14 May 2018), The Future of Justice, UCL Laws, available at https://www.judiciary.uk/wp-content/uploads/2018/05/speech-ryder-spt-ucl-may-2018.pdf (accessed 24 April 2019).

Salter, Shannon, 'Online Dispute Resolution and Justice System Integration: British Columbia's Civil Resolution Tribunal' (2017) *Windsor Yearbook of Access to Justice* 34: 112.

Sandel, Michael, *Justice* (London: Penguin, 2009).

Saville, Lord, 'Information Technology and a Public Inquiry', in M. Saville and R. Susskind, eds, *Essays in Honour of Sir Brian Neill: The Quintessential Judge* (London: Lexis-Nexis, 2003).

Schiavetta, Susan, 'The Relationship Between e-ADR and Article 6 of the European Convention of Human Rights pursuant to the Case Law of the European Court of Human Rights' (2004) *The Journal of Information, Law and Technology* (1), available at http://www2.warwick.ac.uk/fac/soc/law/elj/jilt/2004_1/schiavetta/ (accessed 24 April 2019).

Schubert, Glendon, *The Judicial Mind Revisited* (New York: Oxford University Press, 1974).

Sela, Ayelet, 'Streamlining Justice: How Online Courts Can Resolve the Challenges of Pro Se Litigation' (2016) *Cornell Journal of Law and Public Policy* 6(2): 331.

Sen, Amartya, *The Idea of Justice* (London: Penguin, 2009).

Smith, Adam, *An Inquiry into the Nature and Causes of the Wealth of Nations,* paperback edn (Oxford: Oxford University Press, 1998).

Sorabji, John, *English Civil Justice after the Woolf and Jackson Reforms* (Cambridge: Cambridge University Press, 2014).

Sorabji, John, 'The Online Solutions Court—A Multi-door Courthouse for the 21st Century' (2017) *Civil Justice Quarterly* 36(1): 51.

Susskind, Daniel, *A World Without Work* (London: Allen Lane, 2020, forthcoming).

Susskind, Jamie, *Future Politics* (Oxford: Oxford University Press, 2018).

Susskind, Richard, 'Detmold's Refutation of Positivism and the Computer Judge' (1986) *The Modern Law Review* 49: 125.

Susskind, Richard, *Expert Systems in Law* (Oxford: Oxford University Press, 1987; paperback edn, 1989).

Susskind, Richard, 'Lawyers and Coders Hack Away Dead Wood for Digital Courts' (6 July 2017), *The Times*, available at https://www.thetimes.co.uk/article/lawyers-and-coders-hack-away-dead-wood-for-digital-courts-5qgxbwdd0 (accessed 24 April 2019).

Susskind, Richard, 'Making the Case for Online Courts' (6 December 2018), *The Times*, available at https://www.thetimes.co.uk/article/making-the-case-for-online-courts-gtsrgcwq2 (accessed 24 April 2019).

Susskind, Richard, 'Management and Judges', in Lord Saville and Richard Susskind, eds, *Essays in Honour of Sir Brian Neill* (London: Lexis-Nexis, 2003).

Susskind, Richard, 'Online Disputes: Is it Time to End the 'Day in Court'?' (26 February 2015), *The Times*, available at https://www.thetimes.co.uk/article/online-disputes-is-it-time-to-end-the-day-in-court-6rpxjbtx0x8 (accessed 26 April 2019).

Susskind, Richard, *The End of Lawyers?* (Oxford: Oxford University Press, 2008; paperback edn, 2010).

Susskind, Richard, *The Future of Law* (Oxford: Oxford University Press, 1996; paperback edn, 1998).

Susskind, Richard, *Tomorrow's Lawyers*, 2nd edn (Oxford: Oxford University Press, 2017).

Susskind, Richard, *Transforming the Law* (Oxford: Oxford University Press, 2000; paperback edn, 2003).

Susskind, Richard and Daniel Susskind, *The Future of the Professions* (Oxford: Oxford University Press, 2015).

The Engine Room, *Technology for Legal Empowerment: A Global Review* (2019), available at https://www.theengineroom.org/wp-content/uploads/2019/01/Tech-for-Legal-Empowerment-The-Engine-Room.pdf (accessed 24 April 2019).

Thompson, Darin, 'Creating New Pathways to Justice Using Simple Artificial Intelligence and Online Dispute Resolution' (2015) *Osgoode Legal Studies Research Paper Series* 152, available at http://digitalcommons.osgoode.yorku.ca/olsrps/152 (accessed 26 April 2019).

Thomas, Lord, 'Judicial Leadership' (22 June 2015), Conference on the Paradox of Judicial Independence, UCL Constitution Unit, available at https://www.judiciary.uk/wp-content/uploads/2015/06/ucl-judicial-independence-speech-june-2015.pdf (accessed 24 April 2019).

Thomas, Lord, 'The Judiciary with the State—The Relationship between the Branches of the State' (15 June 2017), Michael Ryle Memorial Lecture, available at https://www.judiciary.uk/wp-content/uploads/2017/06/lcj-michael-ryle-memorial-lecture-20170616.pdf (accessed 24 April 2019).

Twining, William, *Karl Llewellyn and the Realist Movement* (London: Weidenfeld & Nicolson, 1973).

Twining, William, 'Some Jobs for Jurisprudence' (1974) *British Journal of Law and Society* 1: 149.

Tyler, Tom R., 'Court Review: Volume 44, Issue 1/2—Procedural Justice and the Courts' (2007) *Court Review: The Journal of the American Judges Association* 217.

Volokh, Eugene, 'Chief Justice Robots' (2019) *Duke Law Journal* 68: 1135.

Vos, Geoffrey, 'Judicial Diversity and LawTech: Do We Need to Change the Way We Litigate Business and Property Disputes?' (18 January, 2018), Chancery Bar Association Annual Conference, available at https://www.judiciary.uk/wp-content/uploads/2019/01/Speech-to-Chancery-Bar-Association-Annual-Conference.pdf (accessed 24 April 2019).

Vos, Geoffrey, 'The Foundation for Science and Technology Debate on How the Adoption of New Technology can be Accelerated to Improve the Efficiency of the Justice System' (20 June 2018), available at https://www.judiciary.uk/wp-content/uploads/2018/06/speech-chc-the-foundation-for-science-and-technology.pdf (accessed 24 April 2019).

Wahab, Mohamed, Ethan Katsh, and Daniel Rainey, (eds), *Online Dispute Resolution: Theory and Practice* (The Hague: Eleven International, 2012).

Weizenbaum, Joseph, *Computer Power and Human Reason*, edn with new preface (Harmondworth: Penguin, 1984).

Woolf, Lord, *Access to Justice—Interim Report* (London: HMSO, 1995).

Woolf, Lord, *Access to Justice—Final Report* (London: HMSO, 1996).

Yalom, Irvin, *Becoming Myself* (London: Piatkus, 2017).

INDEX

Figures are indicated by an italic *f* following the page number.

Note: For the benefit of digital users, indexed terms that span two pages (e.g., 52–53) may, on occasion, appear on only one of those pages.